The Dog Lover's Companion to Chicago

2ND EDITION

Margaret Littman

AVALON TRAVEL

D1444282

THE DOG LOVER'S COMPANION TO CHICAGO
THE INSIDE SCOOP ON WHERE TO TAKE YOUR DOG

AVALON
publishing group incorporated

Published by
Avalon Travel Publishing
1400 65th Street, Suite 250
Emeryville, CA 94608, USA

Avalon Travel Publishing
An Imprint of Avalon Publishing Group, Inc.

Printing History
1st edition—2003
2nd edition—January 2007
5 4 3 2 1

Text © 2007 by Margaret Littman. All rights reserved.
Maps © 2007 by Avalon Travel Publishing. All rights reserved.
Illustrations © 2007 by Phil Frank.
Illustrations are used by permission and are the property of the original
copyright owner.

ISBN-10: 1-56691-870-7
ISBN-13: 978-1-56691-870-1
ISSN: 1545-2182

Editor: Cinnamon Hearst
Acquisitions Manager: Rebecca Browning
Copy Editor: Ellie Behrstock
Designer: Jacob Goolkasian
Graphics Coordinator: Stefano Boni
Production Coordinator: Tabitha Lahr
Map Editor: Kevin Anglin
Cartographers: Kat Bennett, Sheryle Veverka
Indexer: Rachel Kuhn

Cover and Interior Illustrations by Phil Frank

Printed in the USA by Malloy

ABOUT THE AUTHOR

If there is any better assignment than getting to write *The Dog Lover's Companion to Chicago,* it is getting to do it again. Taking her dogs and their friends to their favorite parks while everyone else puts on a suit and goes to the office is Margaret Littman's dream job.

For more than a decade as a Chicago journalist, Margaret has been allowed to explore eclectic topics for *Chicago* magazine, *Entertainment Weekly, Ladies' Home Journal,*

Wine Enthusiast, Crain's Chicago Business, the *Chicago Tribune,* and others. A Chicago correspondent for *Art & Antiques* magazine, Margaret is the author of *VegOut Vegetarian Guide to Chicago* and was a contributor to *Woman's Best Friend: Women Writers on the Dogs in Their Lives.*

Her research assistants, 10-year-old springer spaniel mix Natasha and year-old American foxhound Cooper, enjoyed sniffing out new dog parks for this book more than their previous task of keeping silent during conference calls. Unfortunately, their lack of opposable thumbs prevented them from helping to type the manuscript.

Margaret has a B.A. in fine arts from Vanderbilt University and an M.S.J. from the Medill School of Journalism at Northwestern University. She is a member of the board of trustees of the Fountain Valley School of Colorado and the board of directors of the Friends of the Forest Preserves.

Natasha is adept at sit, down, and rollover. Cooper excels at slipping through gates, sleeping on the human furniture, and barking at the FedEx truck. All three can be reached at www.littmanwrites.com.

To Boris, Trouble, Alex, and Pax

CONTENTS

Beyond the Windy City 211

Resources 227

Indexes 253

Accommodations Index. 254

Restaurant Index. 256

General Index 258

CHICAGO

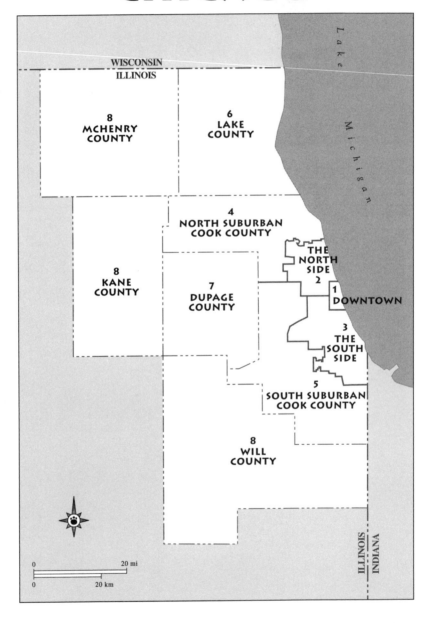

WISCONSIN
ILLINOIS

Lake Michigan

8
MCHENRY
COUNTY

6
LAKE
COUNTY

4
NORTH SUBURBAN
COOK COUNTY

THE
NORTH
SIDE
2

8
KANE
COUNTY

7
DUPAGE
COUNTY

1
DOWNTOWN

3
THE
SOUTH
SIDE

5
SOUTH SUBURBAN
COOK COUNTY

8
WILL
COUNTY

ILLINOIS
INDIANA

0   20 mi

0   20 km

MAPS

Introduction

Most dogs are not particularly interested in poetry. But utter the line calling Chicago "hog butcher for the world," and many pups may become Carl Sandburg fans. Though the Chicago stockyards aren't what they once were, most dogs think any place famous for slabs of meat is going to be their kind of town. (Patient pups who read to the end description of the city as "fierce as a dog with tongue lapping for action" may become even more enchanted with Sandburg.)

There are more than two million dogs living in Cook County. An estimated one million of those live within the Chicago city limits; that's about one dog for every 2.5 people. Add in all the Lake, DuPage, McHenry, Kane, and Will County dogs, not to mention those who fly in on vacation, and that's a lot of tails wagging in expectation of a fresh deli platter.

Vienna sausages aside, many of the things that have attracted people to the Chicago area since settlers arrived in 1850 are the same things that make the area a great place both to be and have a dog. First and foremost is that incredible coastline. The miles and miles of public land along Lake Michigan include sandy beaches, rocky shores, quiet parks, and happening harbors. Farther away from the lake are wide-open spaces and peaceful prairies. Chicago has four distinct seasons, and you'll find dog-friendly places during all of them, from beaches and river cruises for the hottest days, to dog-sledding tracks and indoor play areas for the depths of winter. Few areas are so accessible to nature, yet still offer the sights and smells (mmmm, the smells) of the big city.

In this Midwestern Mecca, there is at least one dog-friendly version of everything: dog newspapers, phone books, and both major and minor league baseball teams. Bakers, photographers, painters, massage therapists, and pet communicators. Carriage rides, summer camps, yoga classes, and church services. Whatever your activity of choice, there's likely a dog-friendly option out here somewhere. In the three years since my springer spaniel Natasha and I wrote the first edition of this book the number of dog-friendly options have only increased. City dogs know this, and Cooper (my American foxhound) and Natasha are always ready to test out another one. Writing is a solitary life, and on more than one day I wouldn't have left my desk if Natasha hadn't planted her head on my keyboard and suggested that there must be something better to do than wait to bark at Erin, our UPS delivery person (and fellow dog lover). Some days, her excursions didn't get her any farther than the ATM, the mailbox, the video store, or the bookstore. Other days—dog days, she calls them—we got out there and chased squirrels, leapt over tree branches, and rolled in something stinky.

Leashes in hand, Cooper, Natasha, and I explored parts of the city and suburbs that were off our beaten path; we hope you will, too. (A native Idahoan who moved to Chicago more than a decade ago, I was shocked to discover that there are, in fact, hills and valleys in Illinois. As a result, I've stopped making flat jokes. Well, cut back on the flat jokes.) If your dog is an urban hound, jump in the car (rent or borrow one if you typically depend on the El) and brace yourself for the slobbery kisses of gratitude when you show your pooch the enormous off-leash spaces in the Lake and DuPage County Forest Preserves. If your dog is the suburban sort, he'll be equally appreciative of the trip into the big city where he'll meet so many of his species. I only ask that as you venture out, you remember to be respectful. Wherever you're going may not be your neighborhood, but it's somebody's neighborhood. Treat any new area as you want visitors to treat your street: don't block driveways or alleys, pick up after your dog, and be quiet early in the morning and late at night, and there won't be any dogfights or turf wars.

Chicago and its environs are generally considered safe areas to live and visit, both for people and their furry friends. I haven't included any destinations in this book that I personally have not and would not go to alone with Cooper and Natasha. That said, a word about street smarts is in order. Chicago is an urban area, and being alert to your surroundings is a necessity. While violent crime doesn't run rampant in the parks I've visited, people do get pickpocketed in public places (and not just in the city; I saw as many shady situations in the suburbs). Many of Chicago's parks and forest preserves have beautiful trails with secluded paths. These areas are best used during the day. Stick to open ball fields and other well-lit areas during nighttime walks. If a park warrants a special disclaimer, I've included that in its description. If you're concerned about an area, the Chicago Police Department's Citizen ICAM website (http://12.17.79.6) maps reported crime by category in any part of the city.

The Dog Lover's Companion to Chicago is divided into chapters, based on geography. Within the city of Chicago, there are three areas: the North Side, Downtown, and the South Side. Within each chapter, parks, places to eat, and places to stay are grouped by neighborhood, which is how Chicagoans talk. The city of Chicago has 77 officially defined neighborhoods, often named after the ethnic groups who first moved in. Chicago is fiercely proud ("fierce as a dog," you might say) of its various ethnic heritages. There wasn't enough room to write about every neighborhood, and not all of them have dog-worthy diversions. I've grouped neighboring communities together, so that it's easy to see which parks are near one another. As you look at these groupings, you should be able to figure out where to go to make a day of it, even in unfamiliar territory. The county chapters are organized similarly, with nearby suburbs grouped together. Sometimes a park lies in two neighborhoods, in which case, I list it under the community where its entrance is, or with which locals most readily associate it. The helpful maps at the beginning of each chapter will always point you in the right direction. If you're stumped, try the general index in the back of the book. Trust us, follow our lead, and you won't miss a thing.

Local Laws

In the city of Chicago, leashed dogs are permitted in all city parks, but not in Chicago Park District buildings, lagoons, or children's play lots. Since the last edition of this book, the Chicago Park District sadly changed its policy on dogs and beaches. While pups used to be permitted on the city's 15 miles of bathing beaches during the off-season, they're now prohibited year-round. The city still has 18 miles of bike paths, in addition to 7,300 acres of parkland. City parks are open dawn–11 P.M., and as long as you pick up after your pet, you're invited to play. Most county forest preserves are open sunrise–sunset. Dogs are generally not welcome on Chicago Public Schools property. Off-leash, Chicago is making progress, but still has a ways to go to compete with New York, a city with the same number of dogs, but four times the number of off-leash dog parks. At press time, there were 12 off-leash Dog-Friendly Areas (DFAs) in the city (11 parks and one beach), and several others are in the works. DFAs are community-petitioned projects; each one can take several years to get approved, and the neighborhood that supports it must help raise funds to build and maintain the park. All Park District DFAs have dog gates (a double-door system to prevent Houdini breeds from getting out), as well as hard surfaces to prevent bacteria growth, facilitate cleanup, and reduce odors.

In 2005 a Cook County Animal and Rabies Control Ordinance was passed that raised the fur on the necks of many local dogs and their owners. Though new, the ordinance is not outrageous. It requires forest preserves, municipalities, park districts, and others to work with the Cook County Department of Animal Control to create fenced dog parks, and stipulates that animals must be immunized, vaccinated, and have a veterinarian's letter to prove it. But no one likes change, and some of the other stipulations, such as requiring dog areas to be fenced on all sides, resulted in change at many suburbs and at the city of Chicago's only off-leash beach. Dog lovers and veterinarians also became concerned about the costs of required veterinarian visits for off-leash permits. After a year of contentious meetings, a new permit system was developed. Any dog wanting to use a Cook County DFA must have a permit. The permits require signed forms from veterinarians, vouching for vaccinations and healthy stool samples. In Chicago, most local vets will issue and process the permit applications, which are $5, in addition to the modest cost of a city dog license (see below). Because the current permits require a Chicago dog license and a local vet visit, they aren't practical for dogs visiting Chicago for just a short period of time. The Chicago Park District is working with the Cook County Department of Animal Control to develop ways to accept licenses and vet records from other cities so that healthy, immunized dogs from out-of-town can use the dog parks. Dan Parmer, D.V.M., the director of Cook County Animal Control, is generally satisfied with the compliance to the new ordinance, with the exception of a few areas slow to build permanent fencing.

Parks are living things in more than one way, and the Park District is cognizant of this. As the public's recreation needs change, additions like skate parks and dog runs displace bocce ball and horseshoe pits. Locals hope the $5 fee from the new DFA permits will be used to maintain and improve the existing DFAs, as well as help develop new ones.

"No one likes extra paperwork, but I don't think [a permit] is a bad idea. It is comforting to know that all these dogs have been to a vet within the last year," says Barbara Royal, D.V.M., at Family Pet Animal Hospital and The Royal Treatment Veterinary Spa, both in Chicago.

Other DFA rules remain the same and rooted in common sense: include cleaning up after your pooch; ensuring that your dog is fully immunized, dewormed, licensed, and wearing ID tags; and not bringing puppies under four months, dogs in heat, or children under 12 in DFAs. There are typically plenty of abandoned tennis balls and plastic bags in the DFAs. For apartment-bound hounds, DFAs can be an excellent way to get some exercise and learn to socialize with other dogs. Dr. Royal cautions pet owners to be aware when entering areas with a high-density of dogs, like a DFA. While no one means harm, she says, animals do get into fights, and she sees far too many injured small dogs in her practice as a result of too many dogs in too small a space.

When possible, I've included contact information for neighborhood groups, so you can get involved, make donations for upkeep and new fences, or help create a DFA in your neck of the woods. You'll note that some neighborhoods are underserved when it comes to DFAs and dog-friendly businesses. I'll just encourage you, if you live in one of those areas, to consider starting a dog-friendly initiative in your own backyard. The Park District provides interested communities with information on how to start a DFA. If you live in an area with a DFA, become a member of the neighborhood group to help keep it going. All these neighborhood groups rely on your donations—of time and money.

Research from the Dog Advisory Work Group (D.A.W.G.) found that having a dog-focused community group can help strengthen neighborhood relations, support local small businesses, and reduce street crime. D.A.W.G. was instrumental in getting the Chicago Park District to create the first DFA and now assists in establishing DFAs, reducing dogfighting in the city, encouraging scoop-the-poop programs, and spaying and neutering pets. Contact D.A.W.G. at 312/409-2169; www.dawgsite.org.

Thanks to work by D.A.W.G. and the city's Department of Animal Care and Control, eliminating dogfighting has become a city priority. This cruel activity is a felony in Illinois, but is practiced by street gangs to desensitize younger members to violence. The city of Chicago discourages dog owners from tying their pups to posts while they run inside a non-dog-friendly store, as pets have been stolen for use as bait in dogfights. As much as I don't like to think about such abuse, the truth is that the practice seems as prevalent as when I worked on the first edition of this book. Throughout I've noted as many Fetching Necessities—pet-friendly (and fun) businesses where you can bring your dog inside and get your errands done—as possible.

Like almost everywhere else in a city, the DFAs don't always have enough space to accommodate all the people (and dogs) who want to use them. If you head to a small DFA at 5:30 P.M. on a weekday during the post-work rush, your dog might not have much space to run. I encourage you to think of a DFA as just one component in your dog's overall activity plan. Try to use DFAs when they're less congested (even going for a quick walk after work, and then heading to the DFA after dinner, can make a difference). Explore the magnificent on-leash parks, boulevard strolls, forest preserves, and private dog-daycare play areas (noted in the Resources section), in addition to the dog runs of the urban jungle.

Dog policies vary among suburban municipalities. Almost every village or town, including Chicago, requires dogs to be licensed.Though there are an estimated two million dogs in Cook County, only a few thousand had licenses in 2005. While you may not relish the idea of paying another $5–10 in city fees,

I'd urge you to get your dogs licenses. In Chicago, the applications are now available at your vet's office. Licensing information helps city officials gauge interest in various issues. The more dogs with licenses means the more dogs have a voice. Plus, a license is just another tool (with microchips and ID tags) that can help if, heaven forbid, your pup is ever lost. Some towns prohibit dogs from all parks ("What's a park without dogs?" Cooper asks), while others have designated areas with agility equipment and dog-height water fountains. Specifics of those areas are covered in the corresponding chapters.

The Paws Scale

At some point, we've got to face the facts: Humans and dogs have different tastes. We like eating chocolate and smelling lilacs and covering our bodies with soft cotton. They like eating roadkill and smelling each other's unmentionables and covering their bodies with horse manure.

The parks, beaches, and recreation areas in this book are rated with a dog in mind. Maybe your favorite park has lush gardens, a duck pond, a few acres of perfectly manicured lawns, and sweeping views of a nearby skyline. But unless your dog can run leash-free, swim in the pond, and roll in the grass, that park doesn't deserve a very high rating.

The lowest rating you'll come across in this book is the fire hydrant 🔥. When you see this symbol, it means the park is merely "worth a squat." Visit one of these parks only if your dog just can't hold it any longer. These parks have virtually no other redeeming qualities for canines.

Beyond that, the paws scale starts at one paw 🐾 and goes up to four paws 🐾🐾🐾🐾. A one-paw park isn't a dog's idea of a great time. Maybe it's a tiny park with few trees and too many kids lobbing softballs overhead. Or perhaps it's a magnificent-for-people forest preserve that bans dogs from every inch of land except paved paths and a few grassy parking lots. Four-paw parks, on the other hand, are places your dog will drag you to visit. Some of these areas come as close to dog heaven as you can get. Many have lakes for swimming or zillions of acres for hiking. Some are small, fenced-in, urban areas where leash-free dogs can tear around without danger of running into the road. Just about all four-paw parks give you the option of letting your dog off the leash (although some have restrictions, which, when applicable, are listed in the park description).

In addition to finding paws and hydrants, you'll also notice an occasional foot 👣 symbol in this book. The foot means the park offers something special for the humans in the crowd. You deserve a reward for being such a good chauffeur.

The Dog Lover's Companion is not meant to be a comprehensive guide to all of the parks, dog-friendly hotels, and places to eat in the Chicago area. If I included every single park, this book would be larger than a multi-volume set of the *Encyclopædia Britannica*. Instead, I tried to find the best, dog-friendliest, and most convenient parks. Some counties have so many wonderful parks that Cooper, Natasha, and I ran ourselves ragged deciding which to include and which to leave out. Other areas had such a limited supply of parks that, for the sake of dogs living and visiting there, I ended up listing parks that wouldn't be worth mentioning in other chapters.

Navigating the city of Chicago is typically straightforward, thanks to its basic grid organization. The intersection of State and Madison Streets is considered the center of the city for address purposes—all numbering starts from there. Streets carry either a north or south designation according to their relation to Madison Street. Streets carry an east or west designation (there are far fewer streets with east designations) according to their relation to State Street. Each block starts a new 100. (In terms of distance, eight blocks equals one mile.) For example, River Park is located on Francisco Avenue, 51 blocks north of Madison Street, so it would have the address 5100 N. Francisco Ave.

Chicagoans typically refer to streets in hundreds: Fullerton Avenue is "twenty-four hundred north," not "two thousand, four hundred north." Addresses on diagonal streets lie on the grid as well, and major street signs display the grid coordinate as well as the street name. For the most part, streets on the North Side have names. Most east–west streets on the South Side are numbered, and that number corresponds to the grid (57th Street is 5700 South). The first Chicagoans settled on the shores of Lake Michigan, and today, the lake is our North Pole. If you know where the lake is, you always know which direction is east.

Knowing where a park or hotel is on the grid makes it easy to find. To help you in your quest for the perfect pooch playground, whether local or far-flung, directions to the parks listed in this book are from the nearest major street in the city, with grid coordinates in parentheses in the three Chicago chapters. In the suburbs and outlying counties, directions are from major expressways, highways, or landmarks. Addresses are less standardized in the suburbs: Each municipality has its own numbering system, so next-door neighbors may have totally different numbers if a border falls between them. Howard Avenue, the border between Evanston and Chicago, is a classic example of this. Businesses on the north side of Howard Street are numbered by Evanston's system, businesses across the street are numbered by Chicago's grid, and the two addresses have little relation to one another.

Although I tried to make getting around as easy as possible (remembering my own missed turns and detours), signposts can be confusing, and construction often necessitates finding a new route. Chicagoans tend to be approachable; if you're lost, don't hesitate to ask for directions. But to spend more time actually at the park and less time getting there, I highly recommend picking up a detailed street map before you and your dog set out.

Transportation

Getting around the city of Chicago without a car is simple if you're human. You can hop on a bus, grab the elevated train (known as "the El"), or call a cab, and arrive at your destination quickly, cheaply, and without perfecting your parallel-parking skills. With a dog, however, getting from point A to point B can be a little more challenging. Most days, it may not be a hassle. You no doubt walk to the neighborhood park, groomer, and pet-food store. But there are days when a set of wheels is a dog's best friend. You may need to get to the vet or an emergency-care facility. Some days, you just have to get a change of scenery. Many of the best spots in this book require a car to reach them.

Taxi drivers aren't required to transport your pup, but many of them will, particularly if you look sweet and/or desperate. Slip the spiked collar in your pocket, carry a towel or blanket to limit the dog hair you leave behind, and tip well. If you get a dog-friendly cabbie, by all means, remember his or her cab number for future forays.

As far as public transportation goes, well, it doesn't go very far for dog owners. If you have a small dog, you're good to go: The Chicago Transit Authority (CTA) trains and buses allow dogs in a carrier that can be carried by one person. "Carriers are not permitted to occupy seats or impede customer flow; animals are not permitted to annoy customers." I don't know what that last phrase means exactly, but it makes me laugh, given how people annoy one another on the El most days. The suburban PACE buses have the same policy, as does the private Wendella Riverbus (312/337-1446), which provides an eight-minute ride from the Loop to North Michigan Avenue. The suburban Metra trains do not allow any pets, except for guide dogs.

Now that I've told you the bad news, here's the good news. There are pet transport services that will take you and your dog where you want to go. Many full-service dog-care businesses include a pet taxi as one of their

services. Some of these firms are listed in the Resources section in the back of this book. Car-sharing programs are becoming more prevalent as an alternative to renting or owning a car.

In addition to directions, I've included tips for parking in congested areas. Many of the places Cooper, Natasha, and I sniffed out have ample parking, particularly outside of the city limits. But some city neighborhoods have Residential Parking Permits designed to ensure that people who live in popular areas have a place to park. Daily permits are available to their guests, so if you drive to one of these areas, and have friends who live nearby, it's not a bad idea to ask them for a one-time use daily pass (or for permission to use their parking spot). Even using my suggestions, on a warm summer weekend, you'll find it hard to locate an empty spot in a Lincoln Park public lot. That's life in the city. Consider walking when possible. If you do drive, be patient and relax. After all, going to the park is supposed to be fun.

He, She, It

In this book, whether neutered, spayed, or au naturel, dogs are never referred to as "it." They are either "he" or "she." I alternate pronouns so no dog reading this book will feel left out.

To Leash or Not to Leash...

This is not a question that plagues dogs' minds. Ask just about any normal, red-blooded American dog whether she'd prefer to visit a park on the leash or off, and she'll say, "Arf!" (translation: "Duh!"). No question about it, most dogs would give their canine teeth to frolic about without that cumbersome leash.

When you see the running dog ![running dog symbol] symbol in this book, you'll know that under certain circumstances, your dog can run around in leash-free bliss. Fortunately, Chicago and its environs are home to dozens of such parks, and the numbers have only increased since the first edition of this book. The rest of the parks, forest preserves, and neighborhoods require leashes. In the city of Chicago, the fine for off-leash dogs can be hefty and requires a court appearance; you can't just mail the check as you can with a parking ticket. I wish I could write about the parks where dogs often get away with being scofflaws. Unfortunately, those would be the first parks the local police patrol would hit. I don't advocate breaking the law, because, among other things, I think it increases anti-dog sentiment for all of us. But if you're going to, please follow your conscience and use common sense. Be aware of busy streets and other people using the parks, and of course, remove any evidence of your excursion.

Also, just because dogs are permitted off-leash in certain areas doesn't necessarily mean you should let your dog run free. In county forest preserves and other large tracts of wild land, unless you're sure your dog will come back when you call or will never stray more than a few yards from your side, you should consider keeping her leashed. Natasha's "Find me!" command is strong, but given the choice between a deer and me, well, Bambi would win. An otherwise docile homebody can turn into a savage hunter if the right prey is near. Or your curious dog could perturb a contentious critter. In pursuit of a strange scent, your dog could easily get lost in an unfamiliar area. (Some forest rangers recommend having your dog wear a bright orange collar, vest, or backpack when out in the wilderness.) And there are many places where certain animals would love to have your dog for dinner—and not in a way Miss Manners would condone.

Be careful out there. If your dog really needs leash-free exercise but can't be trusted off-leash in remote areas, she'll be happy to know that several beaches permit well-behaved leashless pooches, as do a growing number of beautiful, fenced dog-exercise areas. But pay attention there, too. Observe the other dogs (and owners) roaming leash-free before you unclick. If you have reason to believe your dog won't play well with others, come back in an hour, when the crowd is likely to have changed.

There's No Business Like Dog Business

There's nothing appealing about bending down with a plastic bag or a piece of newspaper on a chilly morning and grabbing the steaming remnants of what your dog ate for dinner the night before. It's disgusting. Worse yet, you have to hang onto it until you can find a trash can. And how about when the newspaper doesn't endure before you can dispose of it? Yuck! It's enough to make you consider one of those battery-operated canine companions instead. But as gross as it can be to scoop the poop, it's worse to step in it. It's really bad if a child falls in it, or—gasp!—starts eating it. And have you ever walked into a park where few people clean up after their dogs? The stench could make a hog want to hibernate.

Unscooped poop is one of a dog's worst enemies. Public policies banning dogs from parks are enacted because of it. At present, a few good Chicago area parks and beaches that permit dogs are in danger of closing their gates to all canines because of the negligent behavior of a few owners. The waste issue is the first one to come up whenever a neighborhood petitions for a new dog-friendly area, and it is the first thing any public official mentions when asked about dogs in the 'hood. The worst-case scenario is already happening in several suburban communities—dogs are banned from all parks. Their only exercise is a leashed sidewalk stroll or a backyard ball toss. That's no way to live.

Just be responsible and clean up after your dog everywhere you go. (And if there's even a remote chance he'll relieve himself inside, skip the hotels and stores that permit dogs.) Any time you take your dog out, stuff plastic bags in your jackets, your purse, your car, and your pants pockets—anywhere you might be able to pull one out when needed. You can now buy leashes with plastic bag dispensers in the handle, or that clip on to the leash, and many suburbs and some city neighborhoods are adding bag dispensers to their lampposts. Or, if plastic isn't your bag, newspapers work. If it makes it more palatable, bring along a paper bag, too, and put the used newspaper or plastic bag in it. That way you don't have to walk around with dripping paper or a plastic bag whose contents are visible to the world. If you don't enjoy the squishy sensation, try one of those cardboard or plastic pooper-scoopers sold at pet stores. If you don't like bending down, buy a long-handled scooper. There's a scooper for every personality.

I've tried not to lecture about picking up poop through this book, because who wants to be known as the author of the poop book? To keep parks pleasant, I should harp on it in every park description, but there are other notable things to write about in that same space. If I mentioned it in some parks and not others, it only means that the waste debate has been particularly fecund in that area. It does not imply that you don't have to pick up in parks where it is not specifically mentioned.

A final note: Don't pretend not to see your dog while he's doing his bit. Don't pretend to look for it without success. And don't fake scooping it up when you're really just covering it with leaves. I see you. Your dog sees you. The other park-goers see you.

Etiquette Rex: The Well-Mannered Mutt

Though cleaning up after your dog is your responsibility, a dog in a public place has his own responsibilities. Of course, it really boils down to your responsibility again, but the burden of action is on your dog. Etiquette for restaurants and hotels is covered in other sections of this chapter. What follows are some fundamental rules of dog etiquette. I'll go through it quickly, but if your dog's a slow reader, he can go over it again: no vicious dogs; no jumping on people; no incessant barking; no leg lifts on backpacks, human legs, or any other personal objects you'll find hanging around beaches and parks; dogs should come when they're called; dogs should stay on command.

Everyone makes mistakes, and dogs are no exception. Do your best to remedy any consistent problems. It takes patience and it's not always easy. If you need professional help, the Resources section of this book includes contact information for some trainers and behaviorists. Sometimes they suggest the simplest things. During a refresher obedience class at the Anti-Cruelty Society, one of Natasha's teachers mentioned that she found her once-obedient dogs no longer seemed to hear the word "come," perhaps because she

overused it in casual conversation. ("Come here." "Want to come outside?" "Guess who's coming over?") Switching to a command like "Find me" made the recall a game to her dog and, I found, to Natasha, too. As a result, her recall is more reliable at the park.

Safety First

A few essentials will keep your traveling dog happy and healthy.

Beat the heat: If you must leave your dog alone in the car for a few minutes, do so only if it's cool out and you can park in the shade. Never, ever, ever leave a dog in a car with the windows rolled up all the way. Even if it seems cool, the sun's heat passing through the window can kill a dog in a matter of minutes. Roll down the window enough so your dog gets air, but also so there's no danger of your dog getting out or someone breaking in. Make sure your dog has plenty of water.

You also have to watch out for heat exposure when your car is in motion. Certain cars, like hatchbacks, can make a dog in the backseat extra hot, even while you feel OK in the driver's seat.

Try to time your vacation so you don't visit a place when it's extremely warm. Dogs and heat don't get along, especially if the dog isn't used to heat. The opposite is also true. If a dog lives in a hot climate and you take him to a freezing place, it may not be a healthy shift. Check with your vet if you have any doubts. Spring and fall are usually the best times to travel.

Water: Water your dog frequently. Dogs on the road may drink even more than they do at home. Take regular water breaks, or bring a heavy bowl and set it on the floor so your dog always has access to water. I like the foldable nylon bowls that can be shoved in a pocket and filled from a water fountain, sink, or bottle. When hiking, be sure to carry enough for you and a thirsty dog.

Rest stops: Stop and unwater your dog. There's nothing more miserable than being stuck in a car when you can't find a rest stop. No matter how tightly you cross your legs and try to think of the desert, you're certain you'll burst within the next minute... so imagine how a dog feels when the urge strikes, and he can't tell you the problem (although Cooper and Natasha seem to have perfected their high-pitched whines to make themselves clear to me). There are plenty of rest stops along the major freeways, many with clearly marked dog areas. I've also included many parks close to expressways for dogs who need a good stretch with their bathroom break.

How frequently you stop depends on your dog's bladder. If your dog is constantly running out the doggy door at home to relieve himself, you may want to stop every hour. Others can go significantly longer without being uncomfortable. Watch for any signs of restlessness and gauge it for yourself.

Car safety: Even the experts differ on how a dog should travel in a car. Some suggest doggy safety belts, available at pet-supply stores. Others firmly believe in keeping a dog kenneled. They say it's safer for the dog if there's an accident, and it's safer for the driver because there's no dog underfoot. Still others say you should just let your dog hang out without straps and boxes. They believe that if there's an accident, at least the dog isn't trapped in a cage. Natasha says that dogs enjoy this more, anyway.

I'm a follower of the last school of thought. Natasha loves sticking her snout out of the windows to smell the world go by. The danger is that if the car kicks up a pebble or bothers a bee, Natasha's nose and eyes could be injured. So far, she's been OK, as has every other dog who has explored Chicago with us, but I've heard about dogs who needed to be treated for bee stings to the nose because of this practice. If in doubt, try opening the window just enough so your dog can't stick out much snout. You'll end up with dog snot on the window, but a trip to the car wash is cheaper than a trip to the vet.

Whatever travel style you choose, your pet will be more comfortable if he has his own blanket or bed with him. One veterinarian brings a faux-sheepskin blanket for his dogs. At night in the hotel, the sheepskin doubles as the dog's bed. On long trips, Cooper lounges on his bed in the back of the station wagon, and then drags it in at night.

Planes: Air travel is even more controversial. Many people think that a dog flying in the cargo hold, like nothing but a piece of luggage, is a kind of animal abuse. Many factors outside of your control, like flight delays, weather emergencies, and luggage intended for Seattle winding up in Saskatchewan, could impact your dog's safe landing. If you decide to transport your dog by plane, there are some basic guidelines to follow. Fly nonstop, and make sure you schedule takeoff and arrival times when the temperature is below 80°F (but not bitterly cold in winter). Be sure to consult the airline about regulations, required certificates, approved carriers, and, of course, fees. Most airlines now prohibit dogs in cargo holds during the hot summer months. Check with your vet to make sure your pooch is healthy enough to fly. If you have a small dog, look into the possibility of having her in a carrier underneath the seat in front of you.

The question of tranquilizing a dog for a plane journey is also difficult. Some vets think it's insane to give a dog a sedative before flying. They say a dog will be calmer and less fearful without a disorienting drug. Others think it's crazy not to afford your dog the little relaxation he might not otherwise get without a tranquilizer. Discuss the issue with your vet, who will take into account the trip length and your dog's personality.

Medical emergencies: Unfortunately, some pet emergencies are unavoidable. My former border collie/shepherd mix, Boris, who died in 2001, once scratched his retina walking through the wilds of Wisconsin. We spent several hours trying to find a veterinarian to help us with an eye patch and some ointment until we got home. My advice: Know the location of the closest vet before you need it. A listing of animal hospitals in and around Chicago, including those open 24 hours, is included in the back of this book. I also recommend taking a copy of *Pet First Aid* (by the American Red Cross) and a first-aid kit with you on your adventures.

The Ultimate Doggy Bag

Your dog can't pack his own bags, and even if he could, he'd probably fill them with rawhide chews and pigs' ears. It's important to stash some of those in your dog's vacation kit, but here are other handy items to bring along: bowls, bedding, a brush, towels (for those muddy days), pooper-scoopers, water, food, prescription drugs, tags, treats, toys, balls, and—of course—this book.

Make sure your dog is wearing his license, identification tag, and rabies tag. On a long trip, you may even want to bring along your dog's rabies certificate. Some parks, hotels, and campgrounds require rabies and licensing information. You never know how particular they'll be.

It's a good idea to snap a disposable ID on your dog's collar, too, showing a cell phone number or the name, address, and phone number of where you'll be vacationing, or of a friend who'll be home to field calls. That way, if your dog should get lost, at least the finder won't be calling your empty house.

Some people think dogs should drink only water brought from home, so their bodies don't have to get used to too many new things. I've never had a problem giving my dogs tap water from other parts of the country, nor has anyone else I know. Most vets think your dog will be fine drinking tap water in most U.S. cities. But if your dog has a particularly sensitive stomach, or you're in parts of Michigan and Wisconsin where the iron content in the water is high, it can't hurt to bring some extra from home.

Bone Appétit

In some European countries, dogs enter restaurants and dine alongside their folks as if they were people, too. (Or at least they sit and watch and drool while their people dine.) Not so in the United States. Rightly or wrongly, dogs are considered a health threat here. But many health inspectors say they see no reason why clean, well-behaved dogs shouldn't be permitted inside a restaurant.

Fortunately, you don't have to take your dog to a foreign country in order to eat together. Chicago is full of restaurants with outdoor tables, and many of them welcome dogs to join their people for an alfresco experience. The law on outdoor dining varies among municipalities, and you'll encounter many interpretations of it. In general, as long as your dog doesn't go inside a restaurant (even to get to a beer garden in the back) and isn't near the food-preparation areas, it's probably legal. The decision is then up to the restaurant proprietor. Some require that your dog be tied to the perimeter fence of the outdoor area. Chicago bars and pubs that don't have full-service kitchens can welcome dogs. In many neighborhoods, these places are the equivalent of a coffeehouse; somewhere to hang out and chat during a long winter afternoon. Some also allow you to order pizza from the restaurant down the block (you know, from the place that can't allow dogs inside). However, some bar owners feel the health department has been arbitrary in enforcing the code. Says one whose establishment was in the first edition of this book, but is no longer

dog-friendly: "We used to let dogs in all the time to roam around the bar with their owners. But one day a dog barked at the wrong guy, and, bam, the health department was here in 10 minutes. So we don't do that anymore."

In 2006 several local restaurant owners and chefs began working with Alderman Walter Burnett, Jr., of the 27th Ward, to clarify Chicago Health Department rules by creating an ordinance that would let dogs eat next to people in outdoor cafés. At press time, the Chicago City Council was still considering the law.

The restaurants, bars, and coffeehouses listed in this book have been double- and triple-checked as dog-friendly eateries. But keep in mind that rules can change and restaurants can close, so I highly recommend phoning before you set your stomach on a particular kind of cuisine. If you can't call first, be sure to ask the manager of the restaurant for permission before you sit down with your sidekick. Remember, it's the restaurant owner, not you, who will be in trouble if someone complains to the health department. Remember, too, that the places to eat included in this book are just a sample. If your furry friend has a friendly face, you'll likely paw your way into many others.

Some fundamental rules of restaurant etiquette: Dogs shouldn't beg from other diners, no matter how delicious the steak looks. They should not attempt to get their snouts (or their entire bodies) up on the table. They should be clean, quiet, and as unobtrusive as possible. If your dog leaves a good impression with the management and other customers, it will help pave the way for all the other dogs who want to dine alongside their best friends in the future.

A Room at the Inn

Good dogs make great hotel guests. They don't steal towels, and they don't get drunk and keep the neighbors up all night. Chicago is full of lodgings whose owners welcome dogs. This book lists dog-friendly accommodations of all types, from motels and cottages to elegant hotels—but the basic etiquette rules are the same everywhere.

Most dogs shouldn't be left alone in a hotel room. Leaving a dog alone in a strange place invites trouble. Scared, nervous dogs may tear apart drapes, carpeting, and furniture. They may even injure themselves. They might also bark nonstop and scare the daylights out of the housekeeper. That said, sometimes there aren't any options. If you're traveling with your dog on a business trip, your boss may not appreciate your taking your companion to your client's office uninvited. Some hotels offer pet-sitting services or dog-walking services if you need to be away. Others have notification systems to alert housekeeping of the presence of a dog in the room. Others require—and provide—crates. Details on these policies are included in the individual hotel descriptions. Some veterinarians recommend some of those sedatives left over from the plane flight. Again, only you know your dog's comfort level with new people and places.

Only bring a house-trained dog to a lodging. How would you like a house-guest to choose the middle of your bedroom as her spot to relieve herself?

Make sure your pooch is flea-free. Otherwise, future guests will be itching to leave.

Even if the hotel provides pet beds, it helps to bring your dog's bed or blanket along for the night. Your dog will feel (and smell) more at home and will be less tempted to jump on the bed. If your dog sleeps on the bed with you at home, bring a sheet or towel and put it on top of the bed so the hotel's bedspread won't get furry or dirty. I carry a lint brush or pet-hair sponge whenever I travel with dogs. In times of desperation, masking tape works to remove pet hair from the furniture. Natasha, Roger (one of our foster dogs), and I used a whole roll at our friends Judy and Rob's cabin one summer weekend. We'll never forget the sponge again.

After a few days in a hotel, some dogs come to think of it as home. They get territorial. When another hotel guest walks by, it's "Bark! Bark!" When the housekeeper knocks, it's "Bark! Snarl! Bark! Gnash!" Keep your dog quiet, or you'll both find yourselves looking for a new home away from home. Cooper and Natasha like to listen to NPR when I'm not at home. (I guess Natasha has a crush on Ira Glass, like every other woman in Chicago.) So, leaving the radio on in a hotel room helps distract them from the possibility that people in other rooms may be ordering room service without her.

For some strange reason, many lodgings prefer small dogs as guests. All I can say is, "Yip! Yap!" It's really ridiculous. Large dogs are often much calmer and quieter than their tiny, high-energy kin. I had some managers say to me, "Well, of course, we can't allow big dogs," but no one could ever explain the rationale. Many managers who had a size limit for pets conceded that they did not have a scale at the front desk and were likely to let in most well-mannered mutts.

If you're in a location where you can't find a hotel that will accept you and your big brute, it's time to try a sell job. Let the manager know how good and quiet your dog is (if he is). Promise he won't eat the bathtub or run around and shake all over the hotel. Offer a deposit or sign a waiver, even if they're not required for small dogs. It helps if your sweet, soppy-eyed pooch is at your side to convince the decision-maker.

You could sneak your dog into hotels, but I don't recommend trying it… unless you enjoy racing in and out of your room as if you're ducking the dog-catcher. It's better to avoid feeling like a criminal and move on to a more dog-friendly location, particularly because there are so many. It's helpful to know that just about every La Quinta hotel welcomes dogs under 50 pounds without an extra fee. Some have more lenient rules than others. I also found that a healthy percentage of two budget chains, Red Roof Inn and Motel 6, permit pooches. On the other end of the price scale, Kimpton Boutique Hotels, W, and Loews pride themselves on being pet-friendly. Space precludes me from listing all the locations, but if you find yourself in a town anywhere in the United States, and you don't know where to look for a dog-friendly lodging, those are good starting points.

The lodgings described in this book are for dogs who obey all the rules. When possible, I provide a range of rates for each lodging, from the least expensive room during low season to the priciest room during high season. When a room price gets into the thousands of dollars, you know we're talking about apartment-sized suites, not the standard double bed.

Some lodgings charge extra for your dog. Some charge a daily fee, others assess one fee for the entire length of a dog's stay, and still others ask for a refundable damage deposit—these details are noted in the lodging description. A few places still ask for nothing more than your dog's promise that you'll be on your best behavior. If no extra charge is mentioned in a listing, it means your dog can stay with you for free.

Also included in this book are websites for those lodgings whose site names aren't too long and convoluted. (When the URL takes up more space than this sentence, I generally don't include it.) Not all lodgings have a website, but when they do, it can be very helpful in deciding where to stay. Sites often provide lots of details, photos, and a way to reserve online. Many managers told me better rates could be found on the Web. But generally, when staying with a pooch, it's a good idea to reserve by phone so you can let the staff know you'll be bringing your beast. I ran into some websites and 800-numbers that promised a specific property was pet-friendly—but when I called the front desk, I heard a different story. Policies do change, and fees are often at the discretion of management. I recommend getting any reservations in writing, so that you don't have problems when you arrive, bags and leash in hand.

Natural Troubles

Chances are your adventuring will go without a hitch, but you should always be prepared to deal with trouble. Make sure you know the basics of animal first aid before you embark on a long journey with your dog.

The more common woes—ticks, mosquitoes, poison oak, and skunks—can make life with a traveling dog a somewhat trying experience. Ticks, which can carry Lyme disease, are hard to avoid in many parts of Wisconsin and Michigan, although they are less common within the Chicago city limits. Always check yourself and your dog all over after a day in tick country. Don't forget to check ears and between the toes. If you see an unattached tick, just pull it straight out with tweezers, not with your bare hands. An attached tick can come out with tweezers, too. By turning the attached tick counterclockwise, the barbs on its mouth should bend and widen the opening the tick has bored into the skin. All of this occurs with no pain to the pup. After only a few gentle turns, without any pulling, the tick slides out of the pet and becomes detached. A good tick check feels like petting to Cooper and Natasha, so they usually don't put up a fuss. The one time I did find an engorged tick on Natasha's chest I was significantly more disturbed by the removal process than she.

The tiny deer ticks that carry Lyme disease are difficult to find. Consult your veterinarian if your dog is lethargic for a few days, has a fever, loses her appetite, or becomes lame. These symptoms could indicate Lyme disease. Some vets recommend a new vaccine that is supposed to prevent the onset of Lyme disease.

A growing problem in the Chicago area is mosquito-borne illness. One of two diseases dogs can get from mosquito bites is heartworm, a parasite that is transferred from one infected dog to another by the insect. Heartworm is easily prevented with a pill (daily or monthly) given to the dog during mosquito season, June through December. Before being prescribed the preventative, dogs are given a quick blood test to assure that they are free of the parasite. The medication kills any infection. Most veterinarians say dogs living in the area should be on heartworm preventative all summer. If you're visiting the Great Lakes from a drier climate, talk to your vet about what kind of prevention would be appropriate for your dog.

In 2002, there was one case of a dog dying from West Nile virus in the Chicago area. Family Pet's Dr. Royal expects that, though rare, West Nile will continue to be a summertime hazard, particularly for older and infirm dogs. There are many mosquito repellents on the market for dogs. Dr. Royal strongly suggests you discuss the use of any product—homeopathic or not—with your vet before using it on your dog, as not all mosquito repellents have been tested on pets yet. (She cautions that tea tree oil, for example, is toxic to cats.) Common sense applies to dodging mosquitoes: Avoid areas of stagnant, standing water, especially around dusk and dawn. If you're getting bitten, chances are your dog is, too.

Poison oak, ivy, and sumac are also common menaces. Get familiar (but not *too* familiar) with them through a friend who knows nature or through a guided nature walk. Dogs don't generally have reactions to poison oak, but they can easily pass its oils on to people. If you think your dog has made contact with some poison oak, avoid petting her until you can get home and bathe her (preferably with rubber gloves). If you do pet her before you can wash her, wash your hands immediately and don't touch your eyes.

Blastomycosis is a fungal infection found in dogs, people, and sometimes cats that has caused concern in the Great Lakes area in recent years. Dogs contract the disease by inhaling the spores of the fungus from wet soil. While the fungus lives in the lake and river valleys throughout the area, the disease is rare. Dr. Royal says she sees only a few cases each year, and those tend to be young male dogs who like to dig. Blastomycosis is treatable, but its symptoms are often confused with kennel cough, pneumonia, and other illnesses.

poison oak

When left untreated, it can be fatal. Dr. Royal says there's no reason to limit a dog's playing in wet areas or swimming in nearby rivers or ponds. But if after doing so, your dog appears ill, mention blastomycosis among the possibilities to your vet.

If your dog loses a contest with a skunk (and she always will), rinse her eyes first with plain warm water, then bathe her with dog shampoo. Towel her off, then apply tomato juice. You can easily go through four gallons of the stuff before a large pup starts smelling less offensive. If you can't get tomato juice, try using a solution of one pint of vinegar per gallon of water to decrease the stink.

Ruffing It Together

Considering that when we're at home, Natasha prefers the cushioned comfort of a wing-back chair to a flimsy dog bed on the floor, the idea of her camping, sleeping on the hard ground in a tent, is, well, about as funny as a cat on a leash. But I understand other people—and dogs—think this sounds like a perfectly good way to spend a vacation. For that reason, we've included limited information on campgrounds and camping destinations in the Beyond the Windy City chapter, as well as some suburban chapters.

All Illinois state parks require dogs to be kept in a tent or vehicle at night, and leashed during the day. If you're camping with your dog, chances are you're also hiking with him. Even if you're not hiking for long, you have to watch your dog's paws, especially the paws of those who are fair of foot. Rough terrain can cause a dog's pads to become raw and painful, making it almost impossible for him to walk. Several types of dog boots are available for such feet. He may feel silly. You may feel silly. But it's easier to carry the booties than to carry your dog home.

Be sure to bring plenty of water for you and your pooch. Stop frequently to wet your whistles. Some veterinarians recommend against letting your dog drink out of a stream because he could ingest giardia or other internal parasites, but it's not always easy to stop a thirsty dog. Some outdoor experts say it's dangerous to leave even a tethered dog outside your tent at night. The dog can escape or become bait for some creature hungry for a late dinner. So, make sure you buy a tent built for two.

A Dog in Need

If you don't currently have a dog but could provide a good home for one, or you have one and have room for two, I'd like to make a plea on behalf of all the unwanted dogs who will be euthanized tomorrow—and the day after that and the day after that. Animal shelters and humane organizations are overflowing with dogs who would devote their lives to being your best buddy, your faithful traveling companion, and a dedicated listener to all your tales.

The City of Chicago's David R. Lee Animal Care Shelter takes in more than 30,000 lost, abandoned, or surrendered animals each year. That works out to more than 82 animals every single day! In the Resources section of this book, I've included information on the David R. Lee Animal Care Shelter, Animal Adoption Associates (Natasha's previous residence), Red Door Animal Shelter, PAWS Chicago, and many other area shelters. If you can't take on another pet permanently, consider fostering a puppy or dog until he finds a new home. Fostering helps dogs learn the kind of behavior that makes them adoptable and opens up one more space for another stray.

Once you have a pup, remember to control the existing pet population by spaying and neutering your dogs. Several groups, including PAWS, the David R. Lee Animal Care Shelter, and the Anti-Cruelty Society offer low-cost spay and neuter programs. A number of low-cost programs operate in the suburbs as well, including through the Evanston Animal Shelter, the South Suburban Humane Society in Chicago Heights, and the People's Animal Welfare Society in Tinley Park. Contact information is in the Resources chapter.

Need one last nudge? Consider the words of Roger Caras, the late host of the annual Westminster Dog Show: "Dogs are not our whole life, but they make our lives whole."

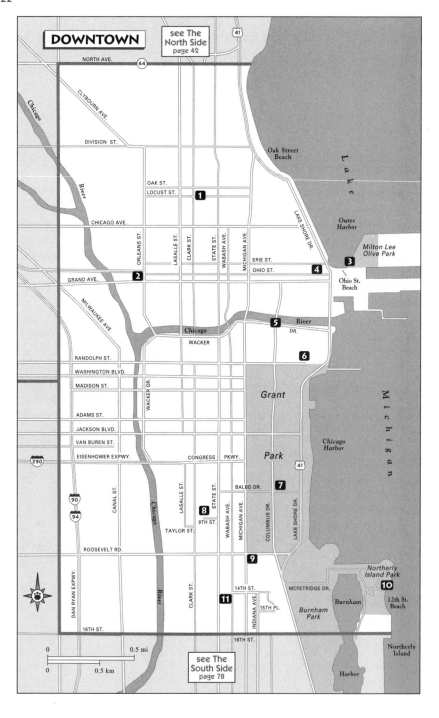

DOWNTOWN

see The North Side page 42

NORTH AVE.

64

CLYBOURN AVE.

DIVISION ST.

Chicago

River

OAK ST.

LOCUST ST.

1

Oak Street Beach

CHICAGO AVE.

ORLEANS ST.

LASALLE ST.

CLARK ST.

STATE ST.

WABASH AVE.

MICHIGAN AVE.

ERIE ST.

OHIO ST.

GRAND AVE.

2

MILWAUKEE AVE.

Chicago

WACKER

River

DR.

5

6

RANDOLPH ST.

WASHINGTON BLVD.

MADISON ST.

WACKER DR.

ADAMS ST.

JACKSON BLVD.

VAN BUREN ST.

EISENHOWER EXPWY.

CONGRESS PKWY.

Grant

Park

LASALLE ST.

STATE ST.

BALBO DR.

7

8

9TH ST.

WABASH AVE.

MICHIGAN AVE.

COLUMBUS DR.

LAKE SHORE DR.

TAYLOR ST.

290

90

94

CANAL ST.

Chicago

River

ROOSEVELT RD.

9

DAN RYAN EXPWY.

CLARK ST.

14TH ST.

11

INDIANA AVE.

15TH PL.

McFETRIDGE DR.

16TH ST.

16TH ST.

LAKE SHORE DR.

41

41

LAKE SHORE DR.

L a k e

Outer Harbor

Milton Lee Olive Park

3

Ohio St. Beach

4

M i c h i g a n

Chicago Harbor

Northerly Island Park

10

12th St. Beach

Burnham

Burnham Park

Northerly Island

Harbor

0   0.5 mi

0   0.5 km

see The South Side page 78

CHAPTER 1

Downtown

When Frank Sinatra sang that Chicago was "my kind of town," it was the Downtown area, with the Magnificent Mile, State Street (that great street), and the rest of the Loop in all its glory, that seem to have first captured his attention. With office high-rises, that loud El train making its loop, and many of the available open spaces dedicated to parking lots rather than parks, Downtown may seem better suited to singers and salespeople than to those with their eyes on a doggy destination.

But the glory of Grant Park alone is more than many dogs get in other cities. And the cosmopolitan air of the shopping and restaurant districts downtown makes most pooches feel wanted. Small dogs are everywhere, especially in the Gold Coast and Streeterville areas, where high-rise apartments don't give larger dogs room to stretch their four legs. On almost any day in these neighborhoods, you'll see floppy ears and little eyes sticking out of striped bags, backpacks, and purses as they take in the sights and sounds.

Recent years have seen more Chicagoans choosing to live in the Loop, particularly the South Loop, instead of taking the train to and from work each

PICK OF THE LITTER—DOWNTOWN

BEST DOG PARKS
Lakeshore East Dog Park, Magnificent Mile (page 31)
Grant Bark Park, South Loop (page 39)

BEST PLACE TO EAT
Brasserie Jo, River North (page 28)

BEST PLACES TO STAY
Hotel Burnham, The Loop (page 37)
W Chicago City Center, The Loop (page 38)

BEST EVENT
Museum of Contemporary Art Family Day, Magnificent
Mile (page 30)

day. That's made these neighborhoods both more people-friendly and more dog-friendly, including pet-centric businesses opening their doors and community efforts to add more dog runs and parks.

As many of the area's eight million residents head here to work, shop, or check out a museum, driving anywhere Downtown can be a challenge. Once you memorize the one-way streets and adjust to the summer schedule of raising the bridges over the river, the weaving and honking of cab drivers can make even a native nervous. But metered parking on the streets does exist, and depending on the day and time—not to mention your luck—you may find a free space. The farther west you are, generally, the easier it is to find one. Parking lots are almost always nearby throughout Downtown, so if you're willing to pay (expect to spend an average of $12 an hour), you'll be able to find a space. Many lots accept credit cards.

Though parking can be difficult, the good news for you and your dog is that walking is not. On a nice day, most of the destinations in this chapter are a decent walk from each other, and there are plenty of distractions to occupy you both along the way. Your dog will likely want to stop and smell the roses. And the popcorn. And the seagulls. And the Frango mints. Maybe Sinatra should have sung that Chicago is a dog's kind of town.

This chapter includes parks, places to stay, places to eat, and other attractions between North Avenue (1600 North) and 16th Street (1600 South), and Lake Michigan and Halsted Street (800 West).

Gold Coast and Old Town

These two neighborhoods are descriptively named: In the fancy Gold Coast, you may well see rhinestone collars and designer leather leashes. In Old Town, your fun and frolic may be in quaint brick courtyards or in front of some of the city's most interesting and historic brownstones and town houses. Nearby Oak Street Beach is a gateway to the southern end of Lincoln Park, and you'll find people and pets hoofing it back and forth to the park most hours of the day and evening here. In fact, thanks to the constant activity, these are considered some of the safest neighborhoods for a nighttime walk, as long as you stay east of Wells Street. The famous (or infamous) intersection of Rush and Division Streets (100 East, 1200 North) is celebratory ground zero on the rare occasions when a Chicago sports team actually wins a title.

These adjacent neighborhoods are well north of Madison Street, the city's north–south border, but they're more often considered part of Downtown than the North Side, although you may also hear locals refer to them as "the Near North." This area is bordered by the lake on the east, Halsted Street (800 West) on the west, Chicago Avenue (800 North) on the south, and North Avenue (1600 North) on the north.

PARKS, BEACHES, AND RECREATION AREAS

1 Washington Square Park

😺😺 (See Downtown map on page 22)

Like Speakers' Corner in London's Hyde Park, Washington Square was once a popular spot for public orators to get up on their soapboxes about any number of issues. Today, the Newberry Library, just north of Washington Square Park, performs Bughouse Square Debates each July, when prominent thinkers from all over the city come to discourse. Public cheers, jeers, and barks are welcome additions to the debates. The rest of the year, this small, friendly park provides a welcome tree-lined respite from the hustle and bustle of the rest of the Gold Coast, particularly for those who live in the neighborhood. The small, square park has a few sidewalks for a promenade, but grass and trees are the attraction for locals.

Look for street parking on the major streets, as the side streets are permit parking for residents; or turn to one of several nearby pay lots. From Chicago Avenue (800 North), take Dearborn Parkway (50 West) north to Walton Street (930 North). 901 N. Clark St.

PLACES TO EAT

Cactus: The bar stool cushions made out of life preservers and the fishnet decor made Natasha think there was swimming nearby. Unfortunately for her, there's about as much water as you'd expect in a place called Cactus. The

outdoor patio is the epicenter of summer action near Rush Street. Cute dogs are likely to be passed some bar food. 1112 N. State St.; 312/642-5999.

Cucina Bella Osteria & Wine Bar: Possibly the city's most beloved dog-friendly eatery, Cucina Bella treats dogs like family. Pups are provided with free pasta, but, of course, only in the outdoor seating in summer. While your dog enjoys her pasta and treats, you ought to order the fried stuffed olives. Cucina Bella Trattoria, the restaurant's North Side outpost (642 W. Diversey Pkwy; 773/868-1119), is equally accommodating. The restaurant is five blocks west of Wells Street, north of North Avenue. 1612 N. Sedgwick; 312/274-1119.

PLACES TO STAY

Sutton Place Hotel: You might like the tucked-away yet central location of this 246-room Gold Coast hotel. But what your dog will like is that the doormen keep dog treats in their pockets. This is such a common practice that even neighborhood pups swing by for a treat on their morning constitutionals. Dogs under 62 pounds (yes, an odd number), are welcome with a $200 refundable damage deposit. Dogs are not allowed to be left alone in the art deco guest rooms, but the hotels will help you make arrangements for a dog walker's outing to nearby Lincoln Park if you have to be away. Rates are $159–395, but website specials are available. The hotel is on the corner of Rush Street and Bellevue Place, just blocks west of Lake Shore Drive. 21 E. Bellevue Pl.; 312/266-2100; www.suttonplace.com.

River North

Cooper thinks the city should change the name of this increasingly friendly area to "Rover North," because there are so many great things for him and his furry friends to do here. Understandably, residents seem to prefer the current moniker, as it's more descriptive of the location of this community north of the Chicago River.

A fan of the good life, Cooper appreciates the way dogs are welcomed into the everyday ebb and flow of the businesses here. On State Street, the new **Perfect Pear Gallery** (720 N. State St.; www.perfectpeargallery.com) is manned by Tina, a well-mannered pug, and hosts many artists who both love and depict dogs. **Bloomingdale's Home + Furniture** store (600 N. Wabash Ave.; 312/324-7500) welcomes leashed dogs of all sizes. Most mutts run for the Bark Avenue department, but Cooper doesn't mind taking a minute to check out the rehabbed landmark Medinah Temple, home to the new store. **Tails in the City** (1 E. Delaware Pl., 312/649-0347; www.tailsinthecity.com) will have anything you forgot to pack for your pampered pet. You might want to run a brush through your fur before you go in; the store hosted an *America's Next Top Dog Model* contest last year.

This area runs from north of the Chicago River to Chicago Avenue (800 North), and from Michigan Avenue (100 East) to Halsted Street (800 West).

PARKS, BEACHES, AND RECREATION AREAS

2 Ohio Place Park

🐾🐾🐾🦮 (See Downtown map on page 22)

This odd, long lot stretches narrowly along the I-90/94 Expressway entrance at Orleans Street. Owned by the city of Chicago, rather than the Chicago Park District, it operates as an unofficial DFA, its sign simply stating, "Responsible pet owners welcome." Because it isn't an official Park District dog area, it doesn't have the reassuring double gates of most DFAs. Few dog-run users here remember to close the gates, meaning a quick glance at both ends of the long park is necessary before unclipping the leash. Locals hope the Park District will acquire the land and convert it to a legal DFA soon.

Given the lack of amenities—double gates, water fountains, and benches, to name a few—this run wouldn't rate very many paws in more spacious suburbs. But given the lack of open space in the heart of Downtown, not to mention off-leash space, most mutts would rather have this than a mere postage stamp–size place to squat. Users seem to pick up the graveled area regularly, and given that there are no adjacent high-rises to trap smells, the run doesn't have that distinctive odor of some runs.

Dogs who love nothing more than to chase tennis balls could play fetch here for hours without any complaints. Unlike some dog runs, the space is

DOG-EAR YOUR CALENDAR

The first Saturday in May, rain or shine (or, occasionally, snow), the Anti-Cruelty Society holds its annual **Bark in the Park.** The 5K walk/run is now one of the oldest and best-known local animal fundraisers, and one of the few in which dogs can actually earn their keep. Bark in the Park is held at Montrose Harbor (4400 North); dogs and their people can solicit pledges for completing the walk or collect a flat donation. The event has become so popular that running the course is difficult for anyone except greyhounds and early birds, but the walk, where dogs often outnumber people, is a dog lover's dream. After the walk, there are agility demonstrations, photo sessions, behaviorists and veterinarians, and human- and canine-appropriate lunch. 157 W. Grand Ave. (Anti-Cruelty Society) 312/644-8338; www.barkinthepark.org.

wide enough to allow several enthusiastic retrievers to chase at once. The run is on the southwest corner of Ohio Street (600 North) and Orleans Street (326 West), north of the Office Depot store.

PLACES TO EAT

Brasserie Jo: Chef Joho gives complimentary servings of steak tartare (unseasoned, nicely paired with a bowl of water) to all canines whose owners have dinner outside at this French bistro. 59 W. Hubbard St.; 312/595-0800.

Brett's Kitchen: After a nice long walk peering through the many basement windows in the River North gallery district, Natasha likes to rest for a few minutes at this long-standing Franklin Street eatery. Visitors on leashes hang out on the wooden benches circling the trees in all but the coldest

weather; a new outdoor seating area gives everyone more room to linger over breakfast in the summer. Natasha may not know much about art, but she knows what she likes: being given a few of Brett's french fries and homemade quick breads. 233 W. Superior St.; 312/664-6354.

Mambo Grill: This 10-year-old Latin American bar and grill features Cuban and Brazilian cuisine, and dogs are welcome to live *la vida loca* at the outdoor café, which seats 20. 412 N. Clark St.; 312/467-9797.

Scoozi: Every Monday in fair weather is "Doggie Dining" on the outdoor patio of this Italian eatery. Dogs mix, mingle, and chow down on a special menu with Muttini, Puppy Pizza, Bow Wow Burger and Polenta Fries, and K-9 Cannoli. 410 W. Huron St.; 312/943-5900.

PLACES TO STAY

Holiday Inn, Mart Plaza: A swankier spot than typically comes to mind when Holiday Inns are mentioned, this 521-room high-rise sits just west of the mammoth Merchandise Mart. All dogs are allowed without any fees or deposits. A Walgreens drugstore is on the first floor of the building, and the lot has plenty of pay parking. Rates start at $144. 350 N. Orleans St.; 312/836-5000; www.holidayinn.com.

House of Blues Hotel: This was once one of the most dog-friendly hotels in the city. Now that House of Blues Hotel is no longer part of the Loews chain, it is simply average. There's no extra charge for coming with your pup, but there's no special treatment either. Room rates range $179–$299. If arriving by cab, tell the driver Marina City, rather than House of Blues Hotel. The Hotel is north of the Chicago River on Dearborn Parkway. The valet area is up the ramp, off the busy street. 333 N. Dearborn Pkwy.; 312/245-0333; www.hob.com or www.loewshotels.com.

Streeterville and the Magnificent Mile

The term "Magnificent Mile" was coined in the 1940s by Arthur Rubloff, the real estate developer responsible for much of the city's grandeur. He meant it to refer to the fancy shops—such as Tiffany and Chanel—that have attracted shoppers to this stretch of Michigan Avenue. The name stuck and has come to apply to the area as a whole, perhaps because so much of it is magnificent. This small area, which runs from the Chicago River (100 North) to Division Street (1200 North) and from Lake Michigan to Michigan Avenue (100 East), is home to a large concentration of dog-loving hoteliers, retailers, and restaurateurs. Streeterville and the Magnificent Mile are home to many stores, like **Neiman Marcus** (737 N. Michigan Ave.; 312/642-5900), that don't seem to worry about an errant tail or a little fur on the floor. For pooches who love

DIVERSION

Your dog's plenty fun to play with, of course. But should you not want to wake him while he sleeps (let sleeping dogs lie and all that), **Dan Crowley** can keep you entertained, dog lover's style. For 17 years Crowley has been sculpting custom finger puppets. You send him printed photos of your pooch, plus a bio about his unique personality. Two weeks later you get a one-of-a-kind puppet portrait out of Fimo clay. Each puppet sculpture comes on a signed wooden base. There's room for your pet's name on the base. But Crowley does such a good job, no ID will be necessary. Put it on the mantle or have a puppet show; it's up to you. Puppets are $40 each. 773/275-8598; www.dancrowleystudio.com.

attention (and Natasha asks, "Who doesn't?"), walking through these streets is a day in dog heaven.

PARKS, BEACHES, AND RECREATION AREAS

🖪 Milton Lee Olive Park

🐾🐾 (See Downtown map on page 22)

Along the lakefront at the Water Filtration Plant (the busiest water-filtration plant in the country, in fact), Ohio Street Beach is now off-limits to dogs all year, but the adjacent park land with grass is still fair game. North of Navy Pier, east of Lake Shore Drive, Milton Lee Olive Park sometimes get overcrowded with tourists spilling over from Navy Pier. But more often than not, particularly October–April, this area is an overlooked Downtown attraction. The grass is green, and life is good.

There's a parking lot on Navy Pier, but a better option is to exit Lake Shore Drive at Grand Avenue (530 North) and park to the west of the drive, where lots will be less expensive and metered parking is a possibility. Signs marking Navy Pier are generally clear and plentiful. 500 N. Lake Shore Dr.

🖪 Lake Shore Park

🐾 (See Downtown map on page 22)

Within view of the stepped terraces of the new **Museum of Contemporary Art** (OK, it opened almost a decade ago, but locals still refer to it as new), Lake Shore Park is the neighborhood gathering place for folks who live in this tourist-heavy area. Any day the weather is decent, you'll see plenty of neighborhood dogs with their families, as well as visiting dogs walking with their hotel concierges. The park has a friendly vibe and an upbeat, urban atmosphere. Be sure to check the MCA's calendar (220 E. Chicago Ave.;

312/280-2660; www.mcachicago.org). The museum offers regular "family days" where the whole family—even dogs—is welcome in the museum's sculpture garden. Family day often includes demonstrations by dogs expert in flyball and other tricks.

If you're staying in the area or Downtown for an event, this is a good, friendly place to escape the concrete jungle, but it doesn't merit a stop if you're not in the neighborhood. The park runs from Fairbanks Court (254 East) to Lake Shore Drive, between Pearson Street (830 North) and Chicago Avenue. 808 N. Lake Shore Dr.

5 River Esplanade Park and Riverwalk

🐾🐾 (See Downtown map on page 22)

The south bank of the Chicago River from Michigan Avenue to Lake Michigan is a lower-level landscaped lair called Riverwalk. The walk, which is home to restaurants, boat tour and river taxi launches, and entrances to some nearby hotels, also sports a flat open space for a roll in the grass. It connects to the lakefront bike path without having to weave through the traffic above. Like many green spaces in the urban heart of the city, this isn't a park in which to run sprints, but instead a place to stretch one's paws, squat, and take in the scents. Riverwalk is also home to the city's largest piece of public art, a 336-foot-long mural showing the history of the Chicago River. The nearby River Esplanade Park at McClurg Court (300 East) is another nice spot for watching the boats go by. Steps down to the Riverwalk are easily spotted at many of the River's major intersections. 401 E. River Dr.

6 Lakeshore East Dog Park

🐾🐾🐾🐾🐕🦴 (See Downtown map on page 22)

If you just stumbled upon this dog park one day while out for a stroll, you'd know right way that something was out-of-the-ordinary. Even the standard wrought iron dog park fence isn't standard: It's curved and allows ample room at each entrance for leashing and unleashing. The park is landscaped with solid surfaces and grass, not to mention plenty of trees, shrubs, and daylilies. Natasha loves the dog drinking fountain that doubles as a decorative fountain. For you, there are human-height water fountains, benches, and remarkable views of the high rises and the landscaped jewel that is Lakeshore East Park.

The reason this park stands out as an urban jewel is that, while it is owned by the park district, it was built by Magellan Development Group and NNP Residential, the real estate firms that created Lakeshore East. They gave both the dog park and the bigger park (which includes an eye-popping kids' playground) to the city, but still handle the maintenance themselves, which is why the amenities are so lush. There are few oases like this in the city, where dogs can run free while their owners look up at the concrete jungle, but no one feels excessively fenced in.

The dog park is at the west end of Lakeshore East Park, north of Randolph Street, east of Michigan Avenue, west of Lake Shore Drive, and south of Wacker Drive. Parking is a challenge here, given the proximity to Millennium Park. The Millennium Park garage is close, but pricey. None of the Lakeshore East side streets permit street parking, but there are a few meters on lower Randolph Street. If you are staying at one of the downtown hotels, though, this should be your first walking-distance stop. 450 E. Benton Pl.

PLACES TO EAT

Bice Ristorante: A replica of its Milan namesake, this authentic Italian eatery is a favorite among the "Mag Mile" crowd. The outdoor seating accommodates 40, which means there's plenty of opportunity for a stray piece of bread to come your small dog's way. Larger dogs are discouraged from joining the crowded outdoor area. 158 E. Ontario St.; 312/664-1474.

Charlie's Ale House: Humans like the chicken pot pie and 55 beer choices. Dogs like the fact that there are select outdoor tables at this Navy Pier location at which they are welcome. 700 E. Grand Ave.; 312/595-1440.

Ghiradelli Chocolate Shop & Soda Fountain: With one of the best seated views of Michigan Avenue's Water Tower, Ghiradelli is a perfect place to rest your weary paws after a day of painting the town red. Dogs, of course, should not share your hot fudge, but the staff will bring water to help them cool off while you indulge. 830 N. Michigan Ave.; 312/337-9330.

PLACES TO STAY

The Drake: The Drake is one of those old-style hotels where you can easily imagine ladies in long white gloves walking in along the red carpet. Today, you and your dog will still get the red-carpet treatment, provided he weighs less than 50 pounds. The 1920s landmark building has decent-sized guest rooms, and even if you don't end up with a room with a view, there will likely be a public sitting area on each floor where you can gaze out at Lake Michigan. Dogs must be leashed in these public areas, and housekeeping would prefer that you not leave them alone with your dog, although crates are not required. A $200 refundable damage deposit is required on check-in; rates range $139–200. The concierge will order special dog food if necessary. The Drake is a tennis ball's throw from Lake Shore Drive. Parking with in-and-out privileges is available. 140 E. Walton Pl.; 312/787-2200; www.thedrakehotel.com.

Four Seasons Hotel Chicago: If you want to pamper your petite pup, the Four Seasons will lavish luxury on your under-15-pound dog. There's no extra fee or required damage deposit, and a special menu, with food and water bowls, will be delivered on request. The high-rise's 343 rooms, with great views and fancy linens, are fit for royalty. Really. The Duchess of York stays here when she's in town. Rates range $480–3,500 for suites, but there are often weekend specials. The Four Seasons is just west of Michigan Avenue, between Delaware Place and Walton Street. 120 E. Delaware Pl.; 312/280-8400; www.fourseasons.com/chicagofs.

Le Méridien: This 17-story hotel sits atop The Shops at Westfield North Bridge, a tony shopping mall that is home to Nordstrom, The Lego Store, and other human distractions. Dogs up to 25 pounds are welcomed with a VIP program including toys, treats, and clean-up supplies for accidents. A special Do Not Disturb sign for a pet guest alerts housekeeping not to enter unless the pet is in a crate. The Shops at Westfield North Bridge is between Michigan Avenue and Rush Street and is accessible from plenty of parking lots. Rates range $150–1,250 for suites. Packages and Internet deals are frequently available. 521 N. Rush St.; 312/645-1500; www.lemeridien.com.

The Peninsula Chicago: Jennifer Aniston's local pick, The Peninsula Chicago, caters to canines under 20 pounds. An $85 pet massage (45 minutes of rubbing on a special pillow in your guestroom), dog-walking and dog-sitting services, and 24-hour veterinarian services are available. If you have an extra $10 to spend, order the Spaniel Spinach Salad, Chihuahua Chicken & Rice, or a Beagle Burger from the special room-service menu. Rates range $295–1,150. The hotel is on Superior Street west of Michigan Avenue. 108 E. Superior St.; 312/337-2888; www.peninsula.com.

Residence Inn by Marriott: East of Michigan Avenue, this is one of the few hotels in the area with the comforts of home, like refrigerators in the rooms, rather than the opulence of minibars. Any size dog is welcome, with a limit of two dogs per room, plus a $75 fee per dog, per day. Rates are $229–409. 201 E. Walton Pl.; 312/943-9800; www.marriott.com.

Ritz-Carlton Chicago: On top of the Water Tower Place mall, the Ritz-Carlton is everything you would expect from a place called "the Ritz." Posh pooches under 30 pounds are welcome guests. They may not be left unattended in the room, but pet-sitting is available. Rates are $480–565. 160 East Pearson St.; 312/266-1000; www.fourseasons.com/chicagorc.

Sofitel Chicago Water Tower: Canines under 25 pounds are welcome in this 415-room hotel off Lake Shore Drive. Management offers an outdoor dining terrace with an adjacent doggy area for fun in the summer sun, not to mention special plates for dogs. Don't miss the annual dog Halloween costume contest. Rates are $265–575. Packages and Internet deals are frequently available. 20 E. Chestnut St.; 312/324-4000; www.sofitel.com.

W Chicago Lakeshore: You couldn't be closer to Navy Pier unless you slept on the dock. Recently rehabbed, this lakeside hotel requires a one-time $75 cleaning fee from dog lovers who stay with their pets. Dogs under 65 pounds are welcome at this relatively lakeside hotel. Dog-walking services, treats, and pet food are available from the concierge. Rates are $199–339. 644 N. Lake Shore Dr.; 312/943-9200; www.starwood.com.

The Loop

Few cities are lucky enough to have such a prominent visual for their central business district. Named for the shape of the elevated train (El) tracks above, the Loop is technically the area inside that square from Wabash Avenue (50 East) to Wacker Drive (350 West), and Lake Street (200 North) to Van Buren Street (400 South). As with the Magnificent Mile, the term "Loop" is now often used to include the areas to the east, near the Art Institute of Chicago and Grant Park, and to the west toward the Union Station commuter train depot. Skyscrapers are the dominant landmarks in the Loop.

Most dogs become familiar with the Loop for one of two reasons: They bring their people to a festival or event at Grant Park, or they stay in one of the many hotels in the area when visiting the city. Perhaps more of them should come check out **Rain Dog Books** (408 S. Michigan Ave.; 312/922-1200), a dog-friendly used bookstore, or the **Down Town Dog at Macy's on State Street** (111 N. State St., 312/782-4575, www.shopthedog.com), a city outpost of the tony Lake Bluff shop. The area runs from south of the Chicago River to the Congress Parkway/I-290 Expressway (500 South); and from the lake to Halsted Street (800 West).

PARKS, BEACHES, AND RECREATION AREAS

7 Grant Park

🐾🐾🐾 (See Downtown map on page 22)

From Buckingham Fountain to the Petrillo Music Shell, from ball fields to ballroom dancing, Grant Park has it all. Called "Chicago's front yard" by some, this enormous green centerpiece is the first thing many visitors see

DIVERSIONS

Forget going for a walk. Try these modes of transport instead.

Mercury Cruiseline's Canine Cruise: Dogs who would rather sun than swim can't stop barking about this summer tourist attraction for people and their pets. From the south side of the Chicago River at the southeast corner near Michigan Avenue (100 East) and Wacker Drive (300 North), seaworthy dogs line up for tickets to the 90-minute cruises of Lake Michigan and the dog-friendly Navy Pier. The ship's upper deck offers views of all the city's summer sights. Reservations are not accepted and the cruises often sell out, so it pays to be the first dog in line. The Canine Cruises typically run every Sunday through the summer, but if September is warm, they may be extended. Ticket prices are $18 adults, $8 kids, $5 dogs; 312/332-1353; www.mercuryskylinecruiseline.com. Dogs often stop at one of the outdoor food kiosks at Navy Pier (600 E. Grand Ave.; 312/595-PIER) for a bite after boating.

Shoreline Sightseeing Cruises: They don't have a canine-specific cruise, but do welcome leashed pets on tours. The rides leave from Navy Pier every 30 minutes. 474 N. Lake Shore Dr.; 312/222-9328.

Carriage Rides: What could be more romantic than a horse-drawn carriage ride through the city with the one you love? Antique Coach & Carriage Company and Chicago Horse and Carriage Rides make that a possibility by allowing dogs on their two tour routes. Carriages leave from the southeast corner of Huron Street (700 North) and Michigan Avenue (100 East) and trot through the Magnificent Mile, Lincoln Park, or the lakefront. During the winter holidays, tours of the Loop, the decorated Macy's windows, and other downtown sights leave from the corner of State Street (1 East, 1 West) and Randolph (200 North). Carriages hold up to six passengers, so you can bring a two-legged loved one with you as well. Antique Coach & Carriage Company, 773/735-9400; www.antiquecoach-carriage.com. Chicago Horse & Carriage Ltd., 773/395-3950; www.chicagocarriage.com.

when they come to Chicago. Including the Art Institute and the adjacent Museum Campus (described later in this chapter, in the South Loop neighborhood), Grant Park is an impressive 319 acres.

To many people (even those who didn't grow up watching *Married with Children*), few icons say "Chicago" like Buckingham Fountain. From the intersection near Columbus Drive and Congress Parkway, you and your dog can watch its water dance 150 feet in the sky every hour from April to October. During the dog days of summer, its spray is more than welcome. New food kiosks with tables and chairs give dogs and their owners a place to unwind alfresco.

Most of Grant Park's other explorations are far more active. To the south of the fountain is Hutchinson Field, home to softball games, kite flying, and tennis-ball tossing. During softball season or a scheduled event, like July's annual mammoth Taste of Chicago, it can mean a dogfight just to get a blade of grass here. But on most other days, this Downtown destination is an urban oasis. You can have social time or solitude, depending on your mood, given the large expanse of options here for both bipeds and quadrupeds.

To the north is Butler Field and the Petrillo Music Shell, where free concerts fill the summer nights. At the very northwest corner of Grant Park, near Randolph Street, is the new Millennium Park, a huge success with people despite opening four years late, but it is off limits to dogs. The Rose Gardens near the fountain are more formal than many city parks' flower gardens, but like all the others, they are also off limits to dogs. The thick grove of trees near the roses, though, are fair game, and in the summer, they're a four-footed friend's best bet for a shady haven from the hot temperatures.

Police often patrol Grant Park on horseback, contributing to the pastoral feel of the park (unless, like Natasha, you find such giant four-legged beasts intimidating). Because Grant Park is the first place many visitors go, it's exceeding well kept. You're unlikely to encounter trash or even mud puddles in these manicured acres.

Grant Park's grassy green runs from Michigan Avenue (100 East) to Lake Shore Drive and Randolph Street (150 North) to Roosevelt Road (1200 South). Massive mazes of underground parking lie beneath Grant Park and Millennium Park, with entrances on Michigan Avenue, Randolph Street, and Monroe Street (100 South), accessible from either Lake Shore Drive or Michigan Avenue. Mark your location carefully on your ticket, as it can be difficult to remember where the car is after an exhilarating day at the park. 331 E. Randolph St.; 312/742-7648.

PLACES TO STAY

Fairmont Hotel: Views of Lake Michigan and Grant Park grace many of the rooms in this 692-room hotel. The street-level views, which include underground access to the parking garage, aren't nearly as lovely, but the convenience of driving into a warm, available parking spot can't be beat. The guest rooms are larger than in many Downtown hotels and the windows open to allow a breeze, a real rarity in many high-rises. Dogs weighing less than 25 pounds are allowed with a $25 extra fee per night. If you leave your room without your canine companion, she must be crated. Rates range $119–600, but lower weekend rates are often available. 200 N. Columbus Dr.; 312/565-8000; www.fairmont.com.

Hotel Allegro Chicago: The funkiest of Kimpton's three Chicago-area pet-friendly boutique hotels, the Allegro is situated in what folks call the Loop's Theater District, thanks to a renaissance of grand old stages. As at the

Burnham and The Monaco, Kimpton's two other Chicago hotels, pets are welcome—no size restrictions or deposit either. Of the hotel's 483 rooms, all with deco-style furniture, 60 are pet-friendly and plush, with a pet bed. Registered canine guests are welcome to join the wine happy hour every evening in the bar. The hotel is across the street from City Hall. Canine packages range from $269–349. 171 W. Randolph St.; 866/672-6143; www.allegrochicago.com.

Hotel Burnham: The historic Reliance building has been rehabbed right as the new Hotel Burnham. If either you or your dog is an architecture fan, you may be tempted to take your walks inside these halls, gazing at the ornate elevator grates, woodwork, and other detailing. But at the Burnham, you don't have to worry about walking your pup, because they'll gladly dash out with the dog for you. All-sized dogs are welcomed at check-in with a treat. From there, your dog will be escorted to your room (not large, but brightly colored and unlike anywhere you've stayed before), where non-skid bowls and pet beds made of hypoallergenic fleece and cedar chips await. If you do want to jaunt around the Loop on your own, the front desk will give you a map of the area, with grassy spaces marked, and even a doggy raincoat should you need one. When it's time for bed, your pup will have a biscuit on his pillow. On hot summer nights, Cooper recommends ordering a Frosty Paw from room service. There are no pet fees or deposits. Rates range $139–300. Valet parking is available. 1 W. Washington St., 312/782-1111 or 866/690-1986; www. burnhamhotel.com.

Hotel Monaco: Wood armoires, meditation stations, and colorful decor greet guests to this rehabbed 1912 boutique hotel. Dogs of all sizes are welcome (in fact, any animal except "elephants or horses," according to the front desk. The hotel even has a dog mascot, Stevie Nix). Gourmet dog treats, dog-walking services, pet room service, and any other amenity you need will be provided. No fees or deposits are required of dog lovers. The Hotel Monaco is across the street from the Chicago River, where there's a grassy bank for dogs who like the green stuff, and just a few blocks from the lake, perfect for an evening summer stroll. Pet package rates start at $149. The 192-room hotel is on the south side of the street. 225 N. Wabash Ave.; 312/960-8500 or 800/397-7661; www.monaco-chicago.com.

Palmer House Hilton: A State Street landmark and once the city's preeminent hotel, the Palmer House has gotten an undeserved reputation as an also-ran, as newer luxury hotels with larger rooms and high-tech infrastructures have opened. But with its gone-to-the-dogs approach to even large four-footed friends, there are few such high-class, historic accommodations for people and pooches. Where else can Fido take in a fresco mural on a lobby ceiling, restored by hand by an Italian artist flown in to do the job? There is no size restriction, but if the dog can't be carried in its owner's arms then he'll be asked to use the service elevator. A pet waiver to cover damages is required at check-in. 17 W. Monroe St.; 312/726-7500 or 800/445-8667; www.hilton.com.

Renaissance Chicago Hotel: Convenient to both the Loop and the Magnificent Mile, this 27-floor, 553-room hotel gives you easy access to a river stroll and to the bridge over to the River North neighborhood. Dogs under 20 pounds are allowed with a one-time $45 cleaning fee. Hotel management sometimes makes exceptions for larger, "well-trained" dogs who are accustomed to staying in hotels. Room service offers "Doggie Delicacies" of brisket or eggs at $8 each. A parking garage is available for a fee. 1 W. Wacker Dr.; 312/372-7200; www.marriott.com.

W Chicago City Center: When the former Midland Hotel was turned into Chicago's first W, it got a facelift of an unusual sort. The antique elements that made the Midland a classic Chicago stop are still there, with an open lobby perfect for sniffing out new friends, and a remarkably ornate ceiling. But the W also brought its sophistication, with wood paneling, a nightlife crowd, and big-city theme packages. If you and your pup (as long as he weighs less than 100 pounds) like to be in on the action, check in here. He'll even get a biscuit. Rates are $179–499, plus a non-refundable fee of $100 per stay. 172 W. Adams St.; 312/332-1200; www.starwood.com.

South Loop and Printer's Row

Residents of the South Loop, some of the most active dog owners in the city, believe there are more dogs in their little neck of the urban woods than in any other neighborhood in the city. The City Clerk's office doesn't track pet ownership by neighborhood, so there's no way to know for sure, but there's certainly no shortage of friendly furry faces. South Loop DogPAC, a neighborhood group of dog owners that created a dog-friendly oasis in the urban jungle, noticed all the canine action…as well as that dog owners learn each other's dog's names before they bother to learn the human's names. On the South Loop Dogs website (www.southloopdogs.com), photos of the area's four-footed residents are posted, a fun whim that has become a cyberspace dog park and community-building endeavor. Stop by **Animal House Chicago** (843 W. Monroe St.; 312/666-7767), where you're sure to meet a few more pups at the neighborhood pet-food shop.

On the west side of the South Loop is Printer's Row, a mixed-use area of converted lofts with restaurants, law firms, bookstores, and churches. On the north end of Printer's Row is the Harold Washington Library Center, the city's central library. Take in the architectural elements and decorative green roof as you walk to Dearborn Park. For a different kind of architecture, walk east in the South Loop to examine the new Soldier Field addition, which was built inside the existing historic colonnade.

Many churches are known for their annual blessings of the animals (see the DuPage County chapter), but the funky **Makom Shalom** (637 S. Dearborn Ave.; 312/913-9030) in Printer's Row is one of the few Jewish synagogues to welcome pets in prayer. The dog-friendly service usually takes place when the congregation hears the story of Noah and the ark in the fall.

The South Loop tends to have fewer parking problems than the rest of Downtown, but during football games when the Bears are playing at Soldier Field, choose to walk, not drive. The borders of this area are the Congress Parkway/I-290 Expressway (500 South) and 16th Street (1600 South), from Lake Michigan to Halsted Street (800 West).

PARKS, BEACHES, AND RECREATION AREAS

8 Dearborn Park

🐾 (See Downtown map on page 22)

This 1.25-acre park is a magnet for Printer's Row dogs and their owners. Small grassy spaces, pretty winding paths, and plenty of benches characterize this atypical city park. Neighborhood groups, including the Dearborn Park Advisory Council, work to keep this park clean and keep to a minimum any contention between dog owners and those who don't have furry friends. Dearborn Park isn't anything extraordinary, but if you're in the area and want more than a squat in the street, there's certainly nothing to complain about.

The park is north of 9th Street and west of Plymouth Court (32 West). There isn't parking on the side streets surrounding the park, but this neighborhood has plenty of metered parking and pay parking lots on the major roads. 865 S. Park Terrace; wos90@hotmail.com (Dearborn Park Advisory Council).

9 Grant Bark Park

 (See Downtown map on page 22)

With more dogs than the tiny Coliseum Park DFA can accommodate, the South Loop Dog PAC had been working for years to convert the wide-open space under the pedestrian bridge to the trains into a more accommodating DFA. Inside Grant Park their dream is coming true: a premiere off-leash dog park. Ground broke on Grant Bark Park in 2006, with much of the funding (more than half of the $150,000 total) coming from local residents. A commemorative brick donor's circle pays tribute to just a few of those who pitched in.

The 16,000-square-foot space of off-leash fun is meant to be the city's top dog park. The first phase of the park includes plenty of shade trees, a pea gravel surface, drinking fountains (for people and dogs), benches, plenty of lighting, and two entrances. A doggy wading pool and more landscaping are on the South Loop Dog Park Action Cooperative's wish list. (Like all Chicago Park District DFAs, dogs need a permit to enter Grant Bark Park (see Introduction). The dog park is near the 11th Street pedestrian bridge off Michigan Avenue. www.southloopdogpac.org.

🔟 Museum Campus

👣 🐾 (See Downtown map on page 22)

Home to the Shedd Aquarium, the Field Museum, and the Adler Planetarium, Museum Campus is the renovated southern end of Grant Park. Its grassy yards were complemented with stone benches, pathways, and easier access across Lake Shore Drive. Native plantings and sculptures help to make the space a destination park, rather than a mere walkway.

Dogs should be securely leashed in the Museum Campus because of its proximity to the high-speed traffic of Lake Shore Drive. Dogs who want a little more space can keep walking east, behind the planetarium, as long as they stay off the sand. This back area is less known than much of the rest of the Museum Campus and can be a decent place to play, particularly early in the morning before the museums open.

There are parking lots at Soldier Field and all of the museums, accessible from Columbus Drive (150 East) to McFetridge Drive (1400 South). There is some metered parking on Solidarity Drive (1375 South) near the planetarium, or park west of Michigan Avenue and walk through Grant Park.

1️⃣1️⃣ Coliseum Park

👣 🐕 (See Downtown map on page 22)

Truly not more than a dog run, this small, legal off-leash area abuts the small, but prettier, Coliseum Park play lot. The dog area runs underneath the El tracks, which spooks some dogs but goes over the heads (both literally and figuratively) of others. The space is long and narrow—decent for a good ball toss or two if you're the only dog in the lot, but not practical for much more than that. Now that Grant Bark Park is open, many neighborhood dogs will go there. Still most of the area residences are town houses and condos without yards, so Coliseum Park will remain a good alternative for the post-work walk. As with all city DFAs, come during the weekday and you'll have more room to romp than in the after-work hour.

Street parking is usually available on Wabash Avenue (50 East). The park is south of 14th Place, which is south of 14th Street. 1466 S. Wabash Ave.; 312/747-7640.

PLACES TO STAY

Chicago Hilton and Towers: One of the largest hotels in the area, the Chicago Hilton is almost always hosting some kind of event, be it Peace Corps volunteer training or an academic association conference. With more than 1,500 rooms, check-in can seem a bit like a zoo, but things settle down when you get away from the registration area. Located on the central part of South Michigan Avenue, off Balbo Drive (700 South) and across the street from Grant Park, the Chicago Hilton is easy to get to from Lake Shore Drive or the I-90/94 Expressway from O'Hare. Dogs up to 85 pounds are allowed, but their owners must sign a pet agreement form at check-in, agreeing to pay for any damages. Dogs do not have to be caged when alone in the room. Rates are $179–359. 720 S. Michigan Ave.; 312/922-4400; www.hilton.com.

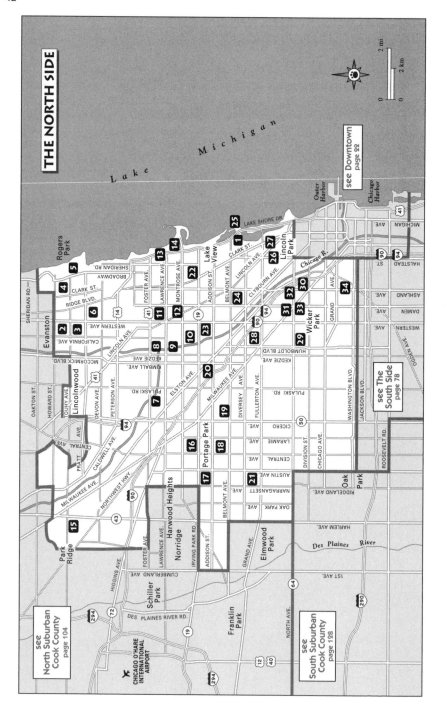

42

THE NORTH SIDE

see Downtown
page 92

see The
South Side
page 78

see North
Suburban
Cook County
page 104

see South
Suburban
Cook County
page 128

CHAPTER 2

The North Side

The North Side of Chicago suffers from its own success. Packed with shops, restaurants, and of, course, people, it has a sometimes well-deserved reputation for traffic congestion. But because of all there is to do, the North Side is a Chicago dog's best friend, thanks to an abundance of lakeside green space and more specialty dog-treat shops than you can shake a stick at.

Sometimes thought of as more affluent than other parts of the city, the North Side has no shortage of places for those who want to pamper their pet. From doggy daycare and spas to canine health-food stores and custom greeting cards with your own pooch on the front, this area has anything the indulgent dog guardian needs. Thanks to Loyola University, DePaul University, and spillover from Evanston's Northwestern University (not to mention a number of other smaller colleges), the North Side also has more than its share of young, hip, athletic collegians, ready to run, swim, or in-line skate with a dog at a moment's notice. It was on the North Side that MTV chose to film its local installment of *The Real World*.

PICK OF THE LITTER—THE NORTH SIDE

BEST CITY PARKS
Lincoln Park (page 45)
Gompers Park, Albany Park (page 50)
Humboldt Park, Humboldt Park (page 72)

BEST DOG PARKS
Puptown/Margate Park, Uptown (page 57)
Wicker Park, Wicker Park (page 76)

BEST BEACH
Montrose Beach, Uptown (page 57)

BEST PLACE TO EAT
Bordo's Eatery and Sauce, Lincoln Park (page 70)

BEST EVENT
Pug Party, Lincoln Park (page 45)

To categorize the North Side as yuppie central is to sell the area short. This chapter, like the other two city of Chicago chapters, is organized—albeit loosely—by neighborhood, because neighborhood affiliation is the way locals identify themselves and their homes. Each neighborhood has its own feel and flavor, sometimes literally, as Swedish pastries, Italian sandwiches, and Polish pierogi perfume the air. With your dog's keen nose leading you (and our maps and suggestions to aid in the inevitable leash correction), you'll be able to sniff out the real North Side, the one locals know and love, with little-known parks and nature trails, dog-friendly shopkeepers, and tempting treats. In fact, nine of the Chicago Park District's official Dog-Friendly Areas (or DFAs, explained in detail in the Introduction) are on the North Side. And because Chicagoans appreciate decent weather when they get it, there are more than a pawful of restaurants that allow dogs to sit and stay at select out-door tables during the summer (Chicago Public Health Department laws are also outlined in the Introduction). In some city neighborhoods, taverns and bars are the coffee-klatch equivalents. Dog-friendly bars are included here when dogs are in regular attendance.

This chapter covers the area from Madison Street (1 North, 1 South) on the south to Howard Avenue (7600 North, the city limits) on the north. Lake

DOG-EAR YOUR CALENDAR

In 1994, while pouring drinks at a local bar, Ben Friedman thought it'd be a funny joke to schedule a "Pug Crawl." He and his pug, Knuckles, along with four or five other pug owners, headed from bar to bar, creating quite a scene as the diminutive dogs walked en masse down the street. Now twice a year, each June and October, more than 1,200 people and 600 pugs are in on the joke. They pug along on the Saturday afternoon event, often dressing their dogs in costumes and winning prizes for the most creative. The sheer number of crawling pugs has forced Friedman and Curly Joe (Knuckles passed away at age 17 in 2002) to schedule a **Pug Party** at one giant venue. They may not trot from one bar to another, but they always share beer, water, and plenty of pug stories. www.pugparty.com.

Michigan is the easternmost boundary (as always—this is Chicago, after all) and the city limits the westernmost. The exceptions are the Magnificent Mile, Gold Coast, River North, and Streeterville neighborhoods near Lake Michigan, which are included in the Downtown chapter.

PARKS, BEACHES, AND RECREATION AREAS

1 Lincoln Park

🐾🐾🐾🐾 (See North Side map on page 42)

When people say, "Let's meet in the park," or, "Let's go to the lake," on the North Side, they mean Lincoln Park, which runs approximately six miles along Lake Michigan's shores from North Avenue (1600 North) to Foster Avenue (5200 North). With more than 1,200 acres, Lincoln Park (the park—not to be confused with Lincoln Park, the neighborhood) spans the city's harborside. As a result, it's a year-round magnet for dogs and their owners, not to mention guys trying to meet girls with dogs, in-line skaters, bicyclists, and other urban outdoors enthusiasts who care nothing about the canine kind except when they're in the way.

It was once the city's cemetery, but these days, Lincoln Park is one of the liveliest and loveliest stretches of parkland in the nation, filled with block-long flowerbeds, tree-shaded esplanades, lush lawns, playing fields, a lily pond, historic field houses, lagoons, a marina, running paths, restaurants, and cafés. Named after Abraham Lincoln (like many things in the great state of Illinois), Lincoln Park offers something for everyone, from winding paths and bird sanctuaries to soccer fields, golf courses, beach volleyball, and even a theater. Dogs aren't allowed in the Lincoln Park Zoo, the golf courses, beaches, or play lots, but there is still a vast expanse of dog-friendliness along Lake Michigan's green shores. On a sunny Sunday morning, you'll see more than one owner and dog splayed out reading the paper, while others jog by on the way to the beach to watch a chess game.

Throughout this chapter, specific dog-worthy areas of Lincoln Park have been highlighted in the neighborhoods where they can be found. If one of those isn't convenient for you and your pooch, you can never go wrong on the North Side by heading east, getting to the park, and just seeing what you find. It won't be long before you run into other local dog owners discussing dog walkers, pet foods, or other pet issues. Because Lincoln Park draws tourists as well as locals, it's crowded on all but the dreariest of days. The congestion, combined with its proximity to busy, high-speed Lake Shore Drive, makes keeping your dog under leash control an absolute must, unless you're in one of the designated enclosed off-leash areas.

There are countless ways into Lincoln Park, but its formal entrance is at North Avenue (1600 North) and Dearborn Parkway (50 West). There you can check out the full text of the Gettysburg Address at the foot of the Lincoln statue. During the summer, the several parking lots throughout the park and lakefront (including on Stockton Drive, Recreational Drive, and Simonds Drive) fill faster than you can say, "Fetch." Arrive early in the morning or after the afternoon rush, or walk, which is one of the best ways to appreciate Lincoln Park's many charms.

Rogers Park and West Ridge

Rogers Park is home to an abundance of high-rises, brick three-flats, and other apartment buildings. This contributes to Rogers Park's parking problems (more on that later), but it also makes for good doggy living. Without a lot of backyards, Rogers Parkers hit the neighborhood's many parks and green spaces for daily dog romps. On any given day, you'll be able to kibitz about kibble with any number of like-minded dog owners.

East Rogers Park is home to Loyola University. West Rogers Park and neighboring West Ridge are the center of traditional Jewish, Pakistani, and Indian communities. As a result, the area is an active melting pot of students, senior citizens, and everyone in between. While dogs aren't allowed at **Rosenblum's World of Judaica** (2906 W. Devon Ave.; 773/262-1700), Natasha loves the stuffed toy matzo balls and other Jewish-themed dog treats sold there, not to mention the strong scents that waft from the area's Indian restaurants and kosher butchers.

Rogers Park runs from the city's northern border at Howard Street (7600 North) to Devon Avenue (6400 North) and from the lake to Kedzie Avenue (3200 West). If you're looking for specific street addresses along Howard Avenue, keep alert. The north side of Howard is numbered with the Evanston numbering system; the south side of Howard belongs to the city. Near the

lake, parking is at a premium, which the city tried to rectify by designating many of the streets east of Sheridan Road for residential permit parking. Finding a legal spot next to the water is about as likely as finding a pile of rawhide on your morning walk. The area west of Sheridan can still be congested, but isn't designated for permits only. The Loyola University campus and its surrounding blocks are dotted with several pay lots.

PARKS, BEACHES, AND RECREATION AREAS

2 Rogers Avenue Park

🐾🐾🐾 (See North Side map on page 42)

This quiet park is situated on Eastlake Avenue, the prettiest street you've never heard of in Rogers Park. A grove of trees here is a favorite of Natasha's friend (and former Rogers Park resident) Bella. The park is well lit, so balls are easy to see and nighttime safety is less of an issue than it is at other parks, so she can come here after work. A friendly community of dog lovers keeps the park exceptionally clean. If you visit, they ask that you follow their lead. Eastlake Avenue (1300 West) is west of Sheridan Road. 7800 N. Rogers Ave.

3 Indian Boundary Park

🐾🐾 (See North Side map on page 42)

Originally the territorial boundary between the Pottawatomie tribe and the U.S. government, this park still has several details showing its heritage. The field house is decorated with Indian chiefs, along with the more classical lions and other statues.

Though this quaint park in a quiet residential area has few canine-specific amenities, Bella has spent many a happy hour playing in its open grassy spaces, which blend with the front yards of surrounding houses. It's particularly pleasant when there are a few inches of snow on the ground and fewer people to get in the way of her rabbit-chasing. Her owner likes the looks of the park's small pond. The Park District wishes it had a smaller duck population. Bella would be happy to help out with a little doggy-dipping on a hot afternoon, but swimming is not allowed. The park is located at Rockwell Street (2600 West) and Lunt Avenue (7000 North). 2500 W. Lunt Ave.; 312/742-7887.

4 Touhy Park

🐾🐾 (See North Side map on page 42)

Bella hates dodging projectiles (that someone had the nerve not to throw for her), and during warm months, this relatively small park is filled to maximum capacity with multiple softball and pickup soccer games. Touhy Park abuts congested Clark Street on the west, so it's noisy and littered, with a fair amount of stroller traffic to and from the park's modest play lot. In autumn and winter, however, there's an adequate expanse of grass for playing fetch. Bella hears that a loyal contingent of dogs convene there mornings to let their owners drink coffee together while they enjoy an early romp. Rogers Parkers welcome new dog owners and dogs who play well with others. The park is located on Paulina Street (1700 West) and Sherwin Avenue (7342 North). 7348 N. Paulina St.

5 Loyola Park and Street-End Beaches

🐾🐾🐾 (See North Side map on page 42)

There are 18 little street-end parks connected here by a virtually uninterrupted expanse of beach. The 10 streets to the south—from Leone Park and Beach on Touhy Avenue to Hartigan Park and Beach on Albion Avenue—make up Loyola Park; Greenleaf Avenue is the point of entry for Loyola Park, which has the benefit of grass and lots of trees, compared to the rockier beaches at Fargo and Chase Avenues. Better yet, these grassy areas are A-OK for leashed dog strolls. Plenty of benches with murals, a walking path, water fountains, and a summertime concession stand run by the nearby Heartland Café keep bipeds happy, too.

Leash laws are obsessively enforced in this high-traffic beach-and-barbecue bastion during the summer, as even dog lovers don't like to sunbathe or picnic among prancing pups. The nearby Loyola Park baseball field is a popular post-work dog frolic area. 1230 W. Greenleaf Ave.; 312/742-7857.

6 Warren Park

🐾🐾🐾 (See North Side map on page 42)

Once the site of the Edgewater Golf Club, Warren Park is a large expanse in West Rogers Park that has something of a rarity in Illinois: hills. The topography helps give this big space some distinctive areas, without a lot of fences. In the winter, dogs love to run up and down (and up and down) these novel hills, and when the snow falls, sledding is a popular pastime for human and beast. Dogs are not allowed on the nine-hole golf course, and since the Chicago Park District has offices on this property, breaking the rules here is not a good idea. Natasha thinks Warren's size and history of community interaction (the surrounding neighborhood and state preservationists were crucial in preventing developers from building on the land when the private club closed) make it the perfect site for the next DFA. But so far, no one has heeded her bark.

The south edge of the park is bordered by dead-end streets and backyards, not good for driving or parking, but good for a solitary stroll or frolic. There is a parking lot off Western Avenue. If it fills quickly in warm weather, try looking for street spots on Ridge Avenue. Warren Park is south of Pratt Boulevard (6800 North). 6601 N. Western Ave.; 312/742-7888.

PLACES TO EAT

Ennui Café: With a large outdoor seating area and a constantly refilled supply of water for the furrier non-cappuccino-drinking patrons, this coffee shop is a great pit stop on the way to or from a run along a Rogers Park beach. Despite the name (*ennui* is French for "boredom"), visitors should find plenty of variety in the large selection of hot and cold beverages, pastries, and light savories like pizza bread. And the diversity doesn't end with the menu; Ennui caters to a wide audience of students, bohemian Rogers Park–types, beachgoers, and, of course, their dogs. 6981 N. Sheridan Rd.; 773/973-2233.

Max's Italian Beef: Real Chicagoans, both human and canine, crave the wet, greasy classic of Italian beef. They can enjoy it together here at several outdoor tables. 5754 N. Western Ave.; 773/989-8200.

U Lucky Dawg: You pup will feel lucky indeed when you buy him a Vienna Beef hot dog at this local favorite hot dog stand. If you're an old-timer, you'll remember this as Fluky's. The name's different, but the food's the same. 6821 N. Western Ave.; 773/274-3652.

Ravenswood Manor and Albany Park

Natasha still fantasizes that the royalties from her work on the second edition of this book will allow her to buy a house in Ravenswood Manor, where lucky homeowners enjoy all the typical urban spoils, plus private backyard access to the Chicago River, complete with individual boat docks. The quarter-mile Ravenswood Manor (home to Governor Rod Blagojevich) is surrounded by interesting ethnic pockets, so until Natasha gets her secluded swimming spot, she settles for walking around sniffing and tasting the authentic cuisines of this melting pot. The street-level Brown Line El stops and their traffic-halting railroad crossings help make this area feel like Main Street U.S.A.

The Ravenswood Manor and Albany Park neighborhoods are bordered by Western Avenue (2400 West) to the east and the I-90/94 Expressway to the west. Devon Avenue (6400 North) is the northern border and Irving Park Road (4000 North) is the south.

PARKS, BEACHES, AND RECREATION AREAS

7 Gompers Park

🐾🐾🐾 (See North Side map on page 42)

Works Progress Administration (WPA) funds helped pay to rehabilitate the southern portion of this park in the 1920s, constructing tennis courts, a footbridge over the river, a dam, and a spillway for the lower lagoon. More recent ecological work, thanks to the Park District and Friends of the Chicago River, has concentrated on rehabbing the wetlands. You and your loyal companion may see herons, frogs, toads, and dragonflies when walking through Gompers.

As at nearby Horner Park, the river itself is off limits here to dogs, who may be tempted when they see humans fishing along its banks. But the 38-acre park has enough nooks and crannies to keep even the most water-obsessed retriever distracted. 4222 W. Foster Ave.; 312/742-7628.

FETCHING NECESSITIES

Oh, what a dog's life it would be if it consisted of nothing more than going to a park, then a restaurant, and then another park. But sometimes, you have to stock up on the basics. Here are a few places you can hit together.

Barker & Meowsky, a paw firm: This cleverly named store is equally cleverly stocked with high-end food, bowls, picture frames, fancy collars, and many, many toys. All quadruped visitors get a treat. 1003 W. Armitage Ave.; 773/868-0200; www.barker andmeowsky.com.

Dog-A-Holics: Promises everything for your dog addiction. 904 W. Armitage Ave.; 773/857-5787; www.dog-a-holics.com.

Doggy Style: Dress your pup in organic and hemp togs. 2023 W. Division St.; 773/235-9663.

For Dog's Sake: Health food for dogs. The new location will groom, train, or provide holistic veterinary medicine for your pup. 1757 N. Kimball Ave.; 773/278-4355; www.fordogsake.com.

4 Legs: A long-time favorite of Wrigleyville pet lovers. 3809 N. Clark St.; 773/472-5347.

Off the Leash: High-end food, baked dogs, and adoptions events. 4955 N. Damen Ave.; 773/728-7877; www.offtheleashpets.com.

Parkview Pet Store: Parkview moved from Lincoln Park to Edgewater, and switched its focus to healthy pet food and treats. It still hosts an annual Halloween costume contest. 5358 N. Broadway; 773/561-0001.

PETCO: A small but serviceable outpost for basics. 3118 N. Ashland Ave.; 773/935-7388. There's another at 3046 N. Halsted St.; 773/935-7547; and at 2000 N. Clybourn; 773/665-1368.

PetSmart: In addition to the regular stock of food and treats this national chain carries, this location hosts adoption events for local shelters. While here, you can also sign up for obedience classes, get your dog groomed, and make your own pet ID tag. There's plenty of parking, but getting in can be a drag thanks to Target traffic across the street. 2665 N. Elston Ave.; 773/342-1300. Other city locations are at 2832 N. Broadway; 773/549-2393; and, farther west, at 6655 W. Grand Ave.; 773/836-7578.

Sam & Willy's: This storefront is small, but stocked with everything your pooch needs. 3405 N. Paulina St.; 773/404-0400; www .samandwillys.com.

Sit!: Find treats shaped like maki rolls in Lincoln Square. 2316 W. Leland Ave.; 773/784-2741.

🐾 River Park, Paws Park, and Ronan Park

😺😺🐕 (See North Side map on page 42)

The aptly named River Park is divided in half by the Chicago River. The east side of the park offers plenty of grass and shady trees, and tends to be the more dog-centric of the two. Informal canine play groups and dog obedience classes romp here most evenings during the week. A neighborhood group worked hard to create a Park District–approved DFA, called Paws Park, here. Paws Park is smaller than many area backyards. Squeezed between the swimming pool area and the field house, it doesn't get to enjoy much of the leafy attraction of the rest of River Park. But it is easily accessible from the parking spots on the east side of the park and nearby apartment- and condo-dwellers appreciate the off-leash opportunity. Perhaps because it is new, Paws Park tends to be cleaner and less crowded than some other DFAs.

A soccer field and running track dominate the west side of the park, and in the summer, you'll find kayakers putting their boats in the water (it's the location of one of the city's official kayak/canoe launches) and anglers looking to hook lunch. A paved walking path runs along the water, and although dogs could easily access the river, it isn't officially allowed; and in the center of the park, a dam where the river forks could spell danger.

Adjacent to west River Park, just across its southern boundary at Argyle Street (5000 North), lies Ronan Park, former home to the metal and concrete remnants of a City of Chicago pumping station. Prior to the construction of a water reclamation tunnel 200 feet underground, the station used to dump sewer overflow into the river. A joint effort between the Chicago Park District and Water Reclamation District cleared and landscaped the area, dedicating Ronan Park in 1995. A tailored mulch trail winds through trees along the river from Argyle to Lawrence Avenue (4800 North). It's a short walk, but it's set down on the banks, doesn't get crowded, and feels like a getaway from the city. Watson enjoys watching (and wanting to chase) the ducks and geese lounging in the water and confides that he can't understand why they stopped dumping sewage in the river when it created such a nice smell.

Diagonal street parking is available on Francisco Avenue (2900 West) on the east and Albany Street (3100 West) on the west, but fills quickly during soccer and baseball games. 5100 N. Francisco Ave.; 312/742-7516 or 773/960-8494 (Paws Park Advisory Group).

🐾 Ravenswood Manor

😺 (See North Side map on page 42)

This tiny, triangular turf wouldn't warrant the wag of a tail, except that it's meeting place No. 1 for any activity in the Ravenswood Manor neighborhood. Community organizers stop to chat under the pretty pergola, and the play lot is filled with local kids and strollers most days of the week. Meet your canine companions here as a starting point to see the rest of the area. 4626 N. Manor Ave.

10 Horner Park

 (See North Side map on page 42)

There's plenty of grass to sniff, people to meet (sometimes too many), and animals to chase in this large city park. Because the Chicago River forms the eastern border of the Horner, there are rabbits, raccoons, and possums in addition to the standard squirrels. A community group called Friends of the Chicago River is working to create a reclaimed nature river walk. Until that happens, head over to the east bank of the river, to the River Nature Walk at Rockwell Street and Berteau Street. Natasha doesn't mind being leashed on the walk along the small path full of natural flora and fauna, because it's so quiet and isolated she feels like she's trekking.

In recent years the Chicago Park District has hosted a doggy Easter egg hunt at Horner. Dogs must be leashed (imagine what would otherwise happen to the poor Easter bunny), but are encouraged to seek treat-filled eggs. The parking lots off California fill quickly during basketball games and other Park District classes. 2741 W. Montrose Ave.; 312/742-7572.

PLACES TO EAT

Beans & Bagels: An addition to the growing Rockwell Crossing renaissance, this second outpost of the local coffeehouse offers outdoor tables and bowls of water for your dog. While you wait for your shmear, browse the upscale collars, wrought-iron dog beds, dog treats, and toys two doors to the south at **Ruff Haus Pets** (4652 N. Rockwell St.; 773/478-5100; www.ruffhauspets. com). 2601 W. Leland Ave.; 773/478-2666.

Shelly's Freez: A classic Chicago carry-out spot, Shelly's has fries and Vienna beef hot dogs. But its main appeal is chocolate-dipped soft ice cream cones, always available at the first hint of summer. There are two umbrella-topped picnic benches on the south side of Shelly's, and dogs are welcome to sit while you lick. Parking is available (enter from Lincoln Avenue), but Shelly's is perfect for those nights you want an after-dinner walk. Cash only, but you won't need much. 5119 N. Lincoln Ave.; 773/271-2783.

Tre Kronor: Many people head to Andersonville for authentic Swedish cuisine, but farther west on Foster Avenue sits the home of the city's best Swedish pancakes with lingonberries. Also worth trying are the salmon, pickled herring, and assorted sausages, if you go for that sort of thing. Even if you sit outside with your dog, peek in the window at the cottage-style murals. Expect a wait—it's worth it—for Sunday brunch. 3258 W. Foster Ave.; 773/267-9888.

Lincoln Square and Ravenswood

Lincoln Square likes to tout itself as a "touch of Europe in Chicago." Walking through these streets, once home to the Budlong Pickle factory, you're as likely to hear a resident giving directions in German as in any other language. The neighborhood was settled by German immigrants who brought the flavor of their homeland with them. The central retail area, Lincoln Square (not square in shape) is a bricked-in one-way street with European delis, restaurants, and even an apothecary. (Dogs aren't allowed in **Merz Apothecary,** but the store is a good resource for homeopathic pet remedies, and its knowledgeable pharmacist gives good advice. 4716 N. Lincoln Ave.; 773/989-0900.) North Center and Ravenswood are more traditionally residential neighborhoods, now with growing numbers of yoga studios, DVD stores, and coffee shops housed in former industrial lofts. But Lincoln Square's Old World influence extends into these areas: You can almost always find a good beer-soaked brat nearby.

Several metered parking lots surround the Western stop of the Brown Line El. Even if you don't take one of these spots, be sure to check out the mural of Europe painted on the south wall of the Leland Avenue lot. Permit parking is in effect to the west of Western Avenue during the morning commute. This area runs from Ashland Avenue (1600 West) on the east to Western Avenue (2400 West), and from Irving Park Road (4000 North) to Devon Avenue (6400 North).

PARKS, BEACHES, AND RECREATION AREAS

🔟 Winnemac Park

🐾 🐾 (See North Side map on page 42)

A large park bordered by an elementary and high school, Winnemac Park is one of the city parks that embrace the native habitat. In addition to the standard soccer and softball field, it has a central section of winding paths, tall prairie grasses, and other native plants grown and cared for through Park District educational programs. Winnemac is one of many city parks that screen free movies (usually rated G) for human and canine residents during the summer.

Some neighborhood dogs romp here illegally off-leash. Natasha can't afford the fines for such frolic, nor would she want to risk knocking over a local school kid in her excitement. Fortunately, there's so much to see and sniff that Winnemac remains a decent place to play, on leash. Don't miss the nature-like trail toward the south end of the park, away from the play lot and schools. There's a parking lot off Damen Avenue (available only when school is not in session), but street parking, particularly on Leavitt Street to the west, is plentiful. To get to Winnemac, take Foster Avenue (5200 North) to Damen Avenue (2000 West), and turn south. 5101 N. Leavitt St.; 312/742-5101.

12 Welles Park

🐾 🐾 🐾 (See North Side map on page 42)

This Lincoln Square centerpiece is popular among obedience classes and early-morning play sessions. Rumor is that police ticket off-leash dogs and their owners less often at this park than elsewhere because the ward's alderman is dog-friendly. But as an unfenced park surrounded on the east, west, and south by three of the city's busiest streets, safety is as much a deterrent as fines. A gazebo, a gift of the nearby Old Town School of Folk Music, is home to weekly summer concerts, great for leashed dogs who don't howl and others lounging on the grass.

Many of Welles's finest amenities—horseshoes, an indoor pool, a fitness area, and the excellent Folk and Roots Festival from the Old Town School—are strictly no dogs allowed. Natasha massages her bruised ego by chasing the many squirrels and wolfing down tidbits offered to her by the matron of the all-beef hot-dog stand at the south entrance of the park, and then takes a once around the park, on leash, of course. Harlem Globetrotters creator Abe Saperstein used to coach kids on the courts at Welles. Take Western Avenue (2400 West) to Montrose Avenue (4400 North); street parking is best on Lincoln Avenue, where there's also a city pay lot north of Sunnyside Avenue (4500 North). 2333 W. Sunnyside Ave.; 312/742-7511.

PLACES TO EAT

Daily Bar & Grill: The Daily Bar & Grill has one of the neighborhood's most fabulous patios. There your "well-behaved dog" and you can enjoy standard bar food while watching an interesting parade of musicians and their instruments coming and going from the Old Town School of Folk Music. 4560 N. Lincoln Ave.; 773/561-6198.

O'Donovan's: Tasty and extremely cheap daily specials (Watson prefers $2 burgers with fries on Mondays and $9.95 pasta night with $3.50 Warsteiner pints and $7 bottles of wine on Wednesdays) make the two outdoor seating areas at this bar and grill a hive of activity on summer nights. Dogs are not allowed in the giant beer garden, but are greeted with open arms at the sidewalk café. Cramped seating and heavy foot traffic make it not the ideal place for the spatially challenged pet. One-drink minimum with specials. 2100 W. Irving Park Rd.; 773/478-2100.

Scot's: When he visited Scot's, Watson wanted to bark along with the men singing "Diamonds Are a Girl's Best Friend" at the Ravenswood area's only dog-friendly predominantly gay bar. This small, narrow, minimalist establishment features original artwork on the walls and show tunes on the sound system. Watson says, behave yourself and you may get rewarded (as he did) with a dog biscuit from the bartender. A water bowl is set out in the summer. Weekends are the only time for dog folk—if it gets too crowded, four-legged friends are politely asked to come back another time, no matter how melodious their singing voices. 1829 W. Montrose Ave.; 773/528-3253.

Andersonville, Uptown, and Edgewater

Once a remote farming community north of the city, Andersonville is now the preferred urban address for bohemian, intellectual, socially conscious, and gay and lesbian adults. Its main thoroughfare, recently rehabbed, is also a dog destination in and of itself, with an unusually high concentration of dog bakeries, grooming shops, self-washes, veterinarians, and pet-food stores. Many of these Clark Street businesses host adoption events and other pet celebrations throughout the year. For more than 40 years Andersonville has hosted **Midsommarfest** each June. The costumed dog parade is one of the highlights of summer on the North Side.

Andersonville still shows its Swedish roots: Clark Street is home to the Swedish American Museum Center. You'll also find interesting bookstores, gift shops, and authentic Asian, Middle Eastern, Swedish, and Latino grocery stores and restaurants.

Nearby Edgewater (to the north) is home to **Hollywoof Action Committee** (www.hollywoof.org), a local dog group working to build a DFA in the area. They, and the **Edgewater Dog Lovers** group, meet in front of Swift School (5900 N. Winthrop Ave.) weekly to keep up-to-date on dog issues facing the neighborhood. For our purposes, this area runs from Irving Park Road (4000 North) to Devon Avenue (6400 North) and from the lake to Ashland Avenue (1600 West).

DOG-EAR YOUR CALENDAR

Crunch Fitness is giving new meaning to the term "downward-facing dog." The company's **Ruff Yoga Workshop** offers 30-minute outdoor yoga, er, doga, classes to de-stress you and your pooch. The traditional practice encompasses partnering exercises and stretches. Classes are free and held Sundays in summer at Jonquil Park. Intersection of Wrightwood Street and Lincoln Avenue and Sheffield Avenues; 888/227-8624; www.crunch.com.

PARKS, BEACHES, AND RECREATION AREAS

13 Puptown/Margate Park

🐾🐾🐾🐕 (See North Side map on page 42)

One of the largest city dog parks, Puptown (a play on the name of the surrounding neighborhood, Uptown) sits in a self-contained, fenced area called Margate Park in the midst of Chicago's vast lakeside Lincoln Park. Rehabbed by the Chicago Park District several years ago, Puptown now has dog-height water fountains, but it's still waiting for time to help some of the newer trees and shrubs to fill out and fill in. Natasha thinks it's a shame to have an off-leash area so close yet so far from the lake, but once she's there, she usually gets over it, because there's enough room to run and many pebbles to sniff.

Puptown attracts an interesting mix of dog owners and dogs, particularly more small dogs than frequent the other city DFAs. Generally, there is a strong vibe of community cooperation in keeping Puptown clean and safe, and as a result, it's a good place to gab about the dog's life in the city. A supply of plastic bags and tennis balls is always on hand. Dog walkers have "discovered" Puptown, meaning there are occasions when the park has more pups than space to put them. Street parking is also a challenge on weekends, but if you're willing to walk a few blocks, you can typically find something on the neighborhood side streets. Nearby Lawrence Avenue (4800 North) is a major thoroughfare and an on-ramp to Lake Shore Drive, so keep dogs carefully leashed on your way in and out of Puptown. 4921 N. Marine Dr.; www.puptown.org (Puptown Dog Owners Group).

14 Montrose Beach

🐾🐾🐾🐾🐕 (See North Side map on page 42)

Two years of environmental studies and community meetings, not to mention canine whining and begging, resulted in the city's first (and still only) legal off-leash beach. From a steep path along the Old Wilson Boat Launch north to the water's edge, urban dogs enjoy shallow shores and rippling tides of Lake Michigan. Unlike some city DFAs, which are designed to fit into unused corners of parks where no one else would want to go, the Montrose Beach dog beach is an appealing stretch of decent sand and waves, with plenty of room to fetch Frisbees on land or race after them into the water.

MonDog, the community group that made the beach a reality, named the area the Susan Kimmelman Off-Leash Dog Beach, in memory of one of their most active volunteers, and have worked hard to keep the beach open. Since the county animal control ordinance was passed the park district and MonDog have been working together to raise new funds to build the required permanent fencing for the area. The temporary fencing repeatedly falls down and the lack of permanent fencing is a concern of the county administrator. Otherwise, the first off-leash beach seems to be a success. The Chicago Park District is delighted with how clean MonDog has kept the area since its inception. MonDog reminds visitors that the city will be testing the water for bacteria levels, so owners are encouraged to make sure their dogs make pit stops (and to pick them up, of course) before they reach the lake. Extra cleanup efforts are also encouraged for that same reason, and volunteers often stock empty plastic bags near the fence to help out.

If you don't want to take a sandy dog home after a day at the beach, stop for a bath at nearby **Soggy Paws** (1148 W. Leland Ave.; 773/334-7663; www .soggypaws.com).

Despite its name, the Montrose Beach DFA is at Wilson Avenue (4600 North), not Montrose Avenue. Exit on Wilson Avenue off Lake Shore Drive. Parking is available both on the street and in the lot in the park. On days when the lot fills quickly (event-packed weekends in the summer), park to the west of Marine Drive and walk east. Remember to keep your dog leashed while crossing the park to and from the off-leash beach. Neighborhood lore suggests that some of the residents of nearby high-rises see off-leash dogs from their lakeview apartments and call the police immediately. Like all city DFAs, your dog must have a permit to swim here. 4600 N. Lake Shore Dr.; www.mondog.org.

PLACES TO EAT

Driftwood: Bring your iPod playlist and your ipup and you can relax to your favorite tunes, play darts, and order take-out from area restaurants. Making this bar much like home, except with good company, including the owner's two pooches. Don't forget to ask for the bowl of dog treats behind the bar. 1021 W. Montrose Ave.; 773/975-3900.

The Edgewater: You won't be able to take in the live music indoors at The Edgewater with your pooch, but you and he will both enjoy sitting at the summer tables along Bryn Mawr Avenue for some of the best resident people-watching. The design-your-own sandwich with nine different options is popular, as are the hummus, pico de gallo, and other snack-type treats. 5600 N. Ashland Ave.; 773/878-3343.

Kopi Café: Cosmopolitan dogs enjoy the view of two- and four-legged passersby from the small group of sidewalk tables at Kopi Café on busy Clark Street. Kopi takes its name from the Indonesian word for coffee, and on the inside, this café is crammed full of art and merchandise from the owner's many trips to Bali and elsewhere, as well as a sizable array of travel books. Although dogs might not crave the exclusively vegetarian menu, most humans find something to savor among the wide selection of pastries, sandwiches, wraps, and appetizers. Try the Mango Jet tea, which is actually a dairy-free smoothie, perfect for the dog days of summer. As one might expect, Kopi's staff and clientele, while friendly, tend to be pretty laid back. Extra-excitable pooches might not enjoy themselves in these relatively close quarters quite as much as their mellower counterparts. 5317 N. Clark St.; 773/989-5674.

A Taste of Heaven Bakery: As its name suggests, this coffeehouse-cum-hangout is a bakery first, which means its cookies, brownies, and cakes (sold by the slice for one or full-size for parties), are better than average fare. Natasha takes exception to the anti–Valentine's Day cookies. In addition to sayings such as "I hate you" and "Slut," one heart-shaped sugar cookie sports the legend, "Dog." She endures the indignity at the outside tables during the summer. 5401 N. Clark St.; 773/989-0151.

Portage Park, Edison Park, and the Northwest Side

Edison Park is as far northwest as one can live in the city without having a suburban address, with the Metra rail tracks stopping on Olmsted Avenue (one of the neighborhood's many "O" streets). Tagged as popular with police officers, firefighters, and others who are legally required to have a home in the city, this neighborhood has a Mayberry feel.

Portage Park, Jefferson Park, and most other communities of the Northwest Side are home to so many rows of typical Chicago bungalows that the area is often called "the Bungalow Belt," though Old Irving Park is saturated with Victorian homes. There are large Polish and Italian contingents in these neighborhoods and plenty of restaurants and grocery stores dedicated to the cuisines of each. The jewel of the area is Sauganash—an enclave of distinctive homes on larger-than-typical lots tucked away behind Edgebrook Woods. Sauganash is renowned for its Christmas decorations, as neighbors try to top each other in extravagance each year, and makes a great evening holiday walk, weather permitting. If your dog wants to wear antlers, he'll fit right in.

This section covers from the I-90/94 Expressways on the east to the city limits on the west and from Irving Park Road (4000 North) on the south to the city limits on the north.

PARKS, BEACHES, AND RECREATION AREAS

15 Brooks Park

🐾 (See North Side map on page 42)

Its suburban neighbors to the northwest (Des Plaines) and northeast (Niles) don't allow dogs in most of their parks (see the North Suburban Cook County chapter), so Brooks has become the dog destination for those with both 773 and 847 area codes. Brooks is a small but active family park, with soccer, Irish step dancing, softball, and even bocce going on many days a week. Kids flock to the soft-surface playground, field house, and spray pool. A designated walking/jogging path keeps dogs occupied, as do several ball fields and ample grass, surrounded by trees and benches, all buffered from congested Harlem Avenue by the field house. Brooks runs from Harlem Avenue (7200 West) to Odell Avenue (7344 West) at Estes Avenue (7100 North). Parking is not permitted on side streets after 10 P.M. 7100 N. Harlem Ave.; 312/742-7855.

16 Portage Park

🐾🐾🐾 (See North Side map on page 42)

This park is so good, the neighborhood is named after it.

In all seriousness, even during the coldest of bitter Chicago winters, dogs can be found somewhere in Portage Park. Across the street is one of the city's best holistic veterinarians, Julie A. Mayer, at **Portage Park Animal Hospital** (5419 W. Irving Park Rd.; 773/725-0260), and many patients come here before or after an appointment. People like the whimsical stone gateways built during the Works Progress Administration (WPA), and dogs like the nature area on the park's south side, with dirt paths, ground-nesting birds, and small animals to track.

This is a busy place during the summer, as picnickers, snoozers, and soccer players compete with dogs and their owners for a tuft of grass. Your dog may resent giving up some of his winter space, but she'll love the smell of grilled kielbasa floating through the air. Like all city swimming pools, Portage Park's is off-limits to dogs, although it's interesting to note that Olympic gold medalist Mark Spitz set new world records here during trials for the 1972 Olympics. The south border of Irving Park Road gets a lot of auto traffic; a leash is a must. 4100 N. Long Ave.; 312/742-7634.

17 Merrimac Park

🐕 (See North Side map on page 42)

Once known as Kolze's Electric Grove, this was a private wooded park with gas lamps, a nightly orchestra, and beer for a nickel a glass. Unfortunately, none of those amenities remain. Bordered on two sides by busy streets, Merrimac Park today, like nearby Kilbourn Park, doesn't have a lot to recommend it for wet-nosed travelers. Dogs who are in the neighborhood and need to go should head near the two baseball diamonds on the south side. If you're really in the mood for a run, hightail it to Portage Park (see above) or Riis Park (see below). There's a small parking lot behind the field house. Merrimac is bordered by Irving Park Road (4000 North) and Narragansett Avenue (6400 West). 6343 W. Irving Park Rd.; 312/742-7626.

18 Chopin Park

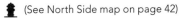 (See North Side map on page 42)

A nice, albeit small, park with plenty of dog essentials (trees and trash cans). Even when there's not another dog in sight at Chopin, there's evidence of them, with "lost dog" flyers papering the park. On the park's southeast side, there's a wading pool, flanked by benches under a roof for that crucial summer shade. Dogs aren't allowed in the water, but are welcome elsewhere on the grassy expanse.

There's a bike rack here, if your dog is one of those who keeps pace with your two-wheeler, but no parking lot. Chopin is at the southwest corner of Long Avenue (5440 West) and Newport Avenue (3434 North). 3420 N. Long Ave.; 312/742-7606.

19 Kilbourn Park

(See North Side map on page 42)

With busy Addison Avenue (3600 North) on the north side and the Metra track flanking the east side, this park isn't big or secluded. There aren't a lot of trees, but there is some open space between three baseball fields, so if you and your pup are in the area and he needs to stretch, there's room to go. A perennial garden and greenhouse have revived neighborhood interest in gardening projects that brighten these environs. Mother's Day weekend the greenhouse hosts an annual organic plant sale. As a result, there's not a parking spot to be found. There's no parking lot, and street parking can be tough near rail lines, but you'd only come here if you were walking around in the neighborhood for other reasons, so it isn't a problem. 3501 N. Kilbourn Ave.; 312/742-7624.

20 Independence Park

(See North Side map on page 42)

The ball fields here were once home to a sunken garden, and though flower fans may miss the old days, dogs don't. Fittingly, Independence Park gives leashed dogs plenty of independence, comprising a several-blocks-wide space in which to run when ballgames are not in session. The park's big open fields take up much of the center of the park, with tall trees, a pretty field house, and flag pole at the perimeter. Natasha encourages you to bat your big, brown dog eyes at the hot-dog vendor who sits on the north side of the park in the summer.

Independence Park is bordered by a particularly busy stretch of Irving Park Road (4000 North), because it's just east of the I-90/94 Expressway and by the

Blue Line El train. Permits are required to park on the side streets, but there are meters on Irving Park. The cross street is Springfield Avenue (3900 West). 3945 N. Springfield Ave.; 312/742-7590.

21 Riis Park

😾 😾 (See North Side map on page 42)

This Northwest Side park is named after reformer Jacob A. Riis, the man Teddy Roosevelt said came nearer to being "the ideal American" than anyone else. Riis advocated inner-city parks, particularly in poorer areas. Riis is probably happy about the diverse community that uses his namesake land, a mix of local schoolchildren, adult softball teams (16-inch Chicago-style softball, of course), and sunbathers. Since 1996, the Park District has spent almost $3 million upgrading the large park, paving basketball courts, installing ice-skating rinks, adding a water park, and renovating the stone-edged lagoon.

To Natasha's dismay, dogs aren't allowed down the water slide, but she likes to sniff out the glacial ridge at Riis Park, said to be a remnant of the shoreline of Lake Michigan. In the winter, the ridge attracts sledders from all over the area. Other dogs like the mix of shady lagoon banks and open sunny meadows, perfect in any of Chicago's ever-changing weather. Riis has had problems with gang activity in the past. Part of the city's investment in the park went to improve security, but a cautious dog lover would stay away after dark, or at least stick to the well-lit areas near the softball fields if a quick nighttime squat is necessary. Riis Park typically has plenty of parking. 6100 W. Fullerton Ave.; 312/746-5363.

PLACES TO EAT

Chief O'Neill's Pub: The beer garden in this classic Irish pub in Avondale seats 250…that's plenty of room for you to bring your canine companion, not to mention his friends from doggy daycare. Monday night is the big dog-friendly evening: Remember to order enough corned beef and cabbage to share. 3471 N. Elston Ave.; 773/473-5263.

Starbucks: Thanks to a dog-loving manager, this Old Irving Park Starbucks is one of the city's most dog-friendly. Dog treats, water bowls, and space at the outdoor café are among the things pups are promised. 4365 W. Irving Park Rd.; 773/736-5226.

SuperDawg Drive-In: Your dog may get all too accustomed to the idea of someone coming out to the car to bring her slabs of meat if you frequent Super-Dawg. A bona fide drive-in, with speakers and carhops who deliver your order, SuperDawg is a Chicago institution and serves some of the city's best franks and fries, delivered in the cutest little colored cardboard box. If you don't want to dine in your car with your dog, there are a few tables under a retro awning along busy Milwaukee Avenue. You may recognize the restaurant's giant icons from the movie *Wayne's World*. 6363 N. Milwaukee Ave.; 773/763-0660.

Lakeview, Wrigleyville, and Roscoe Village

Once several disparate communities, the Lakeview neighborhood has spread out so far that it encompasses a large area, much of which is nowhere near having a lake view. Wrigleyville, as its name suggests, is the area surrounding Wrigley Field, where the Chicago Cubs play, but rarely win. Even non-baseball fans are taken by the physical presence of Wrigley Field, which is settled in snugly amid greystone apartment buildings, restaurants, bars, schools, and other essentials of urban life. Parking in Wrigleyville is never easy. Many of the streets are designated for residential permit parking, and metered spots fill up fast. Under no circumstances should you ever try to drive to or through Wrigleyville during a Cubs game (really, never ever). The rest of the year, the lots used for baseball parking generally have space. Street parking tends to be better the farther west you drive. Roscoe Village, once a little-known enclave marked only by a purple sign on the Metra tracks, is now a culinary confluence, with many of the city's most interesting new restaurants. In inclement weather (of which there is much of in Chicago, unfortunately), locals head to Roscoe Village's **Of Mutts and Men** (2149 W. Belmont Ave.; 773/477-7171). It is essentially an indoor park—requiring a day, month, or annual pass—with room for your pup to run indoors and places for you to play pool or chess.

Having fewer high-rises and more two-flats and single-family homes than Lincoln Park, Lakeview has been able to retain some of the family- and dog-friendliness that made these areas hospitable to so many families for so long. It's not unusual to see impromptu dog play sessions in a neighbor's yard during the after-work walks. Businesses welcoming dogs and selling all-natural, high-end pet foods have opened throughout the area. These

FETCHING NECESSITIES

Calling itself "the people and pet-friendly bank," **North Community Bank** will let you make a deposit—no, not that kind—with dog in tow. This bank, where PAWS Chicago founder Paula J. Fasseas is vice chairman, puts its money where slobbery mouths are. Pets are welcome inside, where tellers keep treats. Adoption events and admonitions to rescue homeless pets are as commonplace here as ATM fees are elsewhere. Main Office, 3639 N. Broadway St.; 773/244-7000; www.northcommunitybank.com.

Among the other North Side locations: 2000 W. Division St., 773/486-7154; 3401 N. Western Ave., 773/244-3245; 3180 N. Broadway St., 773/244-7092; 1555 N. Damen Ave., 773/244-7892; and 3420 N. Clark St., 773/687-5020.

neighborhoods run from Diversey Parkway (2800 North) to Irving Park Road (4000 North) and from the lake to California Avenue (2800 West).

PARKS, BEACHES, AND RECREATION AREAS

22 Challenger Bark

 (See North Side map on page 42)

Nestled between an alley and a cemetery underneath the El tracks near Wrigley Field, Challenger Bark was a plot of land optimistically called Challenger Park that served as a magnet for litter, loitering, and drug dealers... until some neighborhood dog owners turned it into an unofficial dog park. Cautious about leash laws, a group of 15 community activists spent more than a year petitioning the Park District to officially designate the area as a DFA. The fences went up in 2003, and the resulting space is prettier and more peaceful than you'd expect from the street. During Cubs games, the Irving Park Road (4000 North) parking lot is used by baseball fans, so don't drive, unless you're willing to pay to park. Instead, enter by foot (and paw) near the Buena Circle play lot at 1049 W. Buena Avenue, to the northeast of the auto entrance. Challenger Bark is recommended as a small DFA for those in the area already, rather than one worth making a trip from afar, so the pedestrian entrance is one to remember. 1100 W. Irving Park Rd.; 773/477-7933 (Challenger Bark dog group).

23 Revere Park

(See North Side map on page 42)

These nine acres are very kid-friendly, meaning most of the wide-open spaces are typically occupied by baseball and softball teams. Unlike nearby Horner Park, however, there are fewer adult leagues on the field, so there are some early-morning and late-evening windows for canine fun. Revere is one of many city parks that show free family- and dog-friendly movies on summer nights. The park is near the southwest corner of Western Avenue (2400 West) and Irving Park Road (4000 North) in the North Center neighborhood. 2509 W. Irving Park Rd.; 312/742-7594.

24 Hamlin Park

🐾🐾🐕 (See North Side map on page 42)

A well-intentioned city dog park, the Hamlin Park DFA is squeezed in between the sidewalk and the tennis courts in the L-shaped southwest corner at Hoyne and Oakdale. One of the Park District's objectives, when encouraging neighborhood activists to petition for off-leash areas, is to find plots of park land that are otherwise unused. Well, this awkward strip was unused because it isn't very usable. Park District officials now concede it is too linear for dogs to romp freely and vow not to make the same mistake with future DFAs. Year-round mud (courtesy of perennial shade) has been replaced with pea gravel, which improved cleanliness both at the park and helps when you get your pup home.

That said, Cooper thinks a mediocre legal off-leash park is better than being tethered. Plus, because this DFA isn't the best, it's rarely crowded during the workday. After work hours, the small space can house too many dogs at once. Street parking is seldom a problem, particularly on Hoyne Avenue (2100 West). If the trash cans are full (or, as is sometimes oddly the case, missing), walk half a block north to the Dumpster next to the field house.

The rest of Hamlin (leash required) is large, open, and grassy, and thus popular for nighttime obedience classes and impromptu play dates. Mature trees help make this park an oasis just blocks away from the busy Diversey/Damen/Clybourn intersection. Olympic boxer David Diaz trained at the Hamlin Park field house before the 1996 Games. From Diversey Parkway, drive north on Damen Avenue to the park. 3035 N. Hoyne Ave.; 312/742-7785 (Hamlin Park field house) or 773/525-8592 (Hamlin Dog Park Group).

PLACES TO EAT

Brett's Café Americain: A white-tablecloth restaurant that's now less of an anomaly in this area than it once was, Brett's remains one of the few upscale restaurants in a row of casual hangouts. Expect American entrées with ethnic accents, such as Asian, Caribbean, and Southwestern. Dogs are welcomed with water bowls in the outdoor seating, which fits 18. Reservations are a good idea. 2011 W. Roscoe St.; 773/248-0999.

Café Avanti: A favorite neighborhood hangout, Café Avanti is a coffee shop with more. Many locals stop by for dessert after an independent film at the nearby Music Box Theater; the café is open until midnight on weekends. A back room is often used to host community meetings. You and your dog will be perfectly happy sitting out on Southport Avenue, watching the considerable foot and paw traffic on any summer night. Bowls of water and dog biscuits are often offered to canine guests at the outdoor tables. 3706 N. Southport Ave.; 773/880-5959.

Cody's Public House: Dogs roam freely at this corner bar off the main drag—truly a neighborhood tavern with a roster of dog regulars. Even if you arrived sans pooch, you'd guess the place was dog-friendly: The ladies' and men's rooms are designated, respectively, by rear views of a squatting dog and a dog with its hind leg raised. The bar boasts a spacious room for real darts—none of the electronic plastic-tipped variety—but make sure your aim is good enough to avoid Fido. The house rule is "no crapping, no peeing, no lying down… and that goes for the dogs too." There's a backyard beer garden in the summer. 1658 W. Barry Ave.; 773/528-4050.

Costello's Sandwich and Sides: During weekday lunch hours, it's often standing-room-only at Costello's, as neighborhood workers and moms with strollers all clamor for fresh-made sandwiches and sides and the popular kids' menu. The sandwiches exceed the cookie-cutter fare offered at sub chains—in both taste and price. They come with a bag of chips, but Costello's sides ($1.25 extra for a small order of skin-on mashed potatoes, chipotle mac 'n' cheese, cucumber-tomato pasta salad and more) make chips about as appealing as a trip to the vet. The front (Roscoe St.) outdoor tables are open to dogs; the large back patio is not. The restaurant's Lincoln Square location (4647 N. Lincoln Ave.; 773/989-7788) is also dog-friendly. 2015 W. Roscoe St.; 773/929-2323.

Cullen's Bar & Grill: If there's one category of business Chicago has in spades, it's Irish pubs (this is the city that dyes the river green on St. Paddy's Day, after all). At Cullen's, real Irish brogues can be heard from both employees and customers. Dogs are welcomed on the patio with water and treats. Cullen's makes a mean Reuben sandwich, with lots of extra corned beef to share with your pup; keep the Guinness to yourself. Nestled between the Mercury and Music Box Theaters, Cullen's can get crowded after shows, particularly when it's hosting its own live music inside. Windows at Cullen's open out to the street, so if you get a patio table, you and your dog will be able to sing along. 3741 N. Southport Ave.; 773/975-0600.

Deleece: Some of the most solid, consistently good food in Lakeview can be found here. And though it's right next to the hipness that is the Southport strip, its location north of Irving Park Road makes it slightly less known, and therefore a little less hectic. Still, its lamb and Sunday brunch are no secrets, and since you and your dog will have to sit at one of the 35 outdoor seats, you may have to wait. It will be worth it. 4004 N. Southport Ave.; 773/325-1710.

Joey's Brickhouse: Shaded sidewalk tables provide a comfortable spot to hunker down and share some Italian comfort food with Fido. 1258 W. Belmont Ave.; 773/296-1300.

Southport Lanes & Billiards: It still looks like an old Schlitz neighborhood brewery/bar from the outside (such establishments dotted Chicago neighborhoods in the 1930s and '40s), and in many ways that's what it is. A tavern/bowling alley/pool hall has been in business at this corner since 1922. In warm weather, dogs are welcome to join their owners for drinks at the outdoor tables that line Southport Avenue and Henderson Street. Ask a friend to watch your pup long enough to peek inside and see a relic of days gone by: a bowling alley with pin-setters (human beings), rather than a machine to rack the pins. 3325 N. Southport Ave.; 773/472-6600.

Ten Cat Tavern: The farther you walk into this deep, storefront bar, the more pleasant surprises you encounter—mosaics on the walls, poles, an old never-removed sink from a bygone business, two by-the-hour pool tables, a cozy back room with a fireplace, and a beer garden with the flavor of a city backyard. Then there's the comfortable retro furniture, original art on the walls, and pinball. Watson was disappointed that the eponymous 10 cats do not roam the wood floors (the bar got its name because the owner used to own 10 felines), but a more comfortable, homier drinking establishment would be difficult to find. Leashed dogs are welcome in the bar anytime. If they do their business in the beer garden, you will be asked to clean it up. 3931 N. Ashland Ave.; 773/935-5377.

Uncommon Ground: It's labeled a coffee shop, but Uncommon Ground is about as common in coffeehouse circles as finding a Finnish Lapphund at the local dog park. Sure, the place serves an array of coffee and tea drinks, but it packs in the patrons with eclectic American gourmet fare like pumpkin ravioli and Louisiana spiced grilled chicken salad—not to mention a full liquor bar. Up the street from Wrigley Field, it also serves up live music from nationally touring artists and performers from Chicago's Old Town School of Folk Music. Inside is off-limits to canines, but in the summer, dogs can be tied to the outside of the fence while you imbibe. 3800 N. Clark St.; 773/929-3680.

PLACES TO STAY

Best Western Hawthorne Terrace: Once a transient hotel, this 59-room inn is now a remarkably comfortable, boutique-style hotel that welcomes dogs under 25 pounds. Cardio equipment is offered in a makeshift gym with a whirlpool, but you'll have more fun raising your heart rate by walking through this always-active, anything-goes neighborhood. Set in the heart of Boystown, it is within walking distance of Wrigley Field and the lake. Most rooms have refrigerators and microwaves. A $250 damage deposit is refunded upon checkout. Room rates range $139–185; parking (a must in this neighborhood) is extra. 3434 N. Broadway St., 773/244-3434 or 888/675-BEST; www.bestwestern.com/prop_14151.

Lincoln Park

Many consider the Lincoln Park neighborhood, which includes the DePaul University campus, as the heart of the North Side. There's always something going on here, whether it's a mere stroll down Lincoln Avenue (see the **Biograph Theater** at 2433 N. Lincoln Ave., where John Dillinger was shot), or one of the many summer festivals that feed a dog's spirit (and stomach).

Lincoln Park side streets are havens for dogs and their walkers. Beyond the lakefront high-rises, discover streets packed with 19th-century row houses whose tiny front gardens are fenced with fanciful wrought iron. (Look up: You can find evidence of the area's European settlers in some buildings' cornices.) Preservation efforts begun in the 1940s have kept many Lincoln Park streets looking like they did in the late 1800s, while many of the larger thoroughfares are now dotted with newly constructed buildings and 21st-century amenities like parking garages and pet-food stores.

Lincoln Park is known for its retail streets—Clark Street, Wells Street (200 West), Armitage Avenue (2000 North), and Halsted Street (800 West)—and many shops and bars cater to dogs. There's even **The Canine Empire** (866/364-7785; www.canineempire.com), a 100,000-square-foot dog health club. The people bakery **Breadsmith** (1710 N. Wells St.; 312/642-5858) bakes and sells "good dog" biscuits. But even in dog-friendly spots, manners rule: Natasha's buddy Huck got a swift kick out the door for doggy behavior in an Old Town bar.

That was too bad for Huck, as pubs in Lincoln Park aren't just part of the nightlife, they're the town-square equivalent in this urban area. If you want to know what's up with dog lovers in the city, grab a leash and head to

DIVERSION

Braun Drugs looks like a friendly neighborhood pharmacy. And it is—for both four- and two-legged customers. With a valid veterinary prescription, Braun will flavor chewable medications to smell and taste like beef, salmon, chicken, and other tastes your dog will prefer over the proverbial sugar. The custom-made meds can be ready within 24 hours and can be shipped anywhere, or your dog can go with you to pick it up... and get a belly-rub, too. 2075 N. Lincoln Ave.; 773/549-7387.

these picks between North Avenue (1600 North) and Diversey Parkway (2800 North) and from the lake to Ashland Avenue (1600 West).

PARKS, BEACHES, AND RECREATION AREAS

25 Dog Beach

(See North Side map on page 42)

Cooper's been barking himself hoarse on this issue, but no one seems to be listening. This north corner of Belmont Harbor is separated from the rest of the park by a chain-link fence, and as a result it has become the unofficial dog beach. It's so well known that many tour books cite it as a Park District–approved romp. Not only is that not the case—police can and do ticket off-leash dogs here—but area veterinarians discourage their patients from taking a dip here. The shallow sand and lack of wave action, coupled with the high number of urban dogs relieving themselves in such as small space—not to mention boats dumping their waste in the harbor—make the beach a bacteria breeding ground. Some veterinarians say the occasional romp here won't seriously harm your pet, but with a legal dog beach at Montrose Beach, there's no reason to bother with this little patch of sand (which isn't even worth a meager hydrant on the paw scale). No matter who you see swimming here, just keep walking by.

26 Oz Park

🐾🐾 (See North Side map on page 42)

Oz Park's main topographical feature is "the hill," often called "dog hill" because the mini mount is such a popular doggy destination. Leashed dogs are frequent visitors to this grassy 13-acre park, where they lap from the dog-level water fountain. Oz Park is named for the books penned by L. Frank Baum, who lived nearby, and while there's no Toto, one of the park's entrances (Webster Street at Lincoln Avenue) is marked with a yellow brick road and a towering Tin Man.

Many Lincoln Park dog owners swear there's no place like Oz Park. Their dogs pull them to the hill on the south side of the park, near Lincoln Park High School. But heated turf wars over dog rights in the popular, and therefore crowded, neighborhood park have made off-leash ticketing more prevalent here than in many of the other city parks. Early-morning hours, before the play lot fills up, tend to be the dog-friendliest. If you're in the area, try to come by before breakfast. If not, there are other area parks (including the mammoth Lincoln Park and the off-leash Wiggly Field) that rate a special trip before Oz does. Oz Park is just southeast of DePaul University, bordered by Webster Avenue (2200 North) and Larrabee Street (600 West). 2021 N. Burling St.; 312/742-7898.

27 Wiggly Field

🐾🐾🐾🐕 (See North Side map on page 42)

Grace Noethling Park was transformed in 1997 into Wiggly Field, the city's first official DFA, where Rover is allowed to run off-leash. Nestled under the El in trendy Lincoln Park, Wiggly Field is the city dog park with the most amenities: multiple-height water fountains for dogs of all sizes; many benches; plenty of shade; a time-out corner where ill-behaved dogs can go to remember their training; agility equipment; and even a fake mailbox for marking territory.

It is often also the most crowded. If you're looking for a young, energetic crowd to trade training secrets with while watching numerous dogs named Wrigley and Sammy (as in Sosa) wrestle, there's no better spot. Tennis balls, toys, and plastic bags are always left at the park in case you show up empty-handed. If you have a flexible schedule, try the morning, after the 9-to-5ers go to work, and you'll have more room to roam. Even dog lovers who choose less-populated spots for the majority of their off-leash socialization are grateful for the existence of Wiggly Field, as its success (and the hard work of its D.A.W.G. organizers) opened the Chicago Park District's eyes and mind to additional dog parks.

Each October, D.A.W.G. organizes the **Furry, Fun, Fall Festival,** with a dog Halloween costume contest, games, contests, and, of course, edible prizes, at Wiggly Field. Drive south on Sheffield Avenue (1000 West) from Diversey Parkway (2800 North). Metered parking is available on Lincoln Avenue if there are no empty side-street spots. 2645 N. Sheffield Ave.; 773/348-2832; www.dawgsite.org.

PLACES TO EAT

Annette's Homemade Italian Ice: From April–November people like Annette's Italian ice and sundaes. Pooches like to cool off with the soy-based doggy treats. A walk-up window makes it easy to stop on an evening stroll. 2009 N. Bissell St.; 773/868-9000.

Bordo's Eatery and Sauce: There are just 10 outdoor tables along this busy strip of Lincoln Avenue. But if there's a wait for these seats, it's worth it. Dogs are not just tolerated, they're welcomed at this restaurant that serves everything from bar food to Italian entrées. You'll get 15 percent off the check on weekdays just for showing off your pup. 2476–2478 N. Lincoln Ave.; 773/529-6900.

Dunlay's on Clark: Drink specials and better-than-average food have made this new eatery a favorite of people and pups. As in all of Lincoln Park, sidewalk space is at a premium, so dogs who need their space should dine elsewhere. Others will enjoy the outdoor tables on Wrightwood Avenue. 2600 N. Clark St.; 773/883-6000; www.dunlaysonclark.com.

Jake's Pub: With 60 beers (17 of which are on tap) and a website that proclaims it a laid-back, friendly neighborhood bar that encourages you bring your canine best friend, there's nothing not to like. Jake's has been known to host canine birthday parties. 2932 N. Clark St.; 773/248-3318.

PLACES TO STAY

The Inn at Lincoln Park: Dogs under 50 pounds can stay at this historic hotel for a $50 additional fee. It is walking distance to some of the best green spaces in the city. Rates range $149–$265. 601 W. Diversey Pkwy.; 773/348-2810.

Logan Square, Humboldt Park, and West

Logan Square was built by wealthy immigrants in the 1800s, and as a result, this neighborhood and its sister to the south, Humboldt Park, have some of the most impressive mansion-esque homes, wide streets, and beautiful landscaping anywhere in the city. In one walk, you can pass examples of art nouveau, prairie, renaissance revival, Victorian, and gothic architecture.

A century later, gangs and poverty took their toll on these streets, but fortunately, many of the gems remain. In the last 20 years, a preservation- oriented gentrification has occurred. Houses are being rebuilt and rehabbed rather than destroyed. Culinary discoveries lurk at many corners. If you're in the mood for authentic Mexican food, grab your leash and let your nose lead you. This section stretches from Diversey Parkway (2800 North) south to Madison Street (1 North, 1 South) and west from Western Avenue (2400 West) to the city limits.

PARKS, BEACHES, AND RECREATION AREAS

28 Logan Boulevard

🐾 🐾 (See North Side map on page 42)

Not a park per se, Logan Boulevard is one of the city's mighty, but oft-overlooked, boulevards, with lush green medians and housing to match. Walk down this grand boulevard and daydream about living in one of these palatial homes, with a staff of 10 to bring you any chew toy your heart desires. Don't miss the monument at Logan Square commemorating Illinois' first 100 years:

a 68-foot column, topped by an eagle, built in 1918. Your dog will meet many four-footed friends on your midday stroll. Given the traffic on both sides of the street, this is a strictly on-leash outing. Logan Boulevard runs from Kedzie Boulevard to just east of Western Avenue at Elston Avenue. Concentrate your jaunt west of Western (away from the weekend traffic heading toward Target). The Chicago Park District's former chief of staff, Drew Becher, says some dog lovers make a summer day of the city's connected boulevards, stopping at the many outdoor cafés along the way.

29 Humboldt Park

🐾🐾🐾 🐾 (See North Side map on page 42)

One of renowned American master landscape artist Jens Jensen's first gardens, Humboldt Park comprises 207 acres of interesting architecture, prairie grasses, and wide-open spaces. The Boathouse Pavilion at 1301 North Humboldt Boulevard is an excellent example of Prairie School architecture. Make an effort to get to the two bronze buffalo sculptures at the south end of the park (they're one of the few originals left from the World's Columbian Exposition in Chicago in 1893)…unless your dog, like Natasha, is inexplicably afraid of giant fake animals.

Dogs aren't allowed to roam in the remarkable flower gardens or to swim in the lagoons, which, because of their inland beaches, are popular with sunbathers. But there are plenty of winding paths to explore, ducks to watch, and squirrels to chase, not to mention shade trees where you can rest when you're done with all that running. Though safer than it was a few years ago, Humboldt Park is best enjoyed during daylight hours, particularly if you and your dog are walking alone. If you need a nighttime walk, stick to the well-lit sidewalks around the park's exterior.

Humboldt Park is located between North Avenue (1600 North) and Augusta Boulevard (1000 North) and Kedzie Avenue (3200 West) and California Avenue (2800 West). 1400 N. Sacramento Ave.; 312/742-7549.

30 Blackhawk Dog Park/Pulaski Park

🐾🐾🐾 (See North Side map on page 42)

If you walk toward the expressway from the large Pulaski Park, you'd see this little park that looks suspiciously like an official DFA. It is fenced in, has rules posted (not to mention decorative bones hanging all around), and is well cared for by local dog lovers.

Rumors circulate about where this pseudo-DFA came from. One recurring story suggests former congressman Dan Rostenkowski donated the land to neighborhood dog owners. Officially, the Park District is still looking into who owns it and what needs to happen to make it the real deal. But locals think because it is on a patch of land next to the expressway that isn't particularly desirable, the approval process will come quickly. Of course, if you chose to play off-leash here before then, you may be fined and ticketed. If the risk is too high for you, Pulaski Park is a lovely place for a leashed walk. 1419 W. Blackhawk St.

PLACES TO EAT

Dunlay's on the Square: A sister location to Dunlay's on Clark, this Logan Square joint is well located with ample outdoor seating on a wide stretch of sidewalk. Just to prove how dog-friendly Dunlay's is, they serve their own smoked pig ear to canine customers. 3137 W. Logan Blvd.; 773/227-2400; www.dunlaysonthesquare.com.

Wicker Park, Bucktown, and Ukrainian Village

Almost always referred to as "Chicago's SoHo," Wicker Park and Bucktown have lived up to the moniker in ways their residents never imagined. Like SoHo, this area was once a magnet for artists (both aspiring and accomplished) because its inexpensive loft real estate was big enough for painting, sculpting, and performance art. The artists captured the attention of everyone else, who soon realized how convenient the area is to the expressways and public transportation. The area's low rents are gone, but the vibe remains. The neighborhoods (the names of which are used interchangeably, although technically Wicker Park is to the south of Bucktown), have retained a bohemian feel with one-of-a-kind clothing boutiques, recording studios, and other unusual businesses. **Apartment Number 9** (1804 N. Damen Ave.; 773/395-2999) specializes in people fashion, but their dog collars are the talk of the DFA.

The heart of this area is the North, Damen, and Milwaukee intersection, which is always packed with cars, pedestrians, and dogs. These areas are home to three of the city's DFAs. All three are small spots, but their leash-free amenities perk up urban ears.

To the south of Wicker Park is Ukrainian Village, which, as its name suggests, is home to many Ukrainian and Polish Americans. Quieter than its neighbors, Ukrainian Village is a tight-knit community with unusual churches and neighbors who know one another. This area starts from Ashland Avenue (1600 West) on the east and runs to Western Avenue (2400 West); and from Diversey Parkway (2800 North) to Madison Street (1 North, 1 South).

PARKS, BEACHES, AND RECREATION AREAS

❸❶ Churchill Field Park

🐾🐾🐕 (See North Side map on page 42)

Another small DFA crammed next to railroad tracks, Churchill Field Park is frustrating to dogs who see the wide-open spaces of the adjacent baseball field, but aren't allowed to run in the larger space. But the triangular spot

DIVERSION

Hauling a 40-pound bag of dog food home on the El is no fun. Hauling it up four flights of stairs to your apartment is less fun. Fortunately, someone else will do this for you. All you have to say is, "Fetch." **PETCO** in River North (440 N. Orleans St.; 312/670-3747; www.petco.com) offers home delivery service within a five-mile radius of their store. Cost is $15, Monday–Friday, 8 A.M.–5 P.M. Delivery is usually item-by-item but weekly drop-offs can be arranged.

allows for some running and chasing, and the park is equipped with canine-height water fountains for thirsty dogs on hot summer days. The hard surface stops mud and bacteria from going home on your dog's paws, and pea gravel surrounds trees on which he can pee.

Churchill Field Park advocates have self-policed violations of Park District rules, such as dog walkers bringing in more dogs than they can watch. Owners have become more attentive to the potential for overcrowding. With three DFAs in the area, things have improved, as the area's many dogs have a choice of where to play. Churchill Field Park isn't worth a long trip to get here, but if you're in the area, particularly on a weekday, it is a good place to get your ya-yas out. If you enter from Damen Avenue, you'll have to walk behind the baseball bleachers to get to the DFA. Entering from the double gate at Winchester Avenue is easier, but metered parking is available on the Damen Avenue (2000 West) side. 1825 N. Damen Ave.

32 Walsh Park

 (See North Side map on page 42)

This is another DFA that's longer than it is wide, making it hard to chase your own tail, much less one another. This park is so small and narrow there's not much room to get out of the way of dogs in hot pursuit of a tennis ball. What Walsh does have in its favor (besides being a legal off-leash city spot) are running water and a mixture of shade and sun areas for days out in all weather. Because Walsh is one of three DFAs in the Wicker Park/Bucktown area, some of the pressures related to overcrowding have improved in recent years.

Local community groups have worked hard to alleviate early tension between dog lovers and non-dog lovers who use the adjacent Walsh Park. Nonetheless, this isn't a destination DFA, but one to use if you happen to be in the area. Avoid canine congestion during after-work hours during the week and any time on the weekends. Enter the DFA from Marshfield Avenue (1634 West), where street parking is possible. 1722 N. Ashland Ave.; 773/384-0393.

FETCHING NECESSITIES

Sometimes, even humans need to stock up on basics. Here are a few places that will allow you to have your hound by your side when you're running errands.

April Sevens: Rottweiler mix Brooklyn will help you choose a custom frame for Fido's photo. 1945 W. Chicago Ave.; 312/455-1965.

Dark Star Video: This dog-friendly video and DVD rental shop in Lincoln Square classifies flicks in amusing categories, such as Chick Flicks instead of the boring old Comedy. Cooper checks in regularly to see if Classic Dog Dramas has been added yet. 4355 N. Lincoln Ave.; 773/665-7827.

The Denim Lounge: You gotta look good while walking the dog. Bring him here while you pick out the perfect pair of jeans. 2004 W. Roscoe St., 773/935-2820; www.madisonandfriends.com /denimlounge.

Edgewater Antique Mall: Non-clumsy dogs are welcomed in this new treasure trove—and the owners, pups by their sides, may also share some of their favorite secret neighborhood dog stops with four-legged customers. 6314 N. Broadway; 773/262-2525.

Kafka: Store mascot Beakton, a Boston terrier, will help you choose from 250 wines under $15 in this Boystown wine shop. 3325 N. Halsted St.; 773/975-9463.

Krista K Boutique: Krista Kaur Meyers moved to Lakeview from dog-friendly San Francisco. That's where she got the idea of keeping water bowls and a big bag of dog biscuits inside her women's clothing store. 3458 N. Southport Ave.; 773/248-1967.

New Leaf: Dogs like to stop and smell the flowers at this florist because they know they'll get thrown a bone. 2316 W. School St.; 773/327-9068.

Pagoda Red: Small dogs like the pretty courtyard. Their owners like the 8,000 square feet of antiques. Both are welcome inside. 1714 N. Damen Ave.; 773/235-1188.

Unabridged Books: Dog biscuits and belly-rubs greet bibliophiles' beasts in this Lakeview bookstore. 3251 N. Broadway St.; 773/883-9119.

Women & Children First: The specialty at this feminist shop is books by and about women. Dogs of both sexes are equally welcome on leashes. 5233 N. Clark St.; 773/769-9299.

33 Wicker Park

 (See North Side map on page 42)

Natasha likes the size and triangular shape of the off-leash area at Wicker Park because it's perfectly designed for that favorite dog pastime: running and chasing in circles. As the neighborhood residents have changed from artists who could slip out in the afternoons for a romp at the park to folks with 9-to-5 jobs, so has the crowd at the park. Professional dog-walkers, some with more than the sane as well as legal limit of pooches, can take over the DFA on weekday afternoons. Weekday mornings, however, and even early on weekends, the Wicker Park DFA is a great example of what off-leash areas are supposed to be. Owners tend to be friendly with one another, but still keep an eye on what their pooches are doing. Folks pick up after their pups and encourage others to do so, so odor is rarely an issue here.

As its name suggests, the rest of the tree-lined Wicker Park is central to the neighborhood, with farmers markets and kids' classes any time the sun shines. The entire park is just four acres, and it always seems filled with interesting characters from the neighborhood. You and your curious mutt will enjoy sitting on the benches watching the activity, as well as pit-stopping on the grassy patches. During the week, street parking is often possible along Wicker Park Avenue and Schiller Street (1400 North), or in metered spots on Damen Avenue (2000 West). 1425 N. Damen Ave.; 312/742-3647.

34 Union Park

(See North Side map on page 42)

One of Jens Jensen's first gardens is at this odd-shaped park in the West Loop (a neighborhood that spans the Madison Street division, and is covered in greater detail in the South Side chapter). Union Park is also historic for being one of this city's first integrated parks—performers such as Thomas A. Dorsey (the "Father of Gospel Music") and Ramsey Lewis played here in their day. Union Park is still a center of drama and music (including the Pitchfork Music Festival), but much of the activity now goes on inside. That means the fields in the middle of the small park are free for pooches to play in. During early morning and afternoon hours, before high school football and adult intramural teams hit the turf, dog lovers are often the only folks at Union Park. A parking lot is available, but street parking is usually possible. The park is nestled next to Ogden Avenue at Ashland Avenue (1600 West) and Warren Boulevard (36 North). 1501 W. Randolph St.; 312/746-5494.

PLACES TO EAT

Bucktown Pub: Play pinball with your pup at this neighborhood pub. When the bar gets crowded late at night, it is time for dogs to go home. 1658 W. Cortland Ave.; 773/394-9898.

Danny's Tavern: People were sitting on couches in this house-turned-bar long before they did it on *Friends*. Danny's is dark and full of scents your dog can track. Just get him out before it gets too crowded. After 10 P.M., he's sure to get a crushed paw. 1951 W. Dickens Ave.; 773/489-6457.

Enoteca Roma Winebar & Bruschetteria: Saddle up to one of 100 outdoor seats for deals on pizza, pasta, breads, salads, and lots of good wines. 2144 W. Division St.; 773/342-1011; www.enotecaroma.com.

Lemming's: A classic Chicago bar inside and out. Unassuming from the front, dark wood and vintage elements inside. This is another Bucktown bar that has watched its crowd change over the years, but Lemming's is still a laid-back home to pinball, pool, movie nights, drink specials, and dog-friend-liness. 1850 N. Damen Ave.; 773/862-1688.

Rainbo Club: A non-trendy Wicker Park bar sounds like a contradiction in terms these days, but Rainbo Club, just south of the intensity of the neighborhood, is still loyal to its locals. Avoid the rush and bring your pup early on weeknights. Rumor has it that Nelson Algren once drank here. Somehow it seems appropriate, then, that the bar is cash only. 1150 N. Damen Ave.; 773/489-5999.

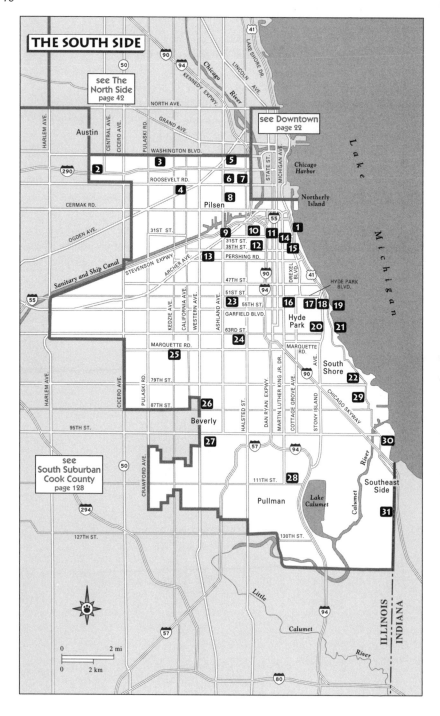

THE SOUTH SIDE

see The
North Side
page 42

see Downtown
page 22

see
South Suburban
Cook County
page 128

Austin

Pilsen

Hyde
Park

Beverly

South
Shore

Southeast
Side

Pullman

Lake Michigan

Chicago Harbor

Northerly Island

Lake Calumet

ILLINOIS
INDIANA

0   2 mi

0   2 km

CHAPTER 3

The South Side

At its most basic, the city of Chicago can be divided into two distinct regions: the North Side and the South Side. The joke goes that South Siders think of North Siders much like Canadians think of the United States, with an air of contempt and moral superiority. And North Siders think of South Siders much like Americans think of Canada, which is to say, not at all.

Like all good jokes, it has bit of truth in it. The North Side is everything you've seen in movies filmed in Chicago: Wrigley Field, Oak Street Beach, even those silly dancing hot dogs from SuperDawg in *Wayne's World* live on the North Side. The South Side gets, well, the car chase scene in *The Blues Brothers* and "Bad, Bad, Leroy Brown." The 2005 World Series–winning Chicago White Sox may have given the South Side some renown, but the stigma sticks.

Certainly no Chicagoan or visitor to Chicago should ignore what might be the city's better half, but that's twice as true for dog lovers. The city's South Side may have fewer fancy pet-pampering businesses (although there are some) and most of the area's hotels—dog-friendly or not—are Downtown. But with expanses of open field, grassy boulevard, and wooded trail, there's

PICK OF THE LITTER—THE SOUTH SIDE

BEST CITY PARKS
Columbus Park, Austin (page 81)
Garfield Park, Garfield Park (page 82)
Sherman Park, New City (page 97)

BEST PLACE TO EAT
Dine, Greektown (page 86)

BEST EVENT
Chicago White Sox Dog Day, Bridgeport (page 88)

no better place for a dog to, well, be a dog. With the exception of a few areas like Hyde Park, Chinatown, and Little Italy, the South Side tends to be less congested than Downtown and the North Side, with easier access to parking. Many dog lovers say there are more unofficial places to let your pup off-leash here. Of course, it's still illegal (the two sides of the city aren't *that* different).

This chapter covers the South Side of the city from Madison Street (1 North, 1 South) on the north to the city's limits on the south (near 138th Street), and from the lake to the western city limits near Cicero Avenue (4800 West). The exceptions are the Loop, South Loop, and Printer's Row neighborhoods, which are included in the Downtown chapter.

PARKS, BEACHES, AND RECREATION AREAS

◳ Burnham Park

🐾🐾🐾 (See South Side map on page 78)

This is the South Side's geographical equivalent to Lincoln Park. True, there's no zoo, no Theater on the Lake, and no neighborhood that abuts the park the way the Lincoln Park community does on the North Side. But there is plenty for an outdoors enthusiast—whether two- or four-legged—to do in Burnham Park, which runs roughly from the Museum Campus north of 16th Street down to 59th Street, where Jackson Park begins.

In flux since its design by Chicago's master architect, Daniel Burnham (hence the name), the park has been modified and redesigned over the years, depending on the city's needs. During the 1930s, Works Progress Administration (WPA) funds were used to shore up additions to the park through landfills, many at Promontory Point (in the Hyde Park section of this chapter).

More recently, the Soldier Field renovation project converted some parking lots back into green space.

The best way to enjoy Burnham Park is to promenade down the long paths that weave through this South Side sanctuary, including the 3.8-mile walking trail that starts at 24th Street. If your dog is a runner, he might enjoy it if you pick up the pace with in-line skates; the two of you won't be alone, as the paths are filled with bicyclists, joggers, and in-line skaters on a warm day. There are plenty of green pastures—very well kept—for a sit in the sun, and many path-side benches for shorter breaks. Along Lake Michigan the winds can pick up, which is refreshing in the summer, but biting in the winter. For obvious reasons, dogs are not welcome in the new bird sanctuary at 21st Street. Throughout this chapter, specific dog-worthy sites in Burnham Park have been highlighted in the neighborhoods where they're located. 425 E. McFetridge Dr.

Lawndale, Garfield Park, and Austin

The West Side neighborhoods are some of Chicago's most frequently forgotten. Austin, for one, often gets lumped with nearby Oak Park, its suburban neighbor in the 708 area code. Racial tensions used to be high between the two areas: so high, in fact, that many Oak Park streets have cul-de-sacs that prevent driving through to Austin (although progress has been made in recent years). Lately, the Garfield Park Conservatory and Lawndale Farmers' Market have drawn increasing numbers of people to explore these neighborhoods. These areas run from Western Avenue (2400 West) to Austin Avenue at the city limits (600 West), and from Madison Street (1 North, 1 South) to Cermak Road (2200 South).

PARKS, BEACHES, AND RECREATION AREAS

❷ Columbus Park

😺😺😺 (See South Side map on page 78)

In 1953, the nine acres at this park's southern end were destroyed to make way for the I-290/Eisenhower Expressway, yet this is still a remarkably large, impressive park that shelters dogs and their people from the sounds of the high-speed traffic nearby. In the Austin neighborhood, these 135 acres are on the National Register of Historic Places, thanks to soothing waterfalls, hills and rock formations, and Jens Jensen's emphasis on native plants.

Jensen designed an outdoor stage that's still used by community theater companies and others, providing free entertainment to the thousands who visit this outpost of nature just seven miles from the Loop. Dogs are greeted gladly at any performance, as they are in the secluded, bench-filled picnic area near the second field house. To the north of Jackson Boulevard, which runs through the park, are a number of benches under a shady grove of trees.

To the south of the boulevard are the main field house, a golf course (no dogs allowed), numerous open patches of grass, interesting walks among the native landscapes, and more than one cozy spot in which to curl up and take a break in the sun. The two giant prairie-style lamps on each side of Jackson Boulevard's four-lane park drive are something to see in and of themselves.

As in all city parks, dogs are not allowed to swim in the goose-filled lagoon. But they still enjoy walking alongside it. With the park's active field house right on the water's edge, you'll get plenty of friendly petting from passersby and likely meet other similarly engaged canines as you stroll. Columbus Park is best visited during the day. The Village of Oak Park would like to create an under- or overpass to connect Columbus Park to green space on the other side of the expressway. If such a project is approved, it may increase visits from nearby Oak Parkers and improve nighttime safety.

Exit the 290 Expressway at Central Avenue (5600 West), to the north. There are several parking lots throughout the park, but entering from Jackson Boulevard (300 South) is the most remarkable route. 500 S. Central Ave.; 312/746-5046.

🖪 Garfield Park

😾 😾 😾 🐾 (See South Side map on page 78)

A few years ago, you would have been hard-pressed to find a Chicagoan outside the 60624 ZIP code who knew thing one about Garfield Park. But a Dale Chihuly glass art exhibit in 2001—extended twice through 2002—changed that. Visitors to the Garfield Park Conservatory "discovered" the extensive gardens, nature walks, Gold Dome Building, and other amenities of this 185-acre park. Now the conservatory is a tourist destination and a weekend farmers market is a favorite of locals.

Dogs aren't allowed in the two fishing lagoons or on the nature walks, but will find plenty to sniff in Jens Jensen's now-historic landmark, all without the crowds of Lincoln Park, even on the busiest days. Time spent here can feel like a vacation from the city, and you don't have to spend an hour on the expressways to do it.

Limited parking is available at both the Gold Dome, which houses a Peace Museum, and the conservatory. But street parking is typically not a problem, even during the conservatory's popular annual Chocolate Fest. The park runs through the North and South Sides, from Kinzie Street (400 North) to Fifth Avenue, but is included only in this chapter, to keep things simple. Unless you're going to a specific event (which will likely be well policed), Garfield Park is best explored during daylight hours. 100 N. Central Park Ave.; 312/746-5100.

4 Douglas Park

😺😺😺 (See South Side map on page 78)

One of the magnificent boulevard-connected parks, this graceful greenery (named after U.S. Senator Stephen A. Douglas) is yet another refuge from busy streets and busy lives. Jens Jensen designed it for just that purpose 100 years ago, and it still delivers today, thanks in part to many recent renovations to both the landscaping and the buildings.

At Ogden Avenue and Sacramento Drive (3000 West), the entrance to the park is Flower Hall, which has a formal reflecting pool. East of the building, the garden is more naturalistic, with a lily pond and unusual prairie-style benches. Farther inside the park, your dog will race to explore the footbridges, soccer fields, walking trails, and other Jensen hallmarks. Both tennis players and anglers flock to this park (the lagoon is stocked with four kinds of fish). The attractive prairie-style light fixtures have been restored here, but the park is still safest during the day.

Douglas Park is between Kedzie Avenue (3200 West) and California Avenue (2800 West); 19th Street and Roosevelt Road (1200 South). 1401 S. Sacramento Blvd.; 312/747-7670.

West Loop, Pilsen, and Little Italy

Once known for not much else besides Oprah's Harpo Studios and the United Center, the West Loop is now a growing residential area, with interesting restaurants and antique stores, in addition to the traditional food-service warehouses that have been here for years. The West Loop is also home to **Mars Gallery** (1139 W. Fulton Market; 312/226-7808), a pet-friendly art gallery that hosts the regular benefits for **Red Door Animal Shelter** (773/764-2242; www.reddoorshelter.org), featuring dog- and cat-themed artworks. Closer to the Loop stands Greektown, home of ouzo, *saganaki* (flaming cheese), and plenty of pay parking lots.

South of the I-290 Expressway are Pilsen, the heart of the city's Mexican community, and Little Italy. Not to foster the Second City complex, but if you think of New York's Little Italy when you hear the term, think again. Think smaller. Not that there's anything wrong with Chicago's Little Italy, which runs along Taylor Street. It's one of the city's most charming residential neighborhoods, with plenty—more than plenty—of authentic Italian eateries, grocery stores, and sandwich shops. The Piazza DiMaggio, at Taylor Street and Bishop Street, is home to a Joe DiMaggio sculpture and the National Italian American Sports Hall of Fame Museum.

This area stretches from Madison Street (1 North, 1 South) to Cermak Road (2200 South), and from Western Avenue (2400 West) to Lake Michigan, with the exception of the South Loop areas covered in the Downtown chapter.

THINK GLOBALLY, BARK LOCALLY

You know how much better you feel after a long day or a bad breakup just by seeing your furry one's friendly face? **Chenny Troupe** tries to bring that experience to people in a variety of rehabilitation venues, like traditional hospitals, residential facilities for the mentally ill, and homes for children who are victims of abuse. The dogs help patients and residents with both emotional and physical rehab exercises. But these aren't special therapy pups, or trained by an outsider. Instead, the owners participate directly in these good works by helping their dogs to pass the tough obedience test, and then to go and work their magic all over the city. Chenny Troupe, 773/404-6467; www.chennytroupe.org.

If you'd prefer to spend your time helping dogs recover, call **PAWS Chicago's Lurie Family Spay/Neuter Clinic.** The city's largest low-cost spay and neuter facility needs volunteers to do everything from cleaning puppies and prepping rooms to taking homeless pooches for foster care until they're adopted at one of the organization's well-publicized adoption events. 1997 N. Clybourn Ave.; 773/521-SPAY; www.pawschicago.org.

PARKS, BEACHES, AND RECREATION AREAS

5 Skinner Park

 (See South Side map on page 78)

Skinner is, in many ways, the park that best evokes the 1950s meaning of the word "park." It was the setting of Theodore Dreiser's novel, *Sister Carrie,* but Skinner's old lake was later filled in to make room for ball fields and a play lot. Next door to Mark T. Skinner Elementary School, Skinner is often full of kids playing in the splash fountain, practicing for sports events, or waiting for a ride or walk home. As a result, this is a busy, family-friendly park, but with few of the dog-versus-kid conflicts some other parks have had.

The Monroe Street (100 South) side of the park is shady, with many trees and grassy spots where you can toss a ball with a long leash or just roll in the lawn. The Adams Street (200 South) side is sunnier and more open, but also often filled with ball players. There's been some talk about adding a DFA here, because the neighborhood has many condos and town houses, few with yards. The movement hasn't yet picked up speed, but Skinner is still a clean, decent stop for dogs who happen to be in the area. The spot directly in front of the elementary school is a popular after-work gathering place for dogs and their owners. Street parking is often available on the roads surrounding this rectangular park. The park is bordered by Loomis Street (1400 West) and Throop Street (1300 West). 1331 W. Adams St.; 312/746-5560.

6 Arrigo Park

🐾 (See South Side map on page 78)

Some locals call this neighborhood park "Peanut Park" because of its shape. Natasha calls it "Frisbee Park," because so many students from the University of Illinois at Chicago (UIC) come here to play Ultimate Frisbee. Plenty of local dogs join in the fun, frolic in the well-maintained grass, and rest in the ample shade. This park doesn't offer a lot of space to explore, but it's a pleasant enough place to pass the time, and if you live in the area, it will likely become a daily stop.

At the south end of the park is Columbus Plaza, where a statue of Christopher Columbus proudly stands. Locals fought to bring the bronze figure to the city's Italian-American neighborhood after its tenure in the Italian pavilion at the 1893 World's Columbian Exposition. A celebration takes place on Columbus Day.

The park is west of Racine Avenue (1200 West), and east of Rush Presbyterian–St. Luke's Medical Center. Polk Street (800 South) dead-ends into the park. Much of the neighborhood is permit parking, but you won't be coming here unless you're already in the neighborhood for another reason. Metered parking is available on Taylor Street. 801 S. Loomis St.; 312/747-7640.

7 UIC Campus

🐾 (See South Side map on page 78)

The L-shaped University of Illinois at Chicago campus graciously allows dogs on its acreage, as long as they're leashed, picked up after, and watched at all times (in other words, don't tie your pup to the bike rack while you run in to use the facilities). A grassy corner on the southwest edge of the campus in front of the Sciences & Engineering Building, surrounded by a tall fence, has been tagged "the dog lot." Many area residents, not all of them UIC-affiliated, come here to swap pooch stories and let their pups get a little grass time. The grounds are well kept and there are plenty of trash cans for keeping them that way. The southwest corner of the campus is at Taylor Street (1000 South) and Morgan Street (1000 West).

8 Addams Park

🔥 (See South Side map on page 78)

This sad little park has virtually no trees, no benches, no water fountains, and really, not much other than a vast swath of well-trod grass. It's nothing more than a place to squat, but when your dog needs to go, he needs to go. This is your only option in this part of Pilsen. The area is well policed during the day, particularly when in use by students from Medill Elementary School next door, but should be avoided at night. If your dog can hold it, head over to Little Italy or the UIC instead. The park is east of Laflin Street (1500 West). 1301 W. 14th St.; 312/746-5487.

PLACES TO EAT

Dine: Adjacent to the new Crowne Plaza Chicago Metro Hotel in Greektown, Dine is a 1940s-style eatery and martini bar. Details that don't interest Cooper. But their outdoor tables, water, treats, and policy on welcoming well-behaved dogs do. 733 W. Madison St.; 312/602-2100.

Phil & Lou's: The 120 outdoor seats here are among the dog-friendliest in the city. Cooper covets the brown sugar–brined pork chop, although he usually gets just water and a treat. 1124 W. Madison St.; 312/455-0070.

Twisted Spoke: Whether or not your dog likes riding on a Hog, he'll be welcomed at this "family biker bar." Many people dine on burgers and breakfast burritos outside while sitting on their Harleys, but there are tables (and benches) for those who don't ride. Bloody Marys here are served with or without meat. Cooper likes meat in almost everything, but he's a teetotaler, so he didn't try them. 501 N. Ogden Ave.; 312/666-1500.

West Gate Coffee House: Pick a uncrowded weeknight and you and your pup are likely to grab one of the prime outdoor tables at this local café. 924 W. Madison Ave.; 312/829-9378.

PLACES TO STAY

Crowne Plaza Chicago Metro Hotel: A trendy new hotel, the Crowne Plaza permits dogs under 35 pounds with a $50 per night extra fee. Rates range $184–599. 733 W. Madison St.; 312/829-5000.

Bridgeport, Chinatown, and Back of the Yards

Today, the Bridgeport neighborhood is best known as the birthplace of the Daley dynasty of mayors. The modest bungalow where "Hizzoner," the late Mayor Richard J. Daley, lived stands at 35th Street and South Lowe Avenue. Bridgeport, still considered a stronghold of Chicago's Irish community, is also home to the Chicago White Sox baseball team and the Illinois Institute of Technology (IIT). Locals say that though there aren't official dog parks in the area, it doesn't discourage the dogs, who are everywhere: Just take a walk through the neighborhood's streets and you're bound to meet a few.

Nearby Chinatown doesn't offer much for dogs other than great sniffing opportunities and the chance to salivate at the many ducks hanging in shop windows. The area is busy with a number of outdoor celebrations: Chinese New Year in the winter, Lantern Festival in the spring, the Moon Festival and Double Ten Day (China's independence day) in the fall. Most of these events feature loads of noisy firecrackers and crowded streets—not exactly a dog's idea of a good time. Back of the Yards takes its name from the old Chicago stockyards, and Natasha was greatly disappointed when she discovered the streets there weren't paved with meat.

This area runs from the city limits on the west to the I-94 Expressway/Dan Ryan Expressway on the east, and from 47th Street to 79th Street.

PARKS, BEACHES, AND RECREATION AREAS

9 Canal Origins Park

🐾 🐾 (See South Side map on page 78)

This river-edge park celebrates Chicago's history as a canal town, and Bridgeport's role in that history. The neighborhood got its name because it was near a low bridge on the Chicago River. Boats couldn't squeeze under it, so instead they unloaded their cargo right there. The state and the Chicago Park District turned this industrial space into wetlands, with open green space and educational information about the canal's history. The space is significantly different from the more recreation-focused parks in this area, and an interesting place for an afternoon walk, although you may enjoy the history more than your pup. 2701 S. Ashland Ave.

10 McGuane Park

🐾 (See South Side map on page 78)

Once called Mark White Square as part of the group of community parks formed with Armour Square Park, McGuane is now the hub of Bridgeport recreational life. A family park, McGuane is home to Little League games, tennis, and on dreary winter days, swimming in an indoor pool.

DOG-EAR YOUR CALENDAR

Every April, the **Chicago White Sox Dog Day** lets handlers take their hounds out to the ball game. One dog per each paid admission is allowed to take a seat in the designated bleachers section at US Cellular Field (333 W. 35th St.; 312/674-1000, ext. 5248 or 866/769-4263; www.whitesox.com). Dog Day always sells out early, even back before the Sox were World Champs, in part because there are lots of extra perks, such as an on-field pet parade, a specially sodded rest area for dogs, pet massages, animal adoptions, and, one year, the chance to try out for the "Stupid Pet Tricks" segment on *The Late Show with David Letterman.* The Sox hope to add another Dog Day in September. It's best to remind retrievers that catching the ball is not their objective for the day: Lots of hot dogs usually do the trick. The North Side's Chicago Cubs don't have their own dog day—although with the crosstown rivalry, it may just be a matter of time. But for now, like the pennant, this is one more thing for which Cubbies fans will have to wait.

The stadium also has a Pet Check facility where you can kennel dogs during games the rest of the baseball season. The cost for the Pet Check is $3; proceeds go to an animal charity. Reservations are suggested. 312/674-5503.

All of this activity doesn't leave a lot of room for pups to frolic unfettered, but like the North Side's Welles Park, it's a friendly place to take a walk on nice, shady paths, with the likelihood of running into a neighbor or friend. For a daily stroll in Bridgeport, it can't be beat; if you're not already in the area, it's probably not worth the drive. Parking is available on most of the nearby side streets. The park is south of 29th Street and west of Halsted Street (800 West). 2901 S. Poplar Ave.; 312/747-6497.

11 Dunbar Park

🐾 (See South Side map on page 78)

To the west of Michael Reese Hospital, near a Chicago Police Department station and adjacent to a high school, Dunbar Park sees a lot of action. But none of it offers much for dogs or their owners. Basketball and tennis are popular activities here, as is climbing at the two play lots. While there are many benches on which to sit, there's not a whole lot to look at. This isn't a particularly attractive park, and the surrounding views are of high-rises. Residents of the nearby Lake Meadows Apartments take up most of the street parking; even on a day when the park is empty, the streets may be full. But if you live in one of these high-rises, this is your best bet for a quick walk. Dunbar Park is at 31st Street and Giles Avenue (318 East). 300 E. 31st St.

12 Armour Square Park

🐾🐾 (See South Side map on page 78)

President Theodore Roosevelt described this square and nine other related properties as "the most notable civic achievement in any American city." Such an accolade may be hard to imagine looking at the park today, without the surrounding tenement districts that made these parks such a novelty in 1908. The park is dedicated to Philip D. Armour of hot-dog fame, a meat-packing industrialist after whom the Armour Institute of Technology was also named. That school is now nearby IIT, home to Mies Van der Rohe's landmark architecture.

Dogs, of course, don't care a whit about the history of this little neighborhood park. Literally in the shadow of US Cellular Field (called "Comiskey Park" by old-timers and "the cell" by newscasters), Armour Square Park gives Bridgeport dogs a much-needed place to stretch all four legs. As befits a park next to where the White Sox play, baseball is the focus here, and much of the park's space is taken up by a baseball diamond. Packed in the summer, these are great places for a long-leashed pup to play fetch in the off-season. The play lot on the north side of the park is fenced, and dogs are not allowed in that area.

Armour Square Park is bordered by 33rd Street and Wells Street (200 West). Street parking is available, except during baseball games (both professional and Little League). 3309 S. Shields Ave.; 312/747-6012.

PLACES TO EAT

Donnie's Pizza: A takeout window on Wells Street—most often used during Sox games—makes Donnie's the perfect place to grab a slice for you and your pup. Then walk across 33rd Street to Armour Square Park for a pizza picnic. 3258 S. Wells St.; 312/326-7960.

Bronzeville, Kenwood, and Prairie Shores

Known as the setting for Cayton and Drake's groundbreaking work of urban sociology, *Black Metropolis*, Bronzeville was the center of African-American life in Chicago for a substantial portion of the 20th century (hence its name), and was at various times home to such luminaries as Gwendolyn Brooks, Ida B. Wells, Richard Wright, Bessie Coleman, Joe Louis, and Louis Armstrong. After a sad period of decline following the 1960s, Bronzeville slowly began a renaissance, and is increasingly home to new businesses, condominium conversions, and city improvement projects. Like many other neighborhoods convenient to the Loop, Bronzeville is rapidly gaining residents and businesses.

Similarly, the Kenwood neighborhood has undergone an incredible transformation in recent years. Once the home of meat-packing magnates like the Armours and the Swifts, Kenwood was Hyde Park's wealthier neighbor to the north in the 1920s (as well as the site of the infamous Leopold and Loeb murder). But like a lot of South Side neighborhoods, much of Kenwood descended into crime and poverty, while the remaining pockets of affluence aligned themselves with bordering neighborhoods. But the economic boom of the 1990s led to a rediscovery of Kenwood's beautiful brownstones and prime location, and today, it's one of the South Side's fastest-growing communities.

The Prairie Shores and Lake Meadows neighborhoods are residential areas with a few small parks that will suffice when you don't have time for a longer trip. This section covers a P-shaped area between the I-94 Expressway/Dan Ryan Expressway and Dr. Martin Luther King Jr. Drive (400 East), from 31st Street to 67th Street, as well as the pocket between 31st Street and 47th Street from the I-94 Expressway/Dan Ryan Expressway to the lake.

PARKS, BEACHES, AND RECREATION AREAS

13 McKinley Park

🐾🐾 (See South Side map on page 78)

McKinley Park, named after the assassinated president, was the South Side's experimental park: the first among the tenements in the area to have a public swimming pool, as well as other amenities typically inaccessible to working families at the turn of the 20th century. With a lagoon on the northeast side, walking trails, footbridges, a field house, ice rink, many barbecue stations, trees, and parking, it's easy to understand why the park has been a huge success for the last 100 years.

Imposing mature trees contribute to McKinley's oasis in the asphalt desert. Like Garfield, Douglas, Washington, and Humboldt Parks, which are connected on the city's impressive boulevard system, McKinley's pretty spaces are divided into distinct areas by pathways and plantings, an element that makes this park seem much bigger than it is.

McKinley is bordered by Damen Avenue (2000 West) and Western Avenue (2400 West), 37th Street and Pershing Road (3900 South). The park's small parking lot closes at 10 P.M. An added bonus: McKinley is the closest park to the city's Animal Care and Control adoption facility at 27th Street and Western Avenue. If you adopt a new best friend, her gratitude will only be magnified if you come here for a first taste of freedom. 2210 W. Pershing Rd.; 312/747-6527.

14 Lake Meadows Park

🐾 (See South Side map on page 78)

Lake Meadows Park, to the south of Michael Reese Hospital, is not much more of a draw for dogs than nearby Dunbar Park, but it has its share of shade trees. Instead of the lovely architecture that graces the field houses at most city parks, Lake Meadows gets a mobile trailer. This park is not worth an extra trip: There's no lake or meadow here. But if you're in the neighborhood and your companion needs to go, it's better than the alley or a parking lot. 3117 S. Rhodes Ave.; 312/747-6287.

15 Douglas Tomb State Historic Site

🐾 🐾 🦮 (See South Side map on page 78)

Thousands of Chicago commuters see the statue atop the column from this state historical site every weekday as they speed past on Lake Shore Drive, yet few ever stop to see what lies beneath. From street level at 35th Street, you'll see the entrance to the Douglas Tomb State Historic Site, the final resting place of U.S. Senator Stephen A. Douglas, best known for his 1858 election campaign debates against Abraham Lincoln.

Here, on land Douglas once owned, is an Illinois state monument that includes his cottage and more outdoor educational materials than you ever imagined existed. As is appropriate for a man nicknamed "The Little Giant," this spot is little in square footage and giant in scope. Many marble benches circle the mammoth tomb, sculpture, and pathways, surrounded by pristine green grass inside a fenced enclave. The grass may be so gorgeous here because no one ever comes by, but Natasha enjoys its velvety condition (even in winter, when grass throughout the state is brown and scratchy). A dog can't get a great run here, but she can get an interesting walk. Douglas Tomb is open Wednesday–Sunday, located at a dead end all the way east on 35th Street. www.illinois.gov.

16 Washington Park

🐾 🐾 🐾 🦮 (See South Side map on page 78)

Walking down the sidewalk to Washington Park, it's hard to grasp just how large this park is. But drive through the park's many roads (enter from 55th Street) to head for a parking lot or a particular amenity, and you'll see it's almost inconceivably large. It was designed that way: Its hills, meadows, and trails were intended to be the rural balance to Jackson Park's lakefront space, connected by the Midway Plaisance. Natasha had heard much about the South Open Green, a pastoral meadow that was once stocked with grazing sheep, and she was disappointed not to be able to test her herding skills. The space is now a great big ball field, which she ultimately found satisfactory.

Dogs aren't allowed to swim in the serene boating lagoon, but there are hours' worth of fun to be had on Washington Park's many walking and running paths. Because of its size and park-within-a-park design, there's an activity here for every imaginable pooch preference: solitary walks, ball tosses, nature trails, or just lying in the sun or shade. The community-supported Washington Park Advisory Council is active in making these grounds as safe and clean as Jackson Park, and serious progress has been made over the years. But the park spans several neighborhoods and is still best enjoyed during the day, unless you're attending a specific event.

Washington Park is near the Green Line's Garfield El stop and home to the DuSable Museum of African American History. Unless you're there on the day of a large museum event, you'll find parking inside the park or street parking on nearby side streets. The park is between Cottage Grove Avenue (800 East) and Dr. Martin Luther King Jr. Drive (400 East), and 51st Street and 60th Street. 5531 S. Martin Luther King Dr.; 312/747-6823 or 773/667-4160 (Washington Park Advisory Council).

Hyde Park and South Shore

Home to the prestigious University of Chicago, Hyde Park was originally founded as an independent municipality in 1853 by New York lawyer Paul Cornell, who drew inspiration from the upscale communities of the same name in New York and London. Forcibly annexed to the city in 1889, the current neighborhood of Hyde Park represents only a small portion of the original town. While the fortunes of surrounding areas have risen and fallen with the economy, Hyde Park has remained a stable, prosperous community for decades, due in large part to strong neighborhood organizations and the influence of the university. In a city with a reputation for segregation, Hyde Park has for years been considered to be one of the most successfully integrated neighborhoods in the country. Cooper has been spending a lot of time in Hyde Park, in part because it's one of the South Side's dog-friendliest areas, with pedestrian-friendly streets and blocks of beaches. He's heard tales of flocks of wild parrots in the trees here, but he hasn't yet seen one green tail feather personally.

FETCHING NECESSITIES

It's nice to hang out together at the sidewalk café, but sometimes dog food is what hits the spot for Spot. Here are some South Side stops you and your leashed pal can hit together to get it (and other things you need).

Archer Bank: Owned by the same group as North Community Bank (see the North Side chapter), this bank doesn't have a box of treats waiting at the teller. But you're welcome to bring your dog in with you, so you can teach him what it takes to bring home the rawhide. 4970 S. Archer Ave.; 773/838-3000. 6859 W. Archer Ave.; 773/788-7001.

Bridgeport Pet Boutique: There aren't any pet superstores in the area, but don't panic. Pet food, collars, and all the other essentials are here. 824 W. 35th St.; 773/247-8977.

Pet Luv Pet Center: A small pet-supply store, with leashes, collars, toys, treats, and, of course, dog food. 8057 S. Cicero Ave.; 773/581-7387.

Given the activist nature of Hyde Parkers, it is surprising that there isn't an off-leash DFA in the area yet. Efforts have evaluated possibilities at a number of neighborhood parks. There are only a limited number of potential spots for such a park, but **Hyde Bark D.O.G.** (www.hydebarkdog.org), a community group, is working on the issue.

One of the neighborhoods carved out of pre-annexation Hyde Park, South Shore has a rich and interesting history as a neighborhood that successfully survived major demographic changes and economic challenges. Nestled along the lake, South Shore is home to some of the city's finest beaches and Park District facilities. Its grand old apartment buildings and the nearby strong retail district of Hyde Park have contributed in recent years to South Shore's comeback as a desirable place to live—and for dogs to play.

This section covers the region between 47th Street and 79th Street, and from the lake to the I-94 Expressway/Dan Ryan Expressway.

PARKS, BEACHES, AND RECREATION AREAS

🐾 Nichols Park

🐾🐾 (See South Side map on page 78)

This small, rectangular park wouldn't rate a hydrant in many other neighborhoods. It's not fenced in, it shares grass with a well-used (and also not fenced) children's play lot, and it's surrounded by narrow but busy side streets.

Nevertheless, Nichols's topographical attraction, a small hill, is popular for dog romps in every season. Hyde Park's pet owners come here daily to chat and share dog stories. This is one of those parks where everyone knows each other's names—or at least each other's dog's names. Residents say there has been very little anti-dog sentiment at Nichols. The park is clean and bright, and if your dog is in need of some social time with others who speak her limited language, Nichols is the best stop in the neighborhood. There have been discussions to make Nichols off-leash certain hours of the day, if they can do so while complying with the Cook County Animal Control Ordinance.

Dogs must not stop to smell the flowers in the native wildflower meadow, but you can see it from the park, and maybe catch a scent or two on the breeze. The park is located between Kimbark Avenue (1300 East) and Kenwood Avenue (1342 East), south of 54th Street. 1300 E. 55th St.

18 Stout Park
🐾🐾 (See South Side map on page 78)

Just three blocks west of hound haven Nichols Park, Stout Park is where the in-the-know Hyde Park dogs go. Stout is a small but neat and trim park with a wide-open grassy clearing, a cement path, and several long benches. The park is surrounded by a ring of trees and a low metal fence. There are playgrounds on each end of the park, but dogs pay those no mind, as they focus on fetch in the center of the park. University of Chicago faculty and staff who live in this area swear by Stout because they say it isn't as chaotic as Nichols, although there's no shortage of happy yips and yaps here, especially before and after the 9-to-5 workday.

Stout Park is southwest on the corner of 54th Street and Greenwood Avenue (1100 East), which is a one-way southbound street with ample parking. 5446 S. Greenwood Ave.

19 Promontory Point
🐾🐾🐾🐾 (See South Side map on page 78)

Even on the absolutely coldest, dreariest days, Promontory Point serves as a gathering place for Hyde Park dog lovers and their canine kin. The rocky point isn't a people beach; in fact, people are prohibited from swimming here because the water is deep, the rocks are jagged, and the beaches are not sandy (many triathletes do take a dip anyway). Dogs don't care about those things (although care should be taken with the rocks) and strong swimmers rush in regardless. Of course, like all other city beaches, this is off-limits to dogs. Hyde Park dog lovers would like to see the point made an official DFA during the off-season, but that hasn't happened yet. Community concerns about bacteria in the water are worsened by dog owners who don't bother to pick up, so be at your most attentive while here.

Dog issues aren't the only conflicts for which Promontory Point is known. During the 1950s, access to the area was limited, as the area was reportedly equipped with radar linked to a missile in Jackson Park. On oppressively hot summer nights, the eastern edge of this peninsula gets a comfortable breeze, so a good percentage of Hyde Park now cools off here.

On-leash, there's plenty of doggy fun on the way to the water, which is accessible only on foot (or paw) by a tunnel under Lake Shore Drive. As you emerge from the underpass at 55th Street, you'll see a fountain with a deer head that has a convenient drinking basin at dog height. From there, you and your dog can enjoy the view of the skyline, the expansive green field, picnic areas, and the camaraderie of other dog lovers. 5491 South Shore Dr.

20 Midway Plaisance

🐾🐾 🐾 (See South Side map on page 78)

The Midway Plaisance is not exactly a park, but to call this block-wide swath of grass a mere median would be insufficient. In the heart of the University of Chicago, this mile-long grassy parkway is home to an ice-skating rink, and many college students play soccer, Frisbee, and football here. The Chicago Bears are nicknamed "The Monsters of the Midway" because years ago, they used to practice here on the former Midway of the World's Fair.

The Chicago Park District and the University have kicked off a $20 million plan to make the Midway even more of a recreational must-see than it is. The once-temporary ice rink is now permanent, with a warming house where the cold-of-nose can ward off a chill. The plan includes seasonal gardens and decorative bridges with spots to pause and look at Lorado Taft's *The Fountain of Time* sculpture. The center of the Midway will remain open space for ball games and running with dogs, while more pathways, curbs, and wildflower gardens will create a better delineation between the streets and the park. Even so, the area's design, squeezed between two busy streets, means this isn't an area for off-leash dogs, even if it were legal, no matter how good their recall. If you're looking for a social stroll with your pup, or just want to take in the sights and sounds of the neighborhood, this is a good place to start.

The Midway Plaisance connects to Jackson Park at Stony Island Avenue (1600 East) and to Washington Park at Cottage Grove Avenue (800 East), nestled between 59th Street and 60th Street. 773/834-4549 (Midway Plaisance Advisory Council).

21 Jackson Park

🐾🐾🐾 🐾 (See South Side map on page 78)

Jackson Park, the site of the 1893 World's Columbian Exposition is among the jewels of the South Side that regularly draw North Siders to the area.

Water-seeking retrievers are disappointed that they can't swim at 63rd Street Beach. Pups who like to sniff better than they like to swim enjoy walking around the doughnut-shaped lagoon in the middle of the park. Dogs are not permitted on Wooded Island or in the Osaka Garden, which are found at the center of the lagoons. Even dexterous dogs with low handicaps aren't allowed on the golf course, either, which was one of the first public courses in the country and the first certified as an Audubon sanctuary. But the walk

around the perimeter and by the South Lagoon is equally interesting, so few dogs feel snubbed by the restrictions.

On the north end of the park, off 57th Street, is the Museum of Science and Industry; on the southwest side is the golf course; and at the center, Wooded Island. Jackson Park spans from 56th Street to 67th Street, on Stony Island Avenue (1600 East). The museum has an underground parking garage and there's also some parking inside the park on Hayes Drive. 6401 S. Stony Island Ave.; 312/747-6187.

22 Rainbow Park and Beach

🐾🐾 (See South Side map on page 78)

This is one of Chicago's great beaches. It might even make you forget that you're lakeside and not oceanside. And, it is so breathtaking that you might be content to stay parkside with your pup, which is where he's legally allowed to be.

Between the two beach areas, west of the filtration plant, are plenty of paths with native grasses, shady trees, open spaces in which to sun yourself, and, in addition to the squirrels found at other parks, giant jet-black crows to chase. Water fountains and trash cans are plentiful throughout the park.

At 75th Street, you'll see another entrance to Rainbow Park and Beach, a remnant from before 1959, when Rainbow was two separate parks. It would be almost impossible to miss the Caution High Waves/High Tide signs here, but just in case: Use caution when parking here or walking with a water-loving pup too close to the shore at this edge of the beach. Rough waters can make it hard for even strong swimmers to get ashore.

To get here, take South Shore Drive to any of the park's entrances, including 75th Street or 79th Street. There's a large parking lot near the bathing beach and street parking on several side streets. 2873 E. 75th St. and 3111 E. 77th St.; 312/745-1479.

PLACES TO EAT

Pizza Capri: Well-behaved dogs who don't lunge for other people's linguine are seated at the outdoor tables of this casual Italian restaurant. The affordable eatery—which also has a dog-friendly outpost on the North Side (962 W. Belmont Ave.; 773/296-6000)—serves eight different interesting salads, perfect if you're feeling healthy after your day at the park. 1501 E. 53rd St.; 773/324-7777.

PLACES TO STAY

Hyde Park House: Dogs are welcome in this bed-and-breakfast, with no additional charge unless extra cleaning is required. Rooms have balconies where your dog can get some fresh air. Rates are $100 for a one-night stay, and $90 a night for two or more nights. 5210 S. Kenwood Ave.; 773/363-4595.

Ramada Lake Shore: This 184-room hotel is one of the only full-service hotels near the University of Chicago campus. Fortunately for those visiting Hyde Park or the South Side, it welcomes dogs of all sizes. Guests traveling with pets must stay in the exterior row-house rooms, rather than in the tower (which has internal hallways). The hotel offers free parking and complimentary shuttles. Dog owners must pay a $50 supplement. Rates start at $50. 4900 S. Lake Shore Dr.; 773/288-5800; www.ramadachicagohotel.com.

New City, Englewood, and Chicago Lawn

Another section of Chicago's Bungalow Belt (so named for its many brick bungalow houses), these West Side communities are strongholds of Chicago's diverse working-class population, and home to much of the city's African-American and Lithuanian populations. The Englewood shopping center, which lined Marquette Road (6700 South), was once the city's second-largest retail area after the Loop. The rail station here was a hub, and Martin Luther King, Jr. arrived there in 1966 when he came to meet with the first Mayor Daley. The city is currently overseeing the first new retail development in Englewood in more than 15 years.

This area runs from the I-90 Expressway/Chicago Skyway to the city limits at Cicero Avenue (4800 West), and from 47th Street and 79th Street.

PARKS, BEACHES, AND RECREATION AREAS

23 Sherman Park

🐾🐾🐾🐾 (See South Side map on page 78)

One of the city's most interesting parks, Sherman has a winding path that follows the shape of its interior lagoon, perfect for a morning walk, afternoon jog, or evening stroll. There are multiple signs all over the area reminding dogs that they must be leashed; Natasha suspects this is because more than one tried to swim in the lovely lagoon. Swimming-deprived pups can walk over the quaint bridges, look out over the beautiful plantings, or explore the curving paths around the water.

Sherman is an active neighborhood park: There's a library on the premises, a driving range, several play lots, and a magnificent outdoor people pool, surrounded by ivy-covered pergolas. In the background is St. John of God Church, sometimes reflected in the swimming pool in a way usually seen only on postcards.

Sherman Park is located between Racine Avenue (1200 West) and Loomis Boulevard (1400 West), and 52nd Street and 55th Street. Enter from 55th Street/Garfield Boulevard. 1307 W. 52nd St.; 312/747-6672.

24 Ogden Park

 (See South Side map on page 78)

Dogs frequently run off-leash in this large park, but given the surrounding area's problems with dogfighting, they may not be dogs with whom you want your pup to frolic. None of these dogs seem to be the sociable sort.

It's too bad, because Ogden is a nice park—the sister to Sherman Park, with its lagoons filled in for more running space. Natasha hopes the city's aggressive efforts to reduce dogfighting will make Ogden a more hospitable environment. She'd like to come back and watch the city's only free merry-go-round do its thing. Until then, come by only if you're in the neighborhood and really have to go. It is recommended that you do so during daylight hours. Stick to the areas on the east side of the park, nearest the unusual-looking field house and play lots. Ogden Park is bordered by Racine Avenue (1200 West) and Loomis Boulevard (1400 West), between 64th Street and 67th Street. 6500 S. Racine Ave.; 312/747-6572.

25 Marquette Park

 (See South Side map on page 78)

Like Columbus Park in Austin, Marquette Park seems inconceivably large: 300 acres of water, shade, sun, and fun for urban pups and their masters. Marquette is divided in half by Kedzie Avenue (3200 West), which makes it seem like two parks in one. To the west is the Marquette Golf Course, circled by lagoons that reach both sides of the park. The lagoons are stocked with largemouth bass, bluegill, crappie, and carp and are a popular destination for city anglers.

There are seven different baseball fields here, so there's no shortage of open space if your dog is in the mood for a good leashed ball toss. Like Douglas, Garfield, and Humboldt Parks, the rounded lagoon paths make pleasant promenades, with a variety of natural landscapes to enjoy.

Marquette Park (and the surrounding neighborhood of the same name) are no longer the racially torn areas of the late 1970s, made infamous by the neo-Nazi demonstrations here. Some gang activity exists, but it shouldn't be a concern for dog lovers as long as the sun is still up.

The park is between Marquette Road/67th Street and 71st Street; Central Park Avenue (3600 West) and California Avenue (2800 West). 6734 S. Kedzie Ave.; 312/747-6469.

Pullman and Beverly

Once called "the world's most perfect town," the Pullman Historic District was George M. Pullman's model community for the workers in his passenger railcar company, Pullman Palace Car. The 600-acre site, with employee housing, an open-air food market, park, church, school, and hotel, was the ideal planned community—until he lowered workers' wages, but not their rents. The events triggered the American Railway Union's first strike, organized by Eugene Debs.

Nearby Beverly is often lumped in with its suburban neighbors, Evergreen Park and Blue Island, rather than thought of as a city neighborhood. Home to some of the city's most interesting houses, in colonial revival, Queen Anne, and Richardsonian romanesque architecture, Beverly is best known as the enclave of the South Side Irish. Come visit on St. Patrick's Day, and you'll hear what is possibly the only neighborhood theme song ("We're the South Side Irish…").

This section covers the region between the I-94 Expressway/Bishop Ford Memorial Parkway and the city limits at Western Avenue, and from 79th Street to the city limits at 119th Street.

PARKS, BEACHES, AND RECREATION AREAS

26 Dan Ryan Woods

(See South Side map on page 78)

Hawks, falcons, and owls are among the regular visitors to this Cook County Forest Preserve property in the southwest corner of the city. Beverly-area volunteers would like to coax even more fauna to the area, and are working with preservationists to plant native habitats to attract grouse, quail, turkeys, prairie chickens, herons, and egrets. What dog wouldn't love to see (and possibly chase) turkeys and chickens roaming around during the morning walk?

For the less conservation-minded mutt, the Dan Ryan Woods are still a great all-out exercise area. People come here in the winter to use the 200-foot tobogganing track (and the warming shelter and bathrooms, too). The hilltops provide great views of the area when you and Fido need to take a breath.

However, care and attentiveness are especially warranted here. In January 2003, a stray dog attacked and killed a woman in the Dan Ryan Woods. Even years later, the forest preserve is understandably concerned about off-leash dogs and pooches that appear to have no owner. The incident is

DIVERSIONS

All play and no baths make Rover a very smelly dog. Few pups would choose the water in a tub over a muddy pond, but these city specialty and do-it-yourself groomers make the choice a little more palatable.

Doggy Dooz Pet Styling: Owner Billy Rafferty primps Oprah's dogs (Sophie and Solomon) here. 1111 W. Belmont Ave., Lakeview; 773/472-9944.

Scrub A Dub Dub: Natasha feels a special bond with owner Teresa Boris. She says it's because of her name, but other neighborhood dogs report the same rapport. Even if you're washing your own pup, Boris will give you helpful hints, a free seasonal bandana for your dog, and treats. Take time to play with her pretty Husky puppies. 1478 W. Summerdale Ave., Andersonville; 773/275-PETS (773/275-7387); www.scrubadubdub.net.

Scrub Your Pup: The city's most popular DIY dog wash. Call ahead to see if there's space in the small parking lot in the back. 2935 N. Clark St., Lakeview; 773/348-6218.

Soggy Paws: There's a locker in which you can put your belongings to keep them dry while you wash. 1148 W. Leland Ave.; 773/334-7663; and 1912 S. State St.; 312/808-0768; www.soggypaws.com.

Three Pups in a Tub: If your dog's the modest sort, she'll like the privacy afforded by the four individual cubicles for bathers here. Street parking is ample, except during White Sox games. 556 W. 37th St., Bridgeport; 773/268-WASH (773/268-9274).

commonly referred to as the reason why the forest preserves became more strident in its leash policies. Suffice to say, breaking the leash laws here is not recommended; this close to the south suburbs, turn to the South Suburban Cook County chapter for nearby off-leash options. The Dan Ryan Woods lie between 83rd Street and 87th Street, east of Western Avenue (2400 West); 800/870-3666 (Forest Preserve District of Cook County).

27 Ridge Park

🐾🐾 (See South Side map on page 78)

Offering up one of the highest hills in the city, Ridge Park is big fun for dogs—and their owners—with healthy lungs and hearts. Families from Beverly congregate here to play ball on one of the many softball fields after the Metra train arrives, and to participate in the annual Memorial Day Ridge Run, which is quite a workout.

The nine-acre Ridge Park is also home to the John H. Vanderpoel Art Gallery, a privately owned museum of American art. Just a block away (9516 S.

Wood St.) is the Ridge Park Wetlands, a protected wooded area. The park is south of 96th Street and east of Wood Street (1800 West). 9625 S. Longwood Dr.; 312/747-6639.

28 Arcade Park and Pullman Park

👣 🐾 (See South Side map on page 78)

These two parks are the central green spaces in the Pullman Historic District. The small, green, well-maintained Arcade Park is one of the first things visitors see when they drive up to the area, right next door to the visitors center. This isn't a big, expansive play park, just a place for a dog to do his duty before embarking on a pleasant walking tour of the historic brick homes that line these streets. More than 80 percent of the original Pullman homes still exist, many now rehabbed by the artists and history buffs who live in the area. The walking tour here is as much fun as the parks. It's easy to be transported back in time; Pullman is somehow insulated from the traffic noises of the nearby expressways. Visit during the day when the streets are safe and when you'll get a good view of the architecture.

Exit the I-94 Expressway/Bishop Ford Memorial Parkway at 111th Street. Drive west four blocks to Cottage Grove Avenue. Street parking is plentiful. 11132 S. Saint Lawrence Ave. and 11113 S. Cottage Grove Ave.; 312/747-7661.

Southeast Side and Hegewisch

A common misconception is that Chicago has a North Side, a South Side, and a West Side, but no East Side. In fact, the East Side and Southeast Side, in the very corner of the city near the Indiana border, are responsible for much of the industrial steel work that made Chicago a manufacturing powerhouse.

Achilles Hegewisch once wanted to build two canals, one shortening the Calumet River, the other connecting Lake Michigan and Wolf Lake. He hoped to create a planned workers' community much like nearby Pullman. Neither of those things happened, but the area that bears his name still has many single-family houses and access to some of the area's most dog-worthy diversions.

This section covers the region from 79th Street to the Indiana border and from Lake Michigan to the I-94 Expressway/Bishop Ford Memorial Parkway.

PARKS, BEACHES, AND RECREATION AREAS

29 Russell Square Park

🐾 (See South Side map on page 78)

This small neighborhood park has plenty of grass and open expanses for dogs who live in the area. It's not worth a trip in and of itself, but if you want somewhere to stretch your paws, this is a nice, safe stop. Off South Shore Drive, it's also a good place for a quick pit stop on the way to or from Wolf Lake, Calumet Park and Beach, or Rainbow Park. Park on 83rd Street or Baker Avenue (3015 East). 3045 E. 83rd St.; 312/747-6651.

30 Calumet Park and Beach
🐾🐾🐾🐾 (See South Side map on page 78)

Standing at the park's south end, you'll see the Chicago Skyway, but if you turn and face east, you'll immediately forget that automobiles and expressways even exist. This 200-acre park and beach is home to seagulls, ducks, geese, and plenty of squirrels, all enjoying the many trees, sandy beaches, and, of course, leftovers from the abundant barbecue pits throughout the park. Shared by the Coast Guard and the Chicago Park District (because this park is so close to the Indiana border, its lakefront strip is frequently patrolled), Calumet Park and Beach is a dog-friendly urban getaway, with a marine sensibility. Like all city beaches, leashed dogs aren't permitted on the bathing beach.

There's plenty for tethered dogs to explore in Calumet Park. Wooded areas with paths and trails make for a good sniff-filled stroll (Cooper claims it just smells different this close to the border), and open meadows and baseball fields are good for a long-leashed ball toss when games aren't in session. There are plenty of amenities for dog lovers, trash cans and water fountains among them—as well as some, like a concession stand at the beach in the summer, that cater to humans. This field house is a particularly beautiful example of classical architecture. Inside is the Southeast Side Historical Museum, an interesting examination of this oft-overlooked area, but, unfortunately, dogs are not allowed.

Calumet Park and Beach is very easy to find, even for those unfamiliar with the area, as long as you remember that the beach is on Lake Michigan, and not Lake Calumet, which is west of here. The park is about 17 miles south of the Loop. South Shore Drive turns into Ewing Avenue, and East 98th Street turns into the park drive east of Ewing Avenue (3634 East). Parking lots are plentiful. Plan to make a day of it. 9801 S. Ave. G; 312/747-6039.

31 Wolf Lake and Eggers Grove
🐾🐾 (See South Side map on page 78)

An 804-acre lake divided by the Illinois–Indiana border, Wolf Lake is on Cook County Forest Preserve land that everyone likes to use. Bicyclists love the trails here, conservationists protect the biodiversity of Wolf Lake, outdoors enthusiasts appreciate the ice fishing, and dogs—well, dogs like anywhere with this many elm, oak, and willow trees.

Dogs aren't permitted to swim in Wolf Lake, and frankly, with the trash that's been pulled out and the nature preserves that have been planted back in, you wouldn't want them to, anyway. You and your best friend can pass the time here without getting wet, taking lovely walks along the various trails.

Take the I-90 Expressway (here called the Indiana Toll Road) to the South Avenue exit. Parking is available at 112th Street. 800/870-3666 (Forest Preserve District of Cook County).

PLACES TO EAT

Skyway Dog House: Of course, you'll be drawn to this appealingly named sandwich shack. There are a few tables on the south side of the restaurant where you can sit and share a Vienna beef dog. But a better bet is to get it to go ("take-outs," as they say in Chicago) and have a picnic at the park. 9480 S. Ewing Ave.; 773/731-2000.

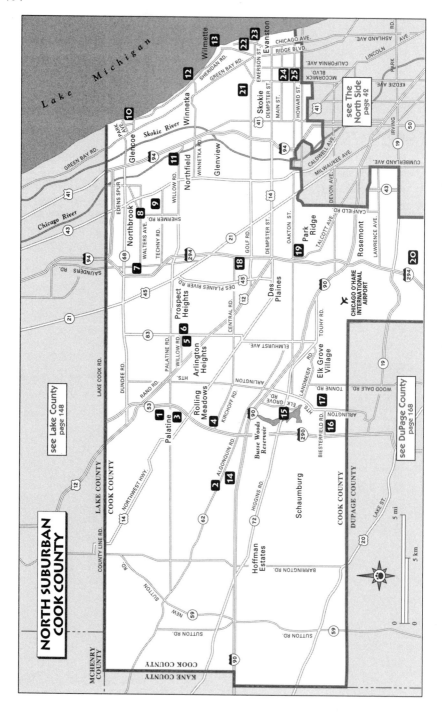

CHAPTER 4

North Suburban Cook County

Spanning 40 miles of land from Northwestern University to O'Hare Airport, North Suburban Cook County comprises vastly different communities and topographies. The North Shore, which hugs the banks and bluffs of Lake Michigan, is among the area's most coveted real estate for both dogs and people. Western Cook County is home to O'Hare International Airport, one of the country's busiest, as well as a confluence of highways and expressways that will take you anywhere your little doggy heart desires.

The Forest Preserve District of Cook County can't match DuPage and Lake Counties in the number of off-leash facilities, pup-friendly events, or general *esprit du chien*. In addition, the two Cook County Dog Training Areas that were included in the first edition of this book have now closed. As they were not true off-leash recreation areas, they haven't been missed. With more than 68,000 acres of open land, however, the Forest Preserves

PICK OF THE LITTER—NORTH SUBURBAN COOK COUNTY

BEST CITY PARKS
Salk Park, Rolling Meadows (page 108)
Wood Oaks Green Park, Northbrook (page 110)

BEST DOG PARKS
E. J. Beck Lake, Des Plaines (page 121)
Pooch Park, Skokie (page 126)

BEST BEACHES
Lakefront Beach and Lakefront Park, Glencoe (page 113)
Centennial Park and Beach, Winnetka (page 114)

BEST PLACES TO STAY
Sofitel Chicago O'Hare, Rosemont (page 121)
The Homestead Hotel, Evanston (page 127)

BEST EVENT
Reindog Parade, Glencoe (page 119)

give dogs and people a little breathing room amidst congested expressways and airport runways.

Though the Forest Preserve properties often span several suburban city limits, each area in this chapter, including municipal parks, is categorized under the suburb where its entrance is most easily found. As in the other chapters, nearby suburbs are grouped geographically to help you plan a day with the most play time and the least driving time. Consequently, suburban Cook County is divided into two separate chapters. This chapter covers the county from Lake Cook Road on the north to the Chicago city limits near Touhy Avenue (7200 North) on the south, and from Lake Michigan to the Lake County line, which is just east of Route 25.

Palatine and Rolling Meadows

Settlers from New England put down roots in Palatine's fertile green prairies as early as 1830, and ever since the railroad first ran here in 1853, it's been a stop on the way and in and out of Chicago. Located 30 miles from the Loop, both Palatine and Rolling Meadows welcome leashed pooches in their parks, as does the Salt Creek Rural Park District, which helps make sure some of the area's best open spaces stay that way. If your pup gets messy and muddy while out for a frolic, stop by **Biscuits & Bows** (1945 Plum Grove Rd., Palatine; 847/202-7877; www.biscuitsandbowsnw.com) for a bath or just for an organic treat before heading on your way.

PARKS, BEACHES, AND RECREATION AREAS

1 Chestnut Park

🔥 (See North Suburban Cook County map on page 104)

Off busy Palatine Road, Chestnut Park has two acres of soccer and football fields and a playground—but not much more. There are few trees, which means lots of big open spaces. But the fumes and the traffic on Palatine Road don't make a good background for a morning run, and the park's busy borders aren't fenced. Chestnut is just west of Arlington Heights, however, and since dogs aren't allowed in that suburb's parks, it's a nearby pit stop if Rover needs to go. The park is on the north side of Palatine Road at Winston Drive, west of Route 53. Palatine Park District; 847/991-0333.

2 Plum Grove Reservoir Dog Park

🐾🐕 (See North Suburban Cook County map on page 104)

The suburb of Palatine's new off-leash place to frolic is limited to 300 regis-trants, guaranteeing this facility is never overcrowded, but making it difficult for non-locals to stretch their four legs. The park is open dawn–dusk, except Wednesday mornings when it is closed for maintenance.

Permits are issued by the Palatine Park District. Unlike at other munici-palities, you should not bring your dog with you to register. Permits are $45 for the first dog, $10 for additional dogs for residents; $90 for the first dog, $20 for additional dogs for nonresidents. You are limited to two dogs per visit. The dog park is at the 44-acre Plum Grove Reservoir on Algon-quin Road south of Harper College. Palatine Park District, 250 E. Wood St.; 847/705-5130; www.palatineparks.org.

3 Twin Lakes Recreation Area

🐾🐾🐾 (See North Suburban Cook County map on page 104)

Natasha felt like Christopher Columbus when she sniffed out this goose-filled gem one warm winter afternoon. Operated by the Salt Creek Rural

Park District rather than the Palatine Park District, Twin Lakes is a little bit of rural paradise in a dense cluster of hotels, condos, and apartment buildings. The main attraction for humans, particularly May–October, is golf. Twin Lakes has an appealing golf course, even for those who don't know a nine iron from a curling iron. Dogs are not allowed on the course itself, nor on the clubhouse patio. But they're welcome to stroll the grounds, which have plenty of narrow trails and grassy enclaves to walk through, not to mention many ducks to chase (and an ample supply of trash cans).

Donut Lake, the easternmost of the twin lakes (and the one that looks less like a doughnut), is stocked with pike, muskie, and other fish. Anglers like the lake, in part because an Illinois Fishing License is not required. Sailboats, paddleboats, and rowboats are available for rental, although dogs like Natasha, who would rather be *in* the water than *on* the water, don't find that much consolation.

The recreation area is just west of Route 53, although it's surprisingly peaceful for being so near a major thoroughfare. The park is just north of the Arlington International Racecourse, east of Northwest Highway/U.S. 14. Parking is not allowed at the clubhouse, except by permit, but there are ample signs directing visitors to parking. The area is open 6 A.M.–10 P.M. Twin Lakes Clubhouse; 1200 East Twin Lakes Dr., Palatine; 847/934-6050; www.saltcreekpd.com.

🞖 Salk Park

🐾🐾🐾 (See North Suburban Cook County map on page 104)

This is actually two long, narrow parks: North Salk Park, which is 17 acres, and South Salk Park, which is 22 acres. Combined, the two parks wind through Rolling Meadows, tucked behind homes and divided in half by Kirchoff Road, site of the Rolling Meadows Shopping Center.

The result is that Salk feels like a giant, fabulous backyard, with many little side-street openings, rather than a large park. Natasha is partial to North Salk Park, home to open soccer fields, a decent smattering of trees, a sledding hill, horseshoe pits, and many winding paths with bridges over Salt Creek (where dogs are not permitted to swim). South Salk Park boasts baseball fields, basketball courts, more lovely jogging paths, a picnic area, and a playground. Next to Arlington Heights, which does not permit pooches in its parks, Salk is a draw for dogs from several surrounding suburbs. You'll find canine companionship here on all but the coldest days.

Salk's only disadvantage is limited parking. Because of the way the park is laid out, neatly between backyards, there are many small entrances and walking paths. One small parking lot off Cardinal Drive is perfect in the winter, as it opens up to many of the best paths in North Salk, but it fills quickly in summer. Another lot on Pheasant serves the Sports Complex in South Salk. Salk Park is south of the Arlington International Racecourse, east of Route 53, west of Wilke Road. Rolling Meadows Park District; 847/818-3202.

Arlington Heights and Prospect Heights

Arlington Heights is best known for Arlington International Racecourse, the Churchill Downs–owned racetrack. Dogs aren't allowed to wager on the ponies, but in the off-season, the facility often hosts dog shows and other specialty events of interest to pet people. In fact, Arlington Heights isn't a lucky place for pooches at all: They're not allowed in the city's parks, except for one event each July. The suburb is mainly included here for its concentration of pup-accommodating hotels.

The suburb of Prospect Heights welcomes wagging tails in all its city parks, as long as the dogs attached to them are leashed, but the River Trails Park District, which runs some recreation areas in the suburb, does not. Parks tend to be well marked, so you shouldn't have a problem figuring out where your dog is not allowed.

PARKS, BEACHES, AND RECREATION AREAS

5 Lions Park

🐾 (See North Suburban Cook County map on page 104)

It doesn't look like much from the busy street. Connected to the Gary Morava Recreation Center, which is home to Prospect Heights' outdoor swimming pool, tennis court, and a playground, Lions Park is a family-focused park, with plenty of year-round activity. Farther north, away from West Camp McDonald Road, are a large picnic grove, a fenced baseball field, and many leafy shade trees that offer a pooch a place to sit back, relax, and bark at the squirrels. Other than the fluffy-tailed friends, there's not much to get excited about here. But if you live in the area, it may be a regular stop, particularly if you have kids enjoying themselves at the Gary Morava Recreation Center.

Lions Park is on the north side of West Camp McDonald Road, between Schoenbeck Road and Elmhurst Road/Route 83. Parking is available next to the center. 847/394-2848.

6 Izaak Walton Park

🐾🐾 (See North Suburban Cook County map on page 104)

Prospect Heights' most lush and scenic spot, Izaak Walton Park, has recently been renovated to every dog's delight. Top of the list for sensitive canines is the sensory garden, highlighting the sights and smells of nature. An oversized picnic shelter—a common feature in Cook County parks—shields human and beast from hot sun in the summer and inclement weather the rest of the year. A viewing area overlooking the park's picturesque wetlands is a nice stop on a walk through this gentle park, but it is not the place for dogs to practice their agility jumps. The park is located on the east side of Elmhurst Road/Route 83 just north of Camp McDonald Road. 847/394-2848.

PLACES TO STAY

Doubletree Arlington Heights: This brand new hotel welcomes you and your dog in all rooms. You'll just need to sign a pet waiver and pay a $100 refundable deposit. Room rates start at $129. Just don't feed Fido one of the Doubletree's famous chocolate chip cookies. 75 W. Algonquin Rd., Arlington Heights; 847/364-7600.

Exel Inn Prospect Heights: This Midwestern budget chain offers dogs weighing less than 25 pounds rooms on the smoking floor. All rooms have free high-speed wireless Internet and come with complimentary breakfast and parking. Rates start at $47. If you and your pooch are staying more than seven days there is a $500 security deposit. The hotel is just south of Willow Road. 540 Milwaukee Ave., Prospect Heights; 847/459-0545; www.exelinns.com.

Red Roof Inn Chicago/Arlington Heights: At the I-90 Expressway and Arlington Heights Road North, this is a clean, convenient stay for people with a dog—only one per room, please. Rates start at $47. 22 W. Algonquin Rd.; 847/228-6650; www.redroof.com.

Northbrook and Glenview

Northbrook is one of the Cook County suburbs that seem to get it. Kids and dogs are actually welcome to romp together at the park, expect at Village Green Park during a community event. Nearby Glenview is the opposite: Dogs are only allowed to walk on the perimeter of certain parks (including Community Park West, Countryside Park, Cunliss Park, and Flick Park). Dogs aren't allowed to check out Wagner Farm, the last working farm on the North Shore. The best canine contribution Glenview has to offer is several hotels that accommodate pets.

PARKS, BEACHES, AND RECREATION AREAS

⁊ Wood Oaks Green Park

🐾🐾🐾🐾 (See North Suburban Cook County map on page 104)

Cooper's friends Jack and Rosie love to run down the hill at this park, and so will almost every other four-footed friend. The big sledding hill is a draw for dog lovers and kids alike. During the winter, it's a snowy slide; in the summer, it's a place to roll and romp. Wood Oaks has nicely delineated 1.25-mile trails, with pickup bags available in case you need extras, and leashed dogs are more than invited to join in the exploring. There are also two baseball diamonds, three soccer fields, and outdoor pay phones for emergencies.

THINK GLOBALLY, BARK LOCALLY

You're not the only one in your family who can help other pets in need of aid. Animal Emergency and Critical Care Center, one of the area's largest pet ER centers, runs an animal **Blood Banking Program.** Dogs who weigh more than 50 pounds and are under eight years old can donate blood to be saved for other pups who may have a rainy day (cats, too, can give if they're so inclined). In exchange for his generosity, your pooch will get a free heartworm test, physical exams, and blood work. Donor dogs must have up-to-date vaccinations, be at a healthy weight, and not bark—at least not too much—at a needle. No word on whether or not there's a doggy lollipop after he's done. Animal Emergency and Critical Care Center;1810 Skokie Blvd., Northbrook; 847/564-5775.

But what gets most tails wagging is that dogs are allowed to swim in Lake Shermerville, the small man-made boating and fishing lake inside the park. Dogs are also welcome to accompany you on a rented canoe ride ($8, $12 for nonresidents), but most opt for the dog paddle instead. The 55-acre park is south of Dundee Road; enter on the west side of Sanders Road; ample parking lots inside the park. 1150 Sanders Rd.; 847/291-2980; www.nbparks.org.

8 Village Green Park

🐾 (See North Suburban Cook County map on page 104)

Families like this 10-acre park because it's one of the few playgrounds in the area with shade. Dogs also like the leafy coverage, as well as the hub of activity that comes from being next to the Park District office and downtown Northbrook. There is a decent-sized field on the east side of the park with paths on which pups can promenade. Village Green is at Shermer Road and Walters Avenue; 847/291-2980; www.nbparks.org.

9 Meadowhill Park, North and Meadowhill Park, South

🐾🐾🐾 (See North Suburban Cook County map on page 104)

These two connected parks combined are Northbrook's biggest, at 80 entertaining acres. Meadowhill Park, North tends to be the kid-focused end, thanks to a water park, lap pool, sun deck, and concession stand. There are four lighted baseball diamonds, a lighted basketball court, three soccer fields, and an in-line hockey/ice hockey rink.

Meadowhill Park, South is where the leashed dogs run, thanks to a tall-grass prairie, native plantings, and one mile of marked hiking trails with arched footbridges. The lighted sled hill is a favorite whether or not there's snow on the ground, and almost any time of year, more than one Northbrook mutt will be sniffing these grounds. Dog lovers here are generally cordial and

clean up after their pets. Bags are provided to make this easy to do. Parking is plentiful. Meadowhill Park is north of Techny Road, west of Waukegan Road/Route 43, and east of Shermer Road. 1700 Techny Rd.; 847/291-2980; www.nbparks.org.

PLACES TO EAT

The Landmark Tavern: A new addition to what locals affectionately call "downtown Northbrook," The Landmark serves solid bar fare and is conveniently located across the street from the Village Green Park. It has a children's menu, and the tables out front invite dogs to join the party. 1352 Shermer Rd.; 847/559-1919.

PLACES TO STAY

Baymont Inn: Pillow-top mattress and free local phone calls await you and your pup at this chain. Rates range $59–129, plus a $50 pet deposit. 1625 Milwaukee Ave., Glenview; 847/635-8300; www.baymontinns.com.

BridgeStreet: Not a hotel, per se, BridgeStreet fulfills temporary housing needs for business travelers and their four-legged friends. This is decent corporate housing—ranging from studio, one-, two-, and three-bedroom fully furnished apartments to condominiums and town houses. You and your pup can rent by the week, month, or longer. BridgeStreet has locations throughout the city and suburbs, but Buffalo Grove is its local headquarters. Pets of all sizes are welcomed with treats, toys, and a list of local dog walkers, groomers, pet parks, and agility courses. Pet deposits vary from property to property. 847/564-3000 or 800/278-7338; www.bridgestreet.com.

Motel 6: This is a clean and safe motel that will welcome you and your "one small, well-behaved pet." Nothing more, nothing less. Rates range $42–55. 1535 Milwaukee Ave., Glenview; 847/390-7200; www.motel6.com.

Glencoe and Northfield

Walk into Glencoe Village headquarters, and you'll see photos of the suburb's slobberiest smiles affixed to a cubicle wall. Chuck, a well-loved U.S. Postal Service employee, has pictures of, and valentines from, local mutts posted above his postal scale. Glencoe is one of the North Shore's prettiest suburbs, sandwiched between the lake and forest preserves, and also has a little downtown filled with dog-friendly boutiques and cafés. Neighboring Northfield ain't as quaint, but it borders the Skokie Lagoons Forest Preserves and welcomes dogs in its city parks. Northfield also hosts a free annual dog show for kids.

PARKS, BEACHES, AND RECREATION AREAS

🔟 Lakefront Beach and Lakefront Park

🐾🐾🐾🐾 (See North Suburban Cook County map on page 104)

Though cited otherwise in many other publications, this beach is not an official dog beach. Glencoe doesn't have an official dog beach. Village Park District officials aren't sure where the confusion started, but they'd like to clear things up.

Even without official status, the Lakefront Beach is a worthy dog destination Labor Day–Memorial Day, when the beach is closed to human beachgoers. The park itself has a carpet of emerald grass, swings and benches, and a neat rock wall overlooking Lake Michigan. From there, dogs, with their masters in tow, climb down the long road to the beach. Officially, dogs must be leashed even when they get to the sandy paradise of Lakefront Beach. But Park District officials concede that no one much minds if dogs are off-leash during the off-season here: They typically have the place to themselves, and because it's such a hike down, there are no worries about car-canine collisions. Dogs and their owners are urged to play nice in order to avoid changes in this civilized coexistence.

Green Bay Road becomes Glencoe Road inside the village. From Glencoe Road, turn east on Park Avenue. Park Avenue dead ends into Lakefront Park, where there is a small parking lot. 847/835-3030.

🔢 Willow Park and Clarkson Park

🐾 (See North Suburban Cook County map on page 104)

The Village of Northfield calls these two parks by two separate names, but only the traffic-heavy Willow Road separates the two. Willow Park is the larger of the two, popular with soccer players and dogs who like to bounce balls off their heads. Clarkson Park, which has an ice-skating rink, is the village gathering spot. Completely renovated, Clarkson has a warming shelter for winter days, a few mature trees, and enough grass for the important tasks. Clarkson Park is home to Northfield's free annual dog show for kids. Neither Willow nor Clarkson is fenced and both abut Willow Road, which is an entrance to the I-94/Edens Expressway.

Willow Park is north of Willow Road, Clarkson Park is south of Willow Road, west of the I-94/Edens Expressway. Northfield Park District; 401 Wagner Rd., Northfield; 847/446-4428.

PLACES TO EAT

Little Red Hen: This family-owned spot features made-from-scratch sandwiches, salads, and pizza—basically anything you and your pup might need for a homemade picnic in the park. There are six outdoor tables, if you choose to stay and eat. 653 Vernon Ave., Glencoe; 847/835-4900.

Winnetka

Although Winnetka has just one park that allows dogs of any size, shape, or breed, residents say the North Shore town is actually very dog-friendly. The name Winnetka, derived from an Indian word meaning "beautiful land," still applies today, both to the landscapes of Lake Michigan and to the well-kept, pedestrian-friendly downtown. Unlike in some other North Shore suburbs, parking in downtown Winnetka is not typically traumatic.

PARKS, BEACHES, AND RECREATION AREAS

🐾 Centennial Park and Beach

🐾🐾🐾🐾🐾 (See North Suburban Cook County map on page 104)
Winnetka's dog beach, like that in neighboring Wilmette, has many rules and regulations, but somehow it doesn't seem as restrictive, or at least not as arbitrary. Permits (called "memberships") are required for access to the dog beach at Centennial Beach, but anyone with a leash is welcome in Centennial Park. Winnetka residents pay $30 for the first dog pass, $10 for each additional dog, and nothing for an annual parking pass. Nonresidents pay $60 for the first dog and $100 for a required nonresident parking sticker. (And you'll want the sticker; it's difficult to park here without it.) Additional nonresident dogs are $35 each. The season pass is good for one year. The park is supervised weekends May–September.

The beach itself leaves nothing to be desired, by either pups or people. Like the one in suburban Lake Bluff (see the Lake County chapter), and others on the North Shore, the beach sits beneath a cliff, sheltered from car-filled streets and boat-filled harbors. The sand is smooth and clean, the water clear (if cold, depending on when you come). Natasha gets a big kick out of the fact that

DIVERSIONS

While royalty often have their dogs included in official portraits, common curs have been left out of the picture. Rectify that oversight by commissioning one of these local animal artists to paint your pet. Most work from photos, which is a good thing, unless your mutt has a remarkably long sit/stay threshold. (Plus, it prevents dog hair from getting stuck to the brush.)

Glenn FujiMori: These small canvases take 6–8 weeks to complete and cost $200. 100 E. Walton St., Chicago; 312/642-4231.

Anne Leuck Feldhaus Studio: Leuck Feldhaus' style is whimsical and animated. Prices for custom commissions vary. 773/772-1085; www.annesart.com.

Keiler Sensenbrenner: Two-foot-wide oil paintings with dogs in scenic backgrounds are Sensenbrenner's specialty. Rates range $300–1,000. 904 Oakton, Evanston; 847/424-0017; www.keilersensenbrenner.com.

Bonnie Siegel: Fine art commissions done in oil paint. 847/291-1728.

dogs are allowed to take a dip here, but people aren't. Particularly since this spot is as pristine as any human beach.

Passes must be purchased in person at the Administrative Office, 540 Hibbard Rd. The dog beach is south of Elder Lane, east of Sheridan Road; 847/501-2040; www.winpark.org.

PLACES TO EAT

Panera Bread: Winnetka locals like to stop for sandwiches at this chain's sidewalk café. In downtown Winnetka, it's the place to catch up with furry friends and then head over to the beach for a swim (remember: Mom told you to wait an hour after eating before jumping into the water). 940 Green Bay Rd.; 847/441-8617.

Wilmette

More than twice the size of neighboring Winnetka, this North Shore town is just 14 miles from the Loop, but worlds away. People move here because of its easy access to the lake and the New Trier school district, often mentioned as one of the country's best. If you're driving north on Sheridan Road to get here from Evanston, you'll know you've made it when you pass the Baha'i Temple, a nine-sided dome that took 40 years to complete and is surrounded by nine fountains and nine flower gardens.

PARKS, BEACHES, AND RECREATION AREAS

13 Gillson Park Dog Beach

🐾🐾🐾🐕 (See North Suburban Cook County map on page 104)

Sitting down? It's going to take a while for you to digest all the many caveats and restrictions for getting to and enjoying Gillson Park Dog Beach.

Dogs are not allowed in the 60-acre Gillson Park, which is the park you have to walk through to get to the dog beach. There is a designated, paved walking route through the park to get to the south end of the park, south of the pier near the Wilmette Harbor. Don't step one paw on a blade of grass on your way down this path. Dogs must be on a leash of six feet or less when walking through Gillson Park to the designated play area. The person on the other end of the leash must be at least 14 years old (or a freshman in high school).

But before you get there, you need a permit ($25 for Wilmette residents, $150 for nonresidents; additional dogs $5 and $50, respectively). Failure to clean up after your dog is subject to a fine and loss of access privileges, but you probably already knew that. The dog beach is open June–August, 6–11:30 A.M. and 5:30–9:30 P.M.; then September–May, 6 A.M.–9:30 P.M.; but closed Memorial Day, Labor Day, and July 4.

Once you've performed all the above tricks (Cooper was prepared with his best roll-over, but that wasn't required), you'll pass through a gate, with a sign that will reiterate all the aforementioned rules (and more). Then, finally, you'll see a grove of trees that separates the triangular beach from the park. This is a lovely fenced beach, with rocks for climbing, sand for digging, and surf for swimming. It's no surprise that residents don't want every dog and her owner coming here all summer.

Gillson Park is east of Sheridan Road, south of Lake Street, just north of the Baha'i Temple. To park at the lakefront, you need a permit ($12 for residents; $80 for nonresidents), but there is open parking on Washington Street, which leads into the designated dog walkway. Wilmette Park District; 1200 Wilmette Ave.; 847/256-6100; www.wilmettepark.org.

PLACES TO EAT

Corner Bakery: Chicago's hometown coffee shop and bakery chain. Dogs are allowed at outside tables, and often do well getting a crumb or two by putting on their most sad-eyed looks. 3232 Lake St.; 847/251-2547.

Hoffman Estates and Schaumburg

Many city-dwellers who make a special trip to Schaumburg have a one-word reason: IKEA. And though it sells plenty of dog bowls, that's not much of a reason for a dog to entertain a trip to the area. Schaumburg's other big draw is the enormous Woodfield Shopping Center. Woodfield department stores Lord & Taylor and Macy's host monthly adoption events for homeless pets from PAWS Chicago (www.pawschicago.org). Other than that, pups find Schaumburg a place to rest their furry heads, because it's home to many hotels, but they go elsewhere to play, such as nearby Hoffman Estates, which hosts an annual Frisbee contest at its Party in the Park. Even office dwellers there get to go fishing regularly, thanks to acres of lake-dotted forest preserves.

PARKS, BEACHES, AND RECREATION AREAS

14 Willow Dog Park

🐾🐾🐕 (See North Suburban Cook County map on page 104)

In 2005, the Hoffman Estates Park District opened a one-half acre off-leash park on a trial basis, giving local dogs who used to go to the nearby Forest Preserves of Cook County dog exercise area an untethered option.

In its first year only 50 lucky local dogs were issued permits to the new facility at the Willow Recreation Center. Everyone kept his paws to himself (at least as much as can be expected), and the park district opened up registration to other locals and nonresidents. However, the district still plans on keeping numbers limited, so that the number of dogs is never overwhelming.

The new facility has five-foot-high fences and plenty of tables and benches so that people can rest while their dogs wear themselves out. Permits are $40 for one dog, $15 for each additional dog for city residents; $60 and $20 for each additional dog for nonresidents.

Willow Dog Park is open 8 A.M.–sunset. Take Algonquin Road east from Barrington Road. The park is at the intersection of Algonquin Road and

Lexington Drive, north of Highland Woods Golf Course. 3600 Lexington Dr.; 847/285-5440; www.heparks.org.

PLACES TO STAY

AmeriSuites Chicago/Schaumburg: Dogs under 20 pounds can stay here, as long as they're on the first or sixth (smoking) floor. Rates range $87–179, plus a $10 dog fee. 1851 McConnor Pkwy., Schaumburg; 847/330-1060; www. amerisuites.com.

Homestead Village Guest Studio, Schaumburg: Most dogs are allowed at this Midwest chain of suite hotels. The staff says there is a 30-pound limit, but they are willing to make exceptions. It's not much to look at, but it offers laundry and kitchens, which can be a blessing after a day at the beach. Rates start at $51. The one-time pet fee ranges $25–75, depending on length of stay. 51 E. State Pkwy., Schaumburg; 847/882-6900; www.homesteadhotels.com.

Residence Inn Chicago, Schaumburg: Near the Woodfield complex, this all-suites hotel gives dog lovers separate living and sleeping areas, as well as kitchens. Rates start at $99, with a $100 one-time fee. Up to two dogs per room are allowed, and there is no weight restriction. 1610 McConnor Pkwy., Schaumburg; 847/517-9200; www.marriott.com.

Elk Grove Village, Franklin Park, and Rosemont

Yes, Virginia, there really are elk in Elk Grove Village. The animals, of course, were native to the area, and give the suburb its name. But in a Cook Country Forest Preserve near O'Hare Airport lives a herd of elk, behind a fence, for people and dogs to see. As partial as people here are to these four-legged legacies, it's no surprise that they welcome dogs in their city parks, some of which also offer obedience classes. The same is not true of nearby Rosemont, which turns a cold shoulder to the cold-nosed in its municipal parks. Both towns are home to many of the O'Hare-area hotels and close to the expressways and access to Forest Preserves and other dog destinations.

Franklin Park prohibits dogs in its parks except for weekly agility classes and an annual New Year's Eve party that includes musical chairs and bobbing for bones.

PARKS, BEACHES, AND RECREATION AREAS

15 Busse Woods

😊😊😊 (See North Suburban Cook County map on page 104)

A green space on the register of national landmarks, Busse Woods is a favorite forest preserve outing for people and pups who live in the northwest suburbs.

DOG-EAR YOUR CALENDAR

Adopt a Pet Program: People often say ice hockey is a sport for animals. In this context, the Chicago Wolves don't mind. The Wolves, the city's "other" hockey team (meaning, not the Chicago Blackhawks), host an Adopt a Pet Program with the Chicago Department of Animal Care and Control on at least eight Saturday night home games throughout the hockey season. Homeless pets are brought to the rink, which is at the Allstate Arena (6920 N. Mannheim Rd., Rosemont). Interested adopters can meet the vaccinated pups and fill out the paperwork on the spot. Animal Care and Control; 312/747-1406; www.ci.chi.il.us/animalcarecontrol. The Wolves; 847/724-GOAL (847/724-4625); www.chicagowolves.com.

Kids' Dog Show: If your dog is a media hound, get her over to Clarkson Park in Northfield. Every summer, the suburb hosts a Kids' Dog Show, with prizes for floppiest ears, best costume, best trick, and other such categories. In addition to the fun of the event itself, winners get fame and fortune. Well, at least dog biscuits and their picture in the local newspaper. There's no charge to enter and the contest is open to the public. Northfield Park District; 401 Wagner Rd.; Northfield; 847/446-4428.

Dog Frisbee Catch and Fetch: Natasha is in training. She plans to take top honors next year at the Dog Frisbee Catch and Fetch, held as part of the Arlington Heights Frontier Days celebration each Fourth of July weekend. Many people say the pooches are the biggest draw of the weekend. The contest is a three-hour extravaganza, open to any dog who thinks he can out-retrieve the area's best retrievers, and spectators fill the park. The weekend also includes a **Pet Parade,** followed by pet tricks, dog look-alike contests, and other fun and frolic. Pups particularly enjoy the events because they're the only two times, during Frontier Days and year-round, when dogs are allowed in Arlington Heights' parks. Local retailer **Catered Canine** (www.cateredcanine.com) sponsors the festivities, with treats and Frisbees for all tail-waggers. Entry is free. Arlington Heights Park District; 410 N. Arlington Heights Rd.; 847/577-8572.

Reindog Parade: Dogs are only permitted in the fabulous **Chicago Botanic Garden** four hours per year. That's all the more reason not to miss the annual holiday costume event, complete with Santa and prizes, the first Saturday in December. Good luck keeping those antlers on for the length of the parade. 1000 Lake Cook Rd., Glencoe; 847/835-5440; www.chicagobotanic.org.

Cradled between the I-90 and I-290 Expressways, Busse Woods is easy to get to and easy to find, which probably contributes to its popularity. But with more than 11 miles of biking and walking trails, dense wooded areas, a fish-filled lake, and proximity to the elk herd, there's plenty to keep everybody busy in Busse. Trails here are paved, which can get hot on the paws in the summer, but makes for fairly easy walking for older or slower dogs. The 437-acre site is well insulated from the noise of cars traveling nearby, so you and Spot will feel you've found a good nature spot, but you'll rarely feel alone, as there are almost always others enjoying the view. On summer weekends, Busse is downright crowded; on weekdays, you'll encounter a few office workers from the area eating lunch alfresco.

There are several entrances to Busse Woods, which are in the Ned Brown Forest Preserve. Adequate parking is available in the preserve. Take one of several entrances on the west side of Arlington Heights Road, east of I-290, west of I-90. Forest Preserve District of Cook County; 536 N. Harlem Ave., River Forest; 800/870-3666.

16 Pirates' Cove

🐾 (See North Suburban Cook County map on page 104)

The real attraction here, at least for people, is the popular Pirates' Cove amusement park. From June to August, don't bother trying to squeeze your body, your car, or your dog into this small parking lot, as it teems with theme-park workers and goers. But in the off-season, the wide-open space behind the amusement park is prime pup territory. There's nothing here except a flat field of grass, adjacent to the Pavilion Fitness Center. This end of the park is hardly a park: There are no benches, trees, or even trash cans. But if your best friend needs to stretch her legs, and you're in the neighborhood, this is as good a spot as any. Park south of Biesterfield Road at Leicester Road, east of the I-290 Expressway. 847/437-9494.

17 Audubon Park

🐾🐾 (See North Suburban Cook County map on page 104)

A pleasant park in central Elk Grove Village, Audubon is far from the noise of O'Hare and the traffic of the I-290 Expressway that many people associate with this town. As befits its name, Audubon is home to quite a few feathered friends. Natasha had never seen so many geese in one spot, particularly geese that seem unfazed by small children, station wagons, or enthusiastic spaniels.

The playground is the main attraction at Audubon, which is next to a junior high school. But the small park has nice, rolling hills, few trees, and ample open space. One could toss a tennis ball here, but Cooper thinks fetch would be more fun with a goose. The park is not fenced and is open sunrise–sunset.

Audubon is at the corner of Elk Grove Boulevard and Ridge Road, south of Route 72 (home of the elk herd). 499 Biesterfield Rd., Elk Grove Village; 847/437-9494.

PLACES TO STAY

Days Inn O'Hare Airport West: It isn't much to look at, but this serviceable hotel welcomes dogs of all sizes, as long as they're kept on a leash. Rates start at $69, with a charge of $10 per pet per night. 1920 East Higgins Rd., Elk Grove Village; 847/437-1650; www.daysinn.com.

Exel Inn of Elk Grove Village: This 113-room budget hotel lies off the I-290 Expressway. All rooms have free high-speed wireless Internet and come with complimentary breakfast and parking. Rates range from $50–65, plus a $500 pet deposit for stays of more than seven days. Dogs under 25 pounds allowed in smoking rooms. 1000 W. Devon Ave., Elk Grove Village; 847/895-2085; www.exelinns.com.

Residence Inn Chicago O'Hare: This 192-room all-suites hotel includes kitchens and shuttle service to the airport. Rates start at $189, with a $75 fee. Up to two dogs per room are allowed. 7101 Chestnut St., Rosemont; 847/375-9000; www.marriott.com.

Sofitel Chicago O'Hare: Calling itself "a touch of France in the heart of America," this hotel has a French bakery inside, not to mention 300 guest rooms, a connection to the Donald E. Stephens Convention Center, and free shuttles to O'Hare. The hotel requires a $50 refundable deposit for dogs over 25 pounds. Average rates range $99–269. 5550 N. River Rd., Rosemont; 847/678-4488; www.sofitel.com.

Des Plaines and Park Ridge

Staying next to the airport in Chicago isn't quite the unpleasantness it is in other cities, partly because there are several pleasant parks in the area. Des Plaines has a lovely park system. Unfortunately, wet-nosed ones are kindly asked to keep away from the city parks. But dogs are welcome in the Forest Preserve of Cook County, whose grasses grow in these two suburbs, as well as in Park Ridge parks.

PARKS, BEACHES, AND RECREATION AREAS

18 E. J. Beck Lake

🐾🐾🐾🐾 (See North Suburban Cook County map on page 104)

The sole off-leash area in the Cook County Forest Preserve is in an area that has long drawn dog lovers: an open, grassy space behind several groves of trees and away from more-traveled picnic areas and campgrounds. It borders the I-294 Expressway on one side, so there is some traffic noise.

The fenced-in space includes a large pond, where dogs have long swum (illegally). When it rains, the area can get boggy, as this is not a sandy beach, but few dogs care about a little muck. This is flat, open space, with plenty of room to run and to watch your dog, even as she picks up speed.

The number of permits issued is limited to 1,000 to prevent overcrowding. Current permit-holders have first crack at renewals before new permits are issued, but so far, anyone who has wanted one has gotten one. The rest of Beck Lake Forest Preserve is open to leashed dogs, and it is a nice place, even when tethered, because there are so many fellow frolickers here. The area is patrolled heavily, and those who are leash-free or without a permit in the dog-friendly area are ticketed. Each person is limited to three (permitted) dogs in the dog area. The gate locks; you will be given a key with your permit.

The Beck Lake dog area is open sunrise–sunset. It is located at Central and East River Roads, just west of the I-294 Expressway and east of Oakton Community College. 536 N. Harlem Ave., River Forest; 800/870-3666 (Forest Preserve District of Cook County); 708/771-1036; www.becklakedogs.org (Beck Lake Dog Area Group).

19 Paws Park

🐾🐾🐾🐕 (See North Suburban Cook County map on page 104)

This L-shaped dog park nestles between the city of Park Ridge's outdoor pool and the railroad tracks, behind the Oakton Sport Complex's loading docks. Airplanes roar overhead from nearby O'Hare. So, it isn't a serene, tranquil place. Despite that, some neighbors have complained about the noise of barking from this decent-sized community dog park. Cooper doesn't really understand what the fuss is about. Even he, with his extraordinary canine hearing, hasn't heard a lot of barking here over the other ambient noise.

Barking or no, he likes it just the same. The entire fenced area, about one-third of an acre, is covered with wood chips, which gives him hours of sniffing pleasure. There's plenty of room to park in front of this fenced area, a picnic bench inside, and a few mature trees around the perimeter, along the railroad tracks. But the main attraction is room to run and a clean, friendly environment in which to do it. A bucket of communal toys (Frisbees, tennis balls, and Kongs) hangs by the double gate, and people and their pups share well.

Because Paws Park is one of the few off-leash dog parks in the area, it can get crowded. Early mornings or afternoons before the 9-to-5 crowd gets home from the office are the best times to come by. Even then, you'll find several friends with whom to wrestle. The standard dog-park rules apply: Pick up after your pet and play well with others. (And bark quietly, Cooper reminds you.) No rawhide is allowed in the park. Paws Park is open Monday–Friday, 7 A.M.–9 P.M., Saturday, 8 A.M.–9 P.M., and Sunday, 9 A.M.–9 P.M. There are adequate lights to help you see your way after dark. Fees are $38 for the first dog, $7.50 for each additional dog for residents, $56 and $12 for nonresidents.

While you may purchase up to three tags, you may only bring two dogs at one time to Paws Park. Fines for violations are as high as $1,000.

The park is on the north side of Oakton Street. Enter the parking lot from Florence Drive, just east of the Algonquin Woods Forest Preserve. Paws Park is located behind the Oakton Sport Complex (keep driving, you'll see signs for Dog Park as you wind through the parking lot). Park Ridge Recreation and Park District; 847/692-5127; www.parkridgeparkdistrict.com.

Northlake

PARKS, BEACHES, AND RECREATION AREAS

20 Northlake Dog Park

(See North Suburban Cook County map on page 104)

As you enter Centerpoint Preserve, look for the flagpole and you'll see the new experimental dog park in Northlake. If you've explored many of the off-leash areas in this book, then you won't find much "experimental" here: grass, fences, dogs with permits frolicking with off-leash abandon. But the experimental status allows the city of Northlake to test the dog park and see how it goes before committing to it for the long-term. Centerpoint Preserve was a popular spot for illegal off-leash activity, leading administrators to believe that it would attract legal off-leash use. The **Friends of the Dog Park** community group helps keep everything on the up-and-up so that the area will become a permanent park of Northlake.

So far, so good. To use the area, your dog must have a Northlake Pet License, $2, as well as a City of Northlake Dog Park Permit, which is $10 for the first dog and $5 for each additional dog up to three total. Nonresidents pay $50 for the first dog and $10 for each additional dog, up to three. This is the only dog park Cooper knows of that claims to be under video surveillance. He made sure his fur was neatly brushed before he arrived. Centerpoint Preserve is at Wolf and Whitehall Roads. City of Northlake, 55 E. North Ave., Northlake; 708/343-8700; www.northlakecity.com.

Evanston and Skokie

Home to Northwestern University, Evanston is the suburb city-dwellers love to love. On the Purple El line, and with the requisite college-town sidewalk cafés, bookstores, and Ultimate Frisbee games, Evanston is the No. 1 stop for dogs who wander north of the city. There are a mind-numbing 91 parks in Evanston, and all of them allow leashed pups on their turf, although some have more anti-dog sentiment than others. Neighboring Skokie is, well, less neighborly when it comes to canines. Dogs are not permitted in Skokie parks, save for one designated dog park, and at Devonshire Cultural Center, where

FETCHING NECESSITIES

So many squirrels to chase, so little time. Take your pup on your errands with you, and you'll have more time to go straight to the beach. Here are a few stores that will help you do it.

Active Endeavors: People love to shop in this outdoor-clothing store. Dogs like it because they get treats and it means their masters are getting geared up to play outside. 694 Vernon Ave., Glencoe; 847/835-3520.

Chalet Nursery and Garden Shops: This organic and environmentally friendly landscape shop will let your pet pick out the plants she wants. 3132 Lake Ave., Wilmette; 847/256-0561; www.chaletnursery.com/retail.html.

The Hungry Pup: A gourmet bakery that makes food for dogs with special dietary needs, on top of the standard treats. Your dog's welcome to come pick up your order, but delivery is also available. 241 Chicago Ave., Evanston; 847/866-9355.

PETCO: Across the street from strip-mall center, this location of the national chain has a veterinary clinic and a photographer, as well as kibble. 5222 Touhy Ave., Skokie; 847/673-7387.

PetSmart: For those on the western side of the county, this is *the* superstore for bags of food, vet services, and grooming. 49 W. Rand Rd., Arlington Heights; 847/253-4488.

Uncle Dan's: Cooper doesn't feel that dogs should have to wear backpacks, but he likes the free treats and water bowl they have waiting for him here. There's plenty of outdoor gear for humans, too. 700 W. Church St., Evanston; 847/475-7100.

---

dogs are allowed, if they are leashed, around the perimeter (on the sidewalk). Skokie residents are limited to two dogs per household. Aside from what Natasha dubs "the park problem," Skokie is an interesting town to visit, with many Jewish delis and leafy side streets to sniff.

PARKS, BEACHES, AND RECREATION AREAS

2️⃣1️⃣ Walter S. Lovelace Park

🐾 🐾 (See North Suburban Cook County map on page 104)

The 18 acres in this northwest corner of Evanston, close to Skokie (where dogs are not allowed in the city parks), attract children, dogs, and anyone else who appreciates a lovely park. Lovelace is laced with many different little areas of enjoyment, such as a fish-stocked pond (in which dogs are not permitted to swim), pathways for walking or jogging, and grassy space for ball-tossing, all of which make the park seem larger than it is. Because it's in the northwestern corner of the village, there are fewer Northwestern students and more families here than in some of the parks closer to the lake. Early in the morning, the soccer field on the west end of the park is the place of impromptu play dates. Cooper likes the fact that he can choose between a solitary walk and social time, according to his mood, all at one city park. Lovelace is west of Gross Point Road, east of Crawford Avenue, and south of Isabella Street; 847/492-7082.

22 Centennial Park

🐾🐾🐾 (See North Suburban Cook County map on page 104)

Much of Evanston is an interesting combination of college-town atmosphere and breathtaking North Shore scenery. The 10 acres of lakefront land in Centennial Park may be the suburb's best example of that combination. Centennial Park is the northernmost patch of grass in a line of seven lakeside parks that stretch from Northwestern University to the suburb's southern border. Each of these parks is connected with sidewalks, walking parks, and meticulously kept turf (a feat of gardening, given the foot traffic it gets). As you and your pup stroll along, it may be difficult to tell when you've crossed from Centennial to Dawes or from Dawes to Burnham Shores, but that won't mar the enjoyment of your outing. During the summer, a favorite pastime is to sit and watch the colorful sailboats on Lake Michigan and talk to the interesting mix of people who are drawn to the shore. The lake is often bluer and more docile here than elsewhere. Dogs are not allowed to set paw in the water, except at the Evanston Dog Beach (see next listing).

Centennial Park runs from Church Street to University Place along Sheridan Road. Street parking (for no more than two hours) can be found on city side streets. 847/492-7082.

23 Evanston Dog Beach

🐾🐾🐕 (See North Suburban Cook County map on page 104)

It may be a surprise to see an off-leash, dog-only beach not rate more paws on Cooper and Natasha's scale. You sort of have to see it to understand, but, in a lot of ways, it's not much worth the trip for nonresidents.

First, there are the rules. The beach is open May–October, 7 A.M.–8 P.M. daily, weather permitting. It is no longer open the rest of the year. You'll need a token to enter the area (this isn't dog discrimination, people need a beach token or daily pass for admission to Evanston's five public beaches, too). Tokens are $40 for residents (of Skokie or Evanston), $80 for nonresidents.

Once you're armed with your token, you and your dog can proceed to the double gate that safely separates this beach from the rest of Evanston's shore. It's a decent stretch of all sand, but there are no rocks or wooded areas and no shade. Dogs jump at the opportunity to swim, and if you live in the area with a water-loving dog, you'll find yourself here often. But Evanston Dog

Beach is not a particularly clean beach. It's not that people don't pick up. They do (although there are no trash cans in the beach area, so many people hang or pile full bags near the exit so they can take them to the park trash cans on the way out, making the entrance particularly... fragrant). Neither the sand, seascape, nor the water is particularly pristine here, and there isn't much to look at other than the many, many Labs who lap up the lake's waves.

The area is policed: If there are dogfights, tokens will be revoked, and dogs without tokens are not admitted. Dog beach tokens may be purchased at the Dempster Street Beach Office, where Dempster meets the lake, or at the city collector's office (2100 Ridge Ave., Evanston).

The dog beach is north of the Church Street launch facility, where Church Street meets the lake. Street parking (for no more than two hours, strictly enforced) can be found on city side streets, and, if you're lucky, on Sheridan Road. 847/866-2900.

24 Pooch Park

🐾🐾🐾🐕 (See North Suburban Cook County map on page 104)

This 2.7-acre off-leash area was a long time coming for Skokie dogs. It's the only option for dogs who want to get out of their own backyards in this quiet suburb. A dog run had been planned at this same spot, but problems with the site and neighborhood concerns postponed it for years. The end result is a successful joint venture between the Skokie Park District and the city of Evanston in Skokie's Channelside Park. Pooch Park's main open expanse is designed for running, fetching, and playing. There are two smaller areas fenced within, one for pups under 35 pounds and another for agility training. The park hosts an annual *Woofstock* event with music, hot dogs, and more.

Permits are required to use Pooch Park. Skokie and Evanston residents pay $35 annually per household (not per dog), and nonresidents pay $70. The Skokie two-dog limit per household applies here. A bone-shaped tag on your dog's collar permits the two of you to enter the area, which is open 5 A.M.– 10 P.M. In addition to the standard rules—no aggressive dogs, pick up after your pet—dogs are specifically prohibited from digging holes, and owners must repair damaged turf. There is ample parking near the Dammrich Rowing Center, north of Oakton Street. Pooch Park is north of Oakton Street, east of McCormick Street. Skokie Park District; 847/674-1500 or 847/866-2900; www .skokieparkdistrict.org or www.poochpark.com.

25 Robert E. James Park

🐾 (See North Suburban Cook County map on page 104)

One of the city of Evanston's largest parks at 45 acres, James Park has eight baseball and softball fields and five soccer and football fields, in addition to playgrounds, basketball courts, and a field house. In southwest Evanston, James gets lots of traffic, young and old. Kids from nearby schools, local football and baseball leagues, and even the Midwest Cricket League flock to the fields, while the new Levy Senior Center welcomes another generation. New lighting and benches have transformed the baseball diamonds, making this the first stop for America's pastime in the summer.

Natasha's not much of a digger, but she's curious to watch the activity in James's community garden, where Evanstonians cultivate vegetables and flowers each summer. When she gets hot from watching all that hard work, she cools off by filling her bowl with water from one of the park's many drinking fountains.

If you live in Evanston, James Park might be an occasional change of walk in your daily routine. If you're coming from outside the area, head to the lakeside parks instead. James Park is south of Oakton Street, west of Dodge Avenue. 847/492-7082.

PLACES TO STAY

The Homestead Hotel: Not to be confused with the chain of Homestead Village hotels, this is an independent hotel in downtown Evanston that caters to long-term guests. Dogs of all sizes are welcome in a limited number of one-bedroom suites, with a $50 refundable deposit for overnight stays, a $300 deposit for month-long guests. Dogs are asked to use the back entrance. Dog room rate is $185. 1625 Hinman Ave., Evanston; 847/475-3300; www .thehomestead.net.

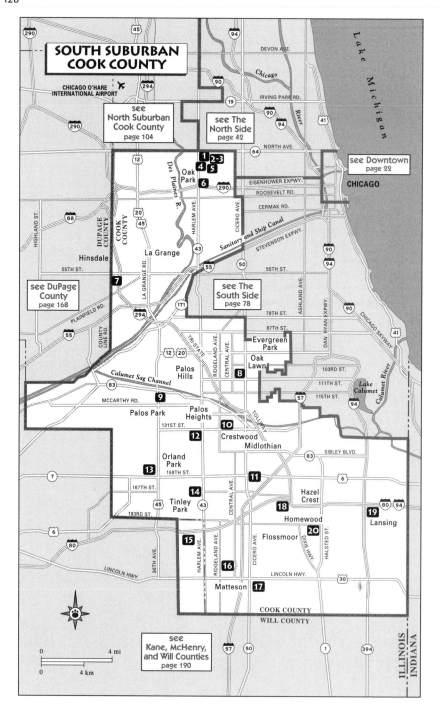

SOUTH SUBURBAN COOK COUNTY

CHICAGO O'HARE
INTERNATIONAL AIRPORT

see
North Suburban
Cook County
page 104

see The
North Side
page 42

see Downtown
page 22

CHICAGO

Oak Park

Lake Michigan

Chicago River

DEVON AVE.

IRVING PARK RD.

NORTH AVE.

EISENHOWER EXPWY.

ROOSEVELT RD.

CERMAK RD.

Des Plaines R.

COOK COUNTY

DUPAGE COUNTY

HIGHLAND ST.

Hinsdale

see DuPage
County
page 168

La Grange

Sanitary and Ship Canal

STEVENSON EXPWY.

55TH ST.

see The
South Side
page 78

79TH ST.

87TH ST.

Evergreen
Park

Oak
Lawn

103RD ST.

111TH ST.

115TH ST.

Lake
Calumet

Calumet Sag Channel

Palos Hills

Palos Park

Palos
Heights

MCCARTHY RD.

131ST ST.

Crestwood
Midlothian

Orland
Park

159TH ST.

167TH ST.

Tinley
Park

183RD ST.

SIBLEY BLVD.

Hazel
Crest

Homewood

Flossmoor

Lansing

Matteson

LINCOLN HWY.

COOK COUNTY
WILL COUNTY

see
Kane, McHenry,
and Will Counties
page 190

ILLINOIS
INDIANA

Calumet River

HARLEM AVE.

CICERO AVE.

ASHLAND AVE.

DAN RYAN EXPWY.

CHICAGO SKYWAY

RIDGELAND AVE.

CENTRAL AVE.

TOLLWAY

TRI-STATE

LA GRANGE RD.

COUNTY LINE RD.

PLAINFIELD RD.

90TH AVE.

DIXIE HWY.

HALSTED ST.

0   4 mi
0   4 km

CHAPTER 5

South Suburban Cook County

This is the land that time forgot. And tourists forget. But a dog never forgets. (Oh wait, that's an elephant.) Although South Suburban Cook County doesn't have the cachet of the North Shore or the farmland of nearby Will County, there's no reason for a dog lover to forget about stopping in this overlooked region.

Many of these suburbs (including Brookfield and Lansing) do not allow dogs in their city parks. The ordinances don't cause a big brown eye to bat, in part because so many locals have acres of land, with winding creeks and swimming pools, that dogs have their own holes to dig. They don't need to go somewhere else to play.

That's not to say there isn't anywhere a visiting pooch can go to let it all hang out. One of Cooper and Natasha's favorite city parks in the entire book is in this chapter, not to mention more than half of the Forest Preserve District of Cook County's 68,000 open acres. The two Cook County Dog Training Areas that were included in the first edition of this book have now closed, but as they were true training areas and not exercise areas or parks, the loss is more symbolic than significant. The Cook County preserves continue to be well used, particularly in the south suburbs. Thanks to wooded trails and multiple entrances, you're likely to find both picnic groves full of people and pooches as well as secluded spots to sniff out. The forest preserves are open sunrise–sunset, and, unless otherwise indicated, free of charge. It would be impossible to list all the forest preserve areas in one book (although Cooper and Natasha would like to try to visit them all). Included are some of the prettiest, most accessible, and, of course, most dog-worthy. Feel free to pull over, grab the leash, and explore others as you drive by; entrances tend to be well-marked.

To help make your exploration easier, suburban Cook County is divided into two separate chapters. The L-shaped area covered in this chapter runs from the city's uneven border near 130th Street on the north to the Will County border at Steger Road on the south, and from the Indiana state line to the DuPage County line, which is just west of the I-55/I-294 Expressway intersection.

Oak Park

Birthplace of Ernest Hemingway and home to the world's largest neighborhood of houses designed by Frank Lloyd Wright, Oak Park is a walking-tour *tour de force*. And where there are walking tours, there are dogs. Like Evanston in North Suburban Cook County, Oak Park is a suburb that city citizens love to visit. It borders the city's West Side, and has plenty of pedestrian attractions, from cafés to brick streets and outdoor benches. Included in this section are several of the parks that attract dogs who live here day in and day out (Natasha would like to point out that a village ordinance states that both dogs and cats must be leashed in these areas). If you're coming for a visit, grab a map of the several walking tours (available from any of the many tourism offices in town) and hit the pavement. If you need to rest your paws for a minute, stop in at **K9 Cookie Co.** (723 South Blvd.; 708/848-K9K9 or 708/848-5959) for an additive-free, cat-shaped dog biscuit.

As delightful as Oak Park is, it may be the suburb that was the most dramatically impacted by the amended Cook County Animal and Rabies Control Ordinance that went into effect in June 2005 (see Introduction). When the first edition of this book was published, off-leash dogs were permitted at Lindberg Park in the early morning hours. The park is not fenced, so the scenario didn't meet the specifications of the new county animal control ordinance, although it seemed to work with little complaint for more than 15 years in Oak Park.

With an estimated 5,000 dogs in its suburb, the Park District of Oak Park considers its current system of a "Dedicated Dog Park" and "Dog Park Plus" to be "temporary." The district is committed to having one or two permanent dog parks that meet the criteria of the ordinance to serve Oak Barkers. Community

PICK OF THE LITTER—SOUTH SUBURBAN COOK COUNTY

BEST CITY PARKS
Wolfe Wildlife Refuge, Oak Lawn (page 136)
Centennial Park, Orland Park (page 142)

BEST DOG PARKS
Simba and Nala's Dog Park, Tinley Park (page 143)
Rover's Run Dog Park, Homewood (page 147)

BEST PLACE TO EAT
Poor Phil's, Oak Park (page 134)

BEST EVENT
LaGrange Pet Parade, LaGrange (page 135)

meetings, surveys, and consultants have evaluated the possibility of dog parks in Maple Park, Stevenson Park, Taylor Park, and Ridgeland Common, as well as working with the Forest Preserve District of Cook County to identify other regional off-leash space. The current options for leashed and off-leash dogs are detailed below. Those who are interested in working with the park district to develop Oak Park–area dog parks before the next edition of this book is published should contact Lisa Lightcap; 708/725-2028; www.oakparkparks.com.

PARKS, BEACHES, AND RECREATION AREAS

1 Lindberg Park

🐾🐾 (See South Suburban Cook County map on page 128)
Once the place where early-bird dogs would get the off-leash worm, Lindberg Park is now exclusively for leashed recreation. It is still a lovely park. Once used as a garbage dump, these 16 acres are now some of Oak Park's prettiest and most fragrant (for humans—dogs probably miss the dump). At the center of the park is Presidential Walk, an area with flowers, prairie grasses, and pathways around a flagpole. To the east, near Woodbine Avenue, are large soccer fields (the destination of the weekend kids). The southwest corner of the park has no shortage of grass either, but it's also home to an interesting grove of trees, including some tall pine trees not often seen in Chicago city parks.

Lindberg Park is not fenced, and is just blocks from Harlem Avenue/Route 43 (7200 West). The park is located in northwest Oak Park, south of North

Avenue/Route 64 (1600 North), at the corners of Marion Street and LeMoyne Parkway. Read the street signs carefully, as parking is permitted only on certain sides of the streets. 708/725-2200; www.oakparkparks.com.

2 Taylor Park

 (See South Suburban Cook County map on page 128)

As the Park District of Oak Park considers possible locations for additional dog parks as part of its new "master plan," Taylor Park continues to be a location up for debate. Because Taylor is one of the area parks designed by Jens Jensen, the landscape artist responsible for many of Chicago's parkland wonders (see the North Side and South Side chapters for more Jensen destinations), some feel it should be restored to its original plans. As Jensen lived from 1860–1951, a dog park was not at the top of his mind (though perhaps it would be if he were designing today). Others are concerned because the proposed site is relatively small and the dog park would be close to an existing play lot.

For now, Taylor is a decent 12-acre place to walk and play on leash. It is the closest park for many who live in the northern part of the suburb and has adequate amounts of shade and sun, as well as paths on which to walk and benches on which to rest. The park is south of North Avenue and west of Ridgeland Avenue. 400 W. Division St.; 708/725-2200; www.oakparkparks.com.

3 Scoville Park

(See South Suburban Cook County map on page 128)

Near Oak Park's downtown, Scoville Park is a landscaping gem to rival the city's other architectural wonders. At the south end of the park is the Horse Show Fountain, designed as a functioning water fountain for horses, people, and dogs, but now just for show. Other decorative elements are courtesy of Jens Jensen. This four-acre site isn't as much of a doggy destination as Ridgeland Common or Maple Park, in part because it's often filled with office workers taking a break for lunch, kids climbing on the playground, and architecture fans taking a tour. But it is a decent place for a stroll or a pit stop on the way to the next Wright facade. Scoville is on Oak Park Avenue (6800 West), between Lake and Ontario Streets. 800 W. Lake St.; 708/725-2200; www.oakparkparks.com.

4 Mills Park

(See South Suburban Cook County map on page 128)

Mills Park is named after the Mills family, who once owned both the land and the historic Farson-Mills House located at the northeast corner of the park (a rare Oak Park landmark not affiliated with Frank Lloyd Wright). It doesn't take much imagination to pretend to be a member of the Mills family when you're walking through these seven acres. There's a high (very high) wrought-iron fence that, combined with the tall, mature trees, makes it easy to lose yourself in the shady lushness of this park.

For an after-work stroll, Mills is popular with Oak Parkers and their dogs. The park is at Randolph and Marion Streets. There's plenty of street parking. 217 S. Home Ave.; 708/725-2200; www.oakparkparks.com.

5 Ridgeland Common Park

🐾🐾🐾🐕 (See South Suburban Cook County map on page 128)

Not much is certain as the Park District of Oak Park evaluates the use of its facilities as part of a new master plan. But presentations at community meetings suggest that Ridgeland Commons will, in one way or another, be a destination for dogs who want to safely run and play off-leash. For now, the temporary situation includes a traditional, albeit small, dog run and early morning hours when more of the park is open for wider untethered play. The Cook County Department of Animal Control approved this tiered use, perhaps because the model had been successful in Oak Park for so long and because the area for expanded play is fenced.

Permits are required in order to use both the Dog Park and Dog Park Plus (see below for explanation) and, unfortunately, they're currently only available to Oak Park residents. They must be purchased in person at Ridgeland Common, 9 A.M.–5 P.M. Monday–Friday; or 9 A.M.–noon on Saturdays. Permits are $39 for the first dog registered, and $5 for each additional dog, with a limit of three dogs (which is the limit the village puts on all its residents). Fines for playing without a permit are considerably higher than they are elsewhere: An illegal off-leash romp could cost you $1,000, which, Cooper will tell you, would pay for a lot of rawhide chews.

The hours and specific rules of the Dog Park and Dog Park Plus are complicated. It might be worth putting down the leash and taking some notes. Dog Park is the dedicated dog off-leash area located in the 8,700-square-foot southeast corner of Ridgeland Common and is open daily sunrise–sunset. The Dog Park Plus area is the fenced-in area of Ridgeland Common that also includes the two ball fields and the sled and ski hill. It is most often used for ball playing and winter sports, and during those times dogs may not be off-leash in the Plus, only in the regular Dog Park. November 1–March 31, the Dog Park Plus is open for off-leash play on Saturdays, Sundays, and national holidays 7 A.M.–9 A.M. April 1–October 31, Dog Park Plus is open for off-leash Saturdays, Sundays, and national holidays 6–8 A.M. Because Ridgeland Common is a major destination for everything from ice skating to swimming, both the parks and the parking lots can be crowded. The park is located at Ridgeland Avenue and Lake Street. 415 W. Lake St.; 708/725-2300; www.oakparkparks.com.

6 Maple Park

🐾 (See South Suburban Cook County map on page 128)

As one of the Oak Park parks not designed by Jens Jensen, some of Maple Park's seven acres are likely to be considered as prime dog park territory under the new master plan. A large part of the park faces busy Harlem Avenue; several of the basketball courts are often unused; and part of the park is already fenced and has access to plumbing. These qualities make it look good to administrators.

All that looks good on paper, and Cooper says the more off-leash parks, the better. For now, Maple Park isn't much of a doggy destination. It is on the far southwest side of the village, meaning it isn't in walking distance of many of Oak Park's charming shops, restaurants, and other parks. If you are in the area and need a place to go, Maple Park will more than suffice. It is one-half block north of Roosevelt Road (1300 South) at Harlem Avenue. 1105 S. Maple, on Harlem Ave.; 708/725-2300; www.oakparkparks.com.

PLACES TO EAT

Poor Phil's: Oak Parkers rush here for the crab legs, sandwiches, and salads, and wash them down with snake bites and black and tans. Natasha isn't really sure what half of those things are, but she likes the fact that she can sit outside here and eat whatever scraps friendly folks throw her way. Water is available in to-go containers upon request. 139 S. Marion St.; 708/848-0871.

Puree's Pizza & Pasta: Locals love this pizza place, where the cheesy stuff is sold whole or by the slice. Slices are available to go, so you can pick up a pie and have a picnic in the park. 1023 Lake St.; 708/386-4949.

Hinsdale and LaGrange

Hinsdale is a North Shore suburb that got misplaced on the South Side. Its property prices, school districts, and society pages are often mentioned in the same breath as those of Highland Park, Wilmette, and Lake Forest. Spilling into both Cook and DuPage Counties, 20 miles from the Loop, even Hinsdale's dog park is more manicured than the forest preserve areas of other south suburbs. Not that there's anything wrong with that. Natasha just likes to freshen up a little before she heads out to Hinsdale.

PARKS, BEACHES, AND RECREATION AREAS

7 Katherine Legge Memorial Park

🐾🐾🐾🐕 (See South Suburban Cook County map on page 128)

First off, if you don't want to sound like a tourist, "Legge" is pronounced "leg." But most area residents just call the place "KLM." KLM is 52 acres of land donated to the Village of Hinsdale in the 1970s. Alexander Legge was the president of International Harvester (and Katherine's husband); they used this spot as their country getaway. Today, their lodge is a favorite place for Hinsdale couples to tie the knot.

Except for *The Brady Bunch*'s Tiger, not too many dogs are welcome at wed-

DOG-EAR YOUR CALENDAR

Since 1947, dogs in tiaras, cats in clown suits, and kids dressed as the superhero of the day have walked down Main Street in suburban LaGrange on the first Saturday of June. What some say is the oldest such event in the country, the **LaGrange Pet Parade** attracts celebrity judges, more than 1,000 entrants, marching bands, and thousands of dollars in scholarships and prizes. The mission of the day is to promote responsible pet ownership. There's no fee to enter, but Cooper warns you that the more creative a costume you pull together, the better your chances are of earning a rawhide or some equally tasty treat. 47 S. Sixth Ave., LaGrange; 708/352-0494; www.lgpetparade.org.

dings. Perhaps for that reason, pooches cannot set paw in KLM during nuptials or other special events. But at other posted times, pups are permitted in the portion of KLM north of the creek. If you park at the south end, you can walk your leashed dog in the area to the west of the paved road. Once you get to the designated area, you can unclip the leash and let Fido free, as long as he remains under your voice control (the rules stipulate that dogs must "heel immediately upon voice command," but in reality, "come," "sit," and "stay" are sufficient). Because KLM is such prized real estate, it's well-maintained, with rich green grass, leafy oak trees, and vibrant flowers not seen in forest preserves and usually off-limits to quadrupeds.

Dogs are allowed in the designated area of KLM Park March–October, 5–9 A.M. and 7–10 P.M.; November–February, 5–10 A.M. and 5–10 P.M. Neither Hinsdale nor KLM have their own permit system, but dogs must wear a dog license tag if it is required in the dog's "domicile." KLM is located at 5091 S. Country Rd., north of I-55, south of I-88, east of Route 83, and west of the Tri-State Tollway/I-294. Village of Hinsdale; 19 E. Chicago Ave., Hinsdale; 630/789-7000; villageofhinsdale.org.

Alsip, Evergreen Park, and Oak Lawn

This cluster of suburbs is conveniently located near the airport... no, the *other* airport. Just south of Chicago Midway Airport and along the I-294/Tri-State Tollway, this region boasts a number of hotel chains that accommodate travelers and their pets, in town for many local dog shows. Evergreen Park, nestled against Chicago's Beverly neighborhood, is often viewed as much as a city neighborhood as it is as a suburb. For the most part, these areas don't permit dogs in their municipal parks. The exception, however, makes a trip worth considering.

PARKS, BEACHES, AND RECREATION AREAS

8 Wolfe Wildlife Refuge

🐾🐾🐾🐾 (See South Suburban Cook County map on page 128)

When setting out to research parks, Natasha was (understandably) skeptical of any parks that were tagged as the sole grassy space in which a city allowed dogs. She pictured yellowed, unkempt grass next to parking lots, congested highways, and loading docks. But when she heard the words "wildlife refuge" in Oak Lawn, her floppy ears perked up.

With good reason, it turns out. This dog-friendly delight is more than 40 acres of fun. A wetlands restoration project, the foliage in Wolfe Wildlife Refuge probably looks a lot like it did before the area was settled more than 100 years ago. A sizeable creek—1.5 miles—runs through the area, along which grow enormous cattails (without actual cats attached to them, Natasha is disappointed to report), as well as other native and prairie grasses. Walkers, bicyclists, and in-line skaters enjoy the paths that wind through this preserve, over footbridges crossing the stream, around little corners where you can stop and listen to native birds above. Stay quiet and you might see frogs, turtles, raccoons, foxes or even monarch butterflies and black-crowned night herons.

Scattered throughout the preserve are amenities that help make it a refuge for people, too. There are plenty of benches and trash cans along the walk, as well as attractive lampposts that light the trails at night. The refuge is open until 10 P.M., and it's a well-illuminated (but not too bright) and safe place to walk the pup after work. On any given night, you and your dog will meet many other smitten canines and their companions along the way. There are other traditional park amenities—like a playground, picnic area, volleyball court, and even a latrine near the parking lot—but none of them will interest your pooch as much as a walk through the refuge.

Wolfe Wildlife Refuge is south of 109th Street, west of Cicero Avenue/Route 50. From Route 50, drive west on Laramie Street, several blocks past the shopping center, to the parking lot. Oak Lawn Park District; 400 S. Kenton Ave., Oak Lawn; 708/857-2222; www.olparks.com.

PLACES TO STAY

Baymont Inn, Chicago Southwest: The Baymont requires a deposit of $50 for all dogs to stay in a first-floor smoking room. If a dog is left in a room unattended, housekeeping will walk on by. Rates start at $80. 12801 S. Cicero Ave., Alsip; 708/597-3900; www.baymontinns.com.

Exel Inn of Bridgeview: This 113-room budget motel is in Bridgeview, just northwest of Oak Lawn, convenient to the I-294 Expressway and Harlem Avenue. Dogs who weigh less than 25 pounds can stay in smoking rooms. A stay of more than seven days requires a $500 security deposit. Parking and breakfast are included. Average rate is $66. 9625 S. 76th Ave., Bridgeview; 708/430-1818; www.exelinns.com.

Palos Heights, Palos Hills, and Palos Park

Don't worry: even people who live here confuse these three similar monikers. When in doubt, just say "Palos," and it'll get you there. As they developed, all three towns have kept elements of the surrounding nature and wildlife. Many homes have large yards with their own groves of trees. Many areas don't have sidewalks, and though the region still adheres to a grid numbering system, the winding streets give it a more countryside feel than most of Chicago's suburbs. The Palos and Sag Valley divisions of the Cook County Forest Preserves cover 15,000 acres. Palos Heights, in particular, comprises some of the south suburbs' most coveted real estate. Many families here have swimming pools in their backyards, which Natasha interprets as the ultimate act of devotion to your dog.

PARKS, BEACHES, AND RECREATION AREAS

🐾 Lake Katherine Nature Preserve

🐾🐾🐾 (See South Suburban Cook County map on page 128)

This is not a romantic beginning to a story: According to city records, in 1985, two thieves tried to steal a car in Palos Heights. When interrupted by the police, they escaped by hiding in the rock- and bush-strewn Calumet–Sag Channel corridor. The then-mayor thought something should be done about this unused area of town, so that it could be something more than a crime getaway.

The result of his brainstorm is the 136-acre Lake Katherine Nature Preserve, named after that mayor's mother. The preserve now protects local wildlife

DIVERSIONS

Alternative therapies have gone to the dogs. Most of these practitioners offer in-home treatments or weekly appointments at a variety of city and suburban veterinarian offices, so their location may not matter. Here are some pet masseurs and communicators who offer more than just heavy petting.

AMTIL (Animal Massage & Therapies): W. Bruce Bregenzer calms stressed-out pets in shelters, as well as those in more luxurious homes. 847/782-1963; www.amtil.com.

Animalspeak: Kim Ogden is an animal communicator, for those times when you can't understand what "arf!" means. 847/681-8743; www.kimogden.com.

Healing Presents for Pets, People and Places: Annette Amelkovich offers *reiki,* a Japanese method of stress reduction, in addition to animal communication. 708/848-6029.

Heeling Arts: In addition to "traditional" pet massage, Pina Sperber offers "Tellington Touch," a pet-specific holistic therapy. 773/539-5499.

K-9 Massage & Kitties 2: Suzen Cook, a certified massage therapist, focuses on increasing circulation and healing from injury. 773/381-1445 or 773/551-7283.

Pam Kuhn, CMT: This pet-massage therapist gives Rover a rubdown. 773/510-2296.

A Path to Wholeness: Susan Dallman performs *reiki* and Tellington Touch. 630/205-0287.

PET-rissage Ltd.: Denise Theobald massages joints after they've taken that agility jump one too many times. petknead@aol.com.

Ruby Room Boutique Spa: At-home pet energy healing. 1743 W. Division St., Chicago; 773/235-2323; www.rubyroom.com.

Carol Schultz: An animal communicator, Schultz offers Bach flower essences, *reiki,* and energy clearings. 815/254-8325; www.carolschultz.com.

Nancy Wallace: A pet psychic, for when the ailments aren't physical. 630/941-6816.

---

and greenery instead of thieves. The 20-acre Lake Katherine portion is the first destination for dogs and their people. Although pups can't swim in the lake (neither can humans) and must be leashed, they like walking around this man-made lake on designated wood-chip trails, and often have the company of many other local dogs. Some pooches particularly like to chase the ducks and geese who call the flat, shallow ponds and meadows here home. There are plenty of observation decks, and people tend to be amazed by the butterflies, dragonflies, and other creatures that share the preserve. Other sections of the preserve that are worth exploring include the aforementioned Cal–Sag Channel, Navajo Creek, waterfalls, and a wetlands project. The Children's Forest is an interesting educational endeavor, with trees planted by local families.

Lake Katherine Nature Preserve is open dawn–dusk, and dog owners must carry with them something with which they can pick up after their pets. If you need to heed the call of nature yourself, the staff will let you bring your dog inside the nature center with you; just be aware of those around you and, of course, make sure your dog is housetrained. The area is located at 119th Street/Route 83 and Harlem Avenue/Route 43. 7402 Lake Katherine Dr., Palos Heights; 708/361-1873 or 708/361-1821 (Friends of Lake Katherine Nature Preserve community group); www.palosheights.org/lake/index.htm.

Crestwood and Midlothian

The little town of Crestwood (population 11,000) borders a forest preserve that covers three times the land area of the community itself. Nearby Midlothian, 22 miles from Downtown, is equally blessed with ample greenery. The Midlothian Park District recently started hosting a **Bone Hunt for Easter** with prizes and take-home goody bags.

PARKS, BEACHES, AND RECREATION AREAS

10 Elizabeth A. Conkey Forest Preserve

🐾🐾🐾 (See South Suburban Cook County map on page 128)

Natasha isn't sure whether or not it's a political commentary that South Suburban dogs have picked a patch of forest preserve named in honor of a long-time female Democratic Convention delegate as their favorite stomping grounds. And, having the one-track mind she does, she doesn't much care. She just wants to get there and play.

Behind what the Cook County Forest Preserve imaginatively calls "Grove Four" stands a mass of tall, mature trees. Through the woods are several walking, running, and biking trails, a small stream, and several hills to climb. The hills are alive, most days, with the quacking of ducks and the barking of dogs. This area is such a popular pup stop that several websites list it as an official (and therefore, off-leash) dog park. Sadly, this is not the case. But everything else you and your dog need is here, including a soccer field for more open space, picnic tables, a "comfort station" (a latrine), and ample parking.

The area is at the southwest corner of 135th Street and Central Avenue in Crestwood, south of the I-294 Expressway. Forest Preserve District of Cook County; 536 North Harlem Ave., River Forest; 800/870-3666.

Midlothian Meadow

😾 (See South Suburban Cook County map on page 128)

This open field isn't the enchanted forest that fills much of the Cook Country Forest Preserves. Instead, it's a wide-open space with a large, much-used picnic area, a bike trail, outhouses, and plenty of parking. If your dog likes no distractions, such as trees or trails, from his leashed ball toss, this is one of the few unobstructed places to go in the area, as most traditional parks are off-limits to the canine kind. Otherwise, there's not much to offer pups here. But drives in the area can be deceiving—what seems like a 10-minute jaunt can turn into an hour—so having a welcoming pit stop not far from two major expressways can be a dog's best friend.

Midlothian Meadow is west of Crawford Avenue and north of 159th Street, between the railroad tracks and I-57. Forest Preserve District of Cook County; 536 N. Harlem Ave., River Forest; 800/870-3666.

PLACES TO STAY

Hampton Inn: There's no size limit or deposit necessary for pets spending the night at this moderate chain, as long as they're well-mannered and on a leash. Room rates include breakfast and use of the health club and swimming pool (for humans only). Average room rate is $99. 13330 Cicero Ave., Crestwood; 708/597-3330; www.hamptoninn.com.

Orland Park, Matteson, and Tinley Park

Most city dwellers head to this area only when they're planning to see an outdoor concert—without their dogs—at the Tweeter Center. On the day of a big show, you definitely want to avoid the area near the southwest corner of the county: Traffic backs up from Route 43 and the I-80 Expressway. Tinley Park allows leashed dogs in only one of its city parks, but the town's limits include many forest preserves. Neighboring Orland Park welcomes leashed dogs in its parks, and though its many shopping malls aren't thought of as a pup's paradise, some have outdoor seating for those who need a break from all their recreating.

PARKS, BEACHES, AND RECREATION AREAS

12 Turtlehead Lake

😾 (See South Suburban Cook County map on page 128)

Turtlehead Lake, like Wampum Lake in Lansing, is one of several forest preserve lakes dug to provide fill for the Tri-State Tollway. The lake is stocked with bass, bluegill, crappie, bullhead, and catfish, and is popular both for ice fishing and its less dangerous summertime counterpart. The 12-acre area has

FETCHING NECESSITIES

Thanks to miles—and miles and miles—of open land, a car is an absolute necessity in this neck of the Chicago woods. This means there are fewer pedestrian-friendly businesses where dogs can paw their way in. If you want to stop for some essentials on the way home from a day at the nature preserve, here are a few places where Rover won't have to wait in the Range Rover.

Animal Care League Resale Shop: Like any thrift shop, the ACL Resale Shop sells jewelry, glassware, toys, books, and clothing. But since it's run by—and proceeds support the work of—this local rescue group, it's a great place for dog-related thrift finds. Locals list orange safety vests, nail clippers, leashes, collars, and toys as some of the things they've picked up here for their best friends. 159 S. Oak Park Ave., Oak Park; 708/383-9660; www.animalcareleague.org.

Bow Wow's Pet Laundry: The entrance to this clever grooming shop is on 122nd Street. 12201 Western Ave., Blue Island; 708/388-7387.

It's a Dog's Life Bakery: In addition to nutrition-packed food, specialty biscuits, clothing, toys, and other treats, this is the place to order your dog a birthday cake. Remember: No chocolate. 3576 W. 95th St., Evergreen Park; 708/424-3993.

K9 Cookie Company: Indulge in cat-shaped biscuits and other treats filled with good humor and fresh ingredients. 723 South Blvd., Oak Park; 708/848-K9K9 (708/848-5959); www.k9cookie company.com.

PETCO: This large chain store has a photo op for your dog, as well as vet services, grooming, kibble, and many different kids of tennis balls. 460 River Oaks West, Lansing; 708/868-1442.

PetSmart: In addition to an adoption center, obedience classes, and an on-site veterinarian, you can stock up on pet food here. 4975 Cal Sag Rd., Crestwood; 708/396-2900.

Scott's Pet Shop: The high-end pet foods and other stock make this one of the city's favorite supply stops, located at 31st Street and Wolf. 3054 Wolf Rd., Westchester; 708/562-5000.

ample grass, meadows, and trees for a decent stroll, but the 500-foot-wide lake is the attraction here. Sailboats are permitted in the lake, so both the water and the parking lot fill quickly on warm summer days. Water-loving dogs may get frustrated about not being allowed to swim here, but others may appreciate the chance to take a walk in the country.

Turtlehead Lake is located on the west side of Harlem Avenue, just south of 135th Street. 13600 S. Harlem Ave., Orland Park. Forest Preserve District of Cook County; 536 N. Harlem Ave., River Forest; 800/870-3666.

13 Centennial Park

☙☙☙ (See South Suburban Cook County map on page 128)

Driving up to this mammoth 236-acre park is deceptive. With its swimming pool, skate park, and other suburban park amenities, you don't get the feeling that you and your dog are going to discover much more than a soccer field or other big expanse of grass. Park in one of the many available parking spots, grab the leash, and get out of the car, because you are in for a treat (and not the bone-shaped kind).

Lake Sedgewick is the centerpiece of Centennial Park. Looking at its nature trails and surrounding flora and fauna, it's hard to believe that Lake Sedgewick is a man-made pond, created on former industrial land. From April–September, Lake Sedgewick is a public boat launch, its parking lot on the south side of the park full of trucks trailing small boats, and people thrilled to have a low-cost place to get in the water. Anglers cast their reels both from boats and from several docks, because the lake is regularly stocked with bass, crappie, and catfish. West of the boat launch are barbecue picnic areas and entrances to the many walking trails that wind through the Ravinia Wetlands, wildflower gardens, and grassland. Plastic bags and trash cans are available all along the trails. Neither pups nor people are allowed to swim in the lake, but both are allowed to dangle toes or paws off of the pier. Shoes with good traction and towels to wipe paws are smart things to bring on this outing: Paths near the lake can be slippery with goose droppings.

The soccer fields, lighted baseball fields, and playground area include a summertime concession stand. Centennial Park is open dawn–10:30 P.M. Centennial is easy to find, even if you aren't familiar with the area, west of LaGrange Road/U.S. Highway 45, east of 108th Avenue, north of 159th Street. The aquatic center is a convenient beacon. 708/403-PARK (708/403-7275).

14 Siemsen Meadow

🐾 (See South Suburban Cook County map on page 128)

This is the only park in Tinley Park that permits even leashed pups to set paw on its turf, so Natasha felt it would be a disservice to the poor dogs who live here not to include it. She acknowledges that if such a big, open meadow existed in the city, there would be much barking in the streets. But this isn't the city. And dogs can't run off-leash here. And, well, there's really nothing to look at on a walk here because, as its name suggests, it's a meadow. In fact, the only view afforded here is across 167th Street, at the several parks in which your dog isn't welcome. If your pooch needs to pee, there's nothing wrong with stopping by, but for a more interesting adventure in the country, choose one of the forest preserve areas instead. Siemsen Meadow is located on 167th Street between Harlem Avenue/Route 43 and 80th Avenue.

15 Simba and Nala's Dog Park

👣👣👣🐕 (See Kane, McHenry, and Will Counties map on page 128)

One of the newest off-leash dog parks in the Chicago area, Simba & Nala's is operated by the Frankfort Square Park District, which is based in Will County, but as the park is located in Tinley Park, it is included in this chapter. The dog park is part of the larger Union Creek Park, which is a 45-acre recreational ground zero in the south suburbs. Union Creek was built thanks to state grant funds, and, as a result, has something for everyone, from ice skating to elevated gardens to skate parks.

Everyone includes dogs. There are both small-dog (30 pounds and under) and large-dog (31 pounds or heavier) play areas, obstacles for agility training and play, plenty of plastic bags and trash cans, and a dog rinsing station, so that you don't have to have quite so much mud in your car at the end of the day. Special events are in the works. Cooper doesn't quite understand why they named a dog park after fictional lions, but as long as there aren't giant cats when he's there, he doesn't care.

Simba and Nala's is open 8 A.M.–dusk. Annual memberships are required for admittance. Membership fees are $25 for Frankfort Square Park District residents and $50 for nonresidents. The dog park is on 80th Avenue just north of the SSSRA building. From I-80 take Harlem Avenue to 191st Street, and 191st to 80th Avenue. 19900 S. 80th Ave., Tinley Park; 815/469-3524; www.fspd.org.

16 Allemong Park

👣 (See South Suburban Cook County map on page 128)

With 25 acres, Allemong Park is one of Matteson's central gathering spots. There are three baseball diamonds, horseshoe pits, soccer fields, picnic areas, drinking fountains, and a lovely gazebo. Dogs and their owners like to walk the half-mile of paths through the hills in this park, although, of course, the dogs would like it better if they were allowed to do so untethered. Allemong isn't a special destination, but it's a decent neighborhood park for dogs who live is within the Matteson city limits.

Parking is not permitted on either the east or west side of Willow Road, and the policy is strictly enforced, as is the leash law here. Park users are allowed to leave their cars in the west or north parking lots at Marya Yates School, and there are additional lots on the east and northwest ends of the park. Allemong is located at Willow and Allemong Roads, east of Ridgeland Avenue and south of Volmer Road, east of the Cook County–Will County border at Harlem Avenue/Route 43.

17 Governors Trail Park

🐾 (See South Suburban Cook County map on page 128)

At more than 20 acres, Governors Trail Park is one of Matteson's largest parks. With two playgrounds, a ball field, a sand volleyball court, horseshoe pits, and a barbecue and picnic shelter, it's a gathering place for the suburb's athletically inclined kids and adults. It boasts well-manicured lawns, despite the foot, paw, and cleat traffic, and plenty of trees, although some are still growing in. There's a small wood-chip trail that leads into the trees.

Many outdoorsy types first experience Matteson as a rest stop along the Old Plank Road Trail. An asphalt-paved running, biking, and walking path, Old Plank turned an abandoned railroad line into a greenway that connects many of these south suburban communities between Chicago Heights and Joliet. Along the way, you see lush forestry and wildflowers and the miles marked on wooden signs. The 20-mile Old Plank Road Trail stretches to Will County and is covered more in that chapter. It's well used by runners (serious running-club-type runners) and bicyclists, so on a sunny weekend, it may not be the best place to take a leashed dog for a leisurely walk. If you're so inclined, however, Governors Trail Park is a great place to pick up Old Plank Road Trail, since there are both a parking lot and restrooms here.

Parking is next to the St. Lawrence O'Toole Parish on the north end of the park. The park, which is open 9 A.M.–dusk, is east of the Lincoln Mall Shopping Center. Crawford Avenue becomes Governors Highway south of Lincoln Highway/U.S. Highway 30. 21402 S. Governors Hwy., Matteson; 708/748-1080.

PLACES TO EAT

Corner Bakery: Panini and other sandwiches, soups, and sweets are the standard fare at this sandwich-shop chain. Started in Chicago, it's a favorite among locals. Ask for water for your thirsty dog. 14650 S. LaGrange Rd., Orland Park; 708/460-8202.

Einstein Bros. Bagels: All locations of this pup-friendly chain sell $1.18 doggy bagels made with dog-safe carob instead of chocolate. Locations with outdoor seating, such as this one, offer fresh water, too. 15837 S. LaGrange Rd., Orland Park; 708/873-9888.

Hazel Crest and Lansing

More than 25 miles from the Loop, Hazel Crest and Lansing are home to a number of manufacturing businesses, hospitals, and other places of business. Dogs think all work and no play makes for dull people, but fortunately, there are plenty of forest preserves and parks nearby. Parks in the city of Lansing are off-limits to dogs entirely, although there are some welcoming forest preserve sites in the area.

PARKS, BEACHES, AND RECREATION AREAS

18 Oak Valley Park

🐾🐾🐾 (See South Suburban Cook County map on page 128)

Ready. Set. Go. It can be a challenge to keep the leash in your hand when you and an active dog get to Hazel Crest's Oak Valley Park. Hold on tight.

Oak Valley Park is actually three separate grassy spaces next to the I-80/294 Expressway interchange, on the north side of suburban Hazel Crest. The one that makes Cooper's doggy heart race is Oak Valley North Park, which is, inexplicably, the southernmost of the three. It's a dramatically steep sledding hill, with a flat path-like area around the top. The walk around this turfed bluff would be pleasant enough, even with the nearby interstate traffic, thanks to a small stand of trees. But most dogs aren't going to settle for the leisurely stroll here, at what turns out to be one of the best places in the south suburbs to get your heart rate up. A few leashed runs up and down this hill, and both you and your dog will be ready to lap up a big bowl of water (bring your own, there aren't any drinking fountains here). You can make yourself dizzy here practicing "roll-over" all the way down the hill, or in winter, bring a sled and be joined on your way down by what seems like most of this suburb's population of 15,000.

With the exception of the trees at the top, this hill is a big, open expanse, without any trash cans or other amenities (that sledders presumably could bonk into). Try to get your dog to go at the top of the hill, where you'll find a trash can near the parking lot, so that you don't have to carry your full baggie, leash, and sled together back up the hill.

Oak Valley Hill Park (again, oddly named, as this is not the park with the sledding hill) lies to the northwest of Oak Valley North Park. It features playgrounds, picnic areas, and ball fields, and in the summer, it's often too crowded for much pup playtime. Swimming in the third park of this trio, the sensibly named Lake Owens, is off-limits to dogs.

Oak Valley North Park is open sunrise–sunset, across from the Hazel Crest community center. If driving from Mahoney Parkway, follow a pretty little stream with grassy banks (themselves good for dog-walking if you live in the area). The parking lot is on the east side of the road, with a hard-to-see sign. If you reach the community center, you've passed it. The park is west of Western Avenue and south of the I-80/294 Expressway in Hazel Crest.

19 Wampum Lake Woods

🐾🐾🐾 (See South Suburban Cook County map on page 128)

Natasha had heard of this winter pastime called ice fishing, but until she pawed up to Wampum Lake one winter afternoon, she had never seen it with her own two brown eyes. This lake was created when tons of earth was dug from the preserve during the construction of the nearby I-294 Expressway/Tri-State

Tollway. Cook County Forest Preserve officials seem to have given in to the fact that this spot, located on the edge of the 75-acre Wampum Lake Woods, is ice-fishing headquarters when the lake freezes. On top of numerous signs that prohibit ice fishing are newer warnings that you fish at your own risk. Many pooches gather here with their people, watching holes drilled through the ice, with or without warming shacks, and wait for bass, bluegill, and other fish to bite. To each her own, Natasha says, but she can think of many other things she'd rather do here.

In addition to fishing, Wampum Lake is a favorite place for locals to go cross-country skiing, biking, and in-line skating. Swimming in the lake, by humans or dogs, is not allowed, partly because of a steep incline. High salt content in the water here has produced more limestone and sandier soil than is typical in this area. This means trees, shrubs, wildflowers, and other plants uncommon in this region are often sought here by conservationists. (Cooper had been told to look for skunk cabbage, but the name made him a little nervous.) Many paths and trails meander through the area, and in every season, there's something different to see. Some visitors swear autumn colors are more vibrant here than in other forest preserve areas, perhaps because the foliage is different. Geese, ducks, and loons sound their way through the area in the winter, and birders report having sighted great blue herons in the spring. While many dog lovers come here, they're diligent about picking up after their pets. Trash cans abound, and you're more likely to step in deer droppings than in dog waste.

To get to Wampum Lake, take the I-94 Expressway/Bishop Ford Freeway to 159th Street East. The entrance is north of Thornton Lansing Road, about a quarter-mile west of the Calumet Expressway, in Lansing. Forest Preserve District of Cook County; 536 N. Harlem Ave., River Forest; 800/870-3666.

PLACES TO STAY

Red Roof Inn Chicago/Lansing: Near the Tri-State Tollway/I-94/I-80 Expressway, this is a clean, convenient stay for people with dogs weighing 80 pounds or less. There is a limit of one pet per room. Rates start at $54. 2450 E. 173rd St., Lansing; 708/895-9570; www.redroof.com.

Homewood and Flossmoor

These two sister suburbs are so much a part of one another that they're most often pronounced as one long word: "Homewoodflossmoor." They even share a park district. The Homewood–Flossmoor Park District owns 33 park sites with more than 220 acres of land. Stop by **Healthy Hounds Dog Barkery & Boutique** (2550 Central Dr., Flossmoor; 708/922-2910; www.healthyhounds dogbarkeryandboutique.com), where not only can you buy baked goods, you can learn to make 'em yourself.

PARKS, BEACHES, AND RECREATION AREAS

20 Rover's Run Dog Park

🐾🐾🐾🐾🐕 (See South Suburban Cook County map on page 128)

When Natasha saw the fire hydrants inside the off-leash dog park in Homewood, she knew she had come to the right place: a dog park with a sense of humor. Tucked behind Apollo and Butterfield Parks, this is a three-acre fenced facility with everything Fido needs. To the left as you approach the park is a separate, fully fenced area for practicing agility, for puppies not ready to run with the big dogs, or for that occasional time-out. That space, with agility equipment, a double gate, and plenty of open earth, is bigger than many of the off-leash dog-friendly areas within the Chicago city limits. But, as they say on late-night TV, that's not all!

The main area has separate double gates, more (and sturdier) agility equipment, the aforementioned hydrants, a walking path around the perimeter of the park, a bulletin board with photos of the park's regular pooches, and toys. Oh, the toys! Natasha was particularly fond of the racquets that sent tennis balls flying faster and farther than a mere toss could.

The only downside she could see is that the trees here are going to need a few more years to fill out. In the summer, there's little shade, something the community group is working to add, along with human toilets. Bottles of water and bowls are left out by users of Rover's Run, and drinking fountains (both human- and dog-height) are on the drawing board. The community keeps this park exceedingly clean, and there are plenty of extra bags to encourage you to do your part. Several benches inside help dog lovers get to know each other, as do ongoing agility classes, dog first-aid courses, and an annual **Haunted Hounds Halloween Event** for dressed-up dogs, as well as the **Great Dog Hunt** held after a traditional children's Easter egg hunt.

There's a $15 annual fee for residents to use the park, $25 for nonresidents, and the tag must be worn by all dogs in the park. Permits can be purchased at the Administrative Office; 3301 Flossmoor Rd.; 708/957-0300. Rover's Run is west of Halsted Street, east of Center Street on 191st Street. There is sufficient parking in the lot in front of the park. 708/957-7275.

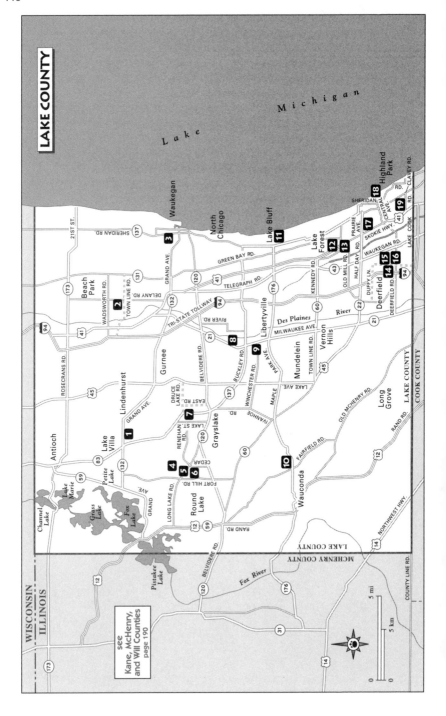

CHAPTER 6

LAKE COUNTY

Lake County

Lake County's striking suburbs have much to offer—sumptuous shopping, countless kinds of cuisine, and breathtaking views—but it's the Lake County Forest Preserve Dog Exercise Areas that have Cooper and Natasha rethinking their urban lifestyle. If only each of these four off-leash areas (and one dogsledding area) were paved with bones, they would call the movers.

Permits (daily or annual) are good for all Lake County Forest Preserve Dog Exercise Areas. All that's required is payment, license plate number, and proof of rabies vaccination, either by mail, online, or in person at the Lake County Forest Preserves Main Office (2000 N. Milwaukee Ave., Libertyville, IL 60048; 847/367-6640; www.lcfpd.org). Annual fees are $44 for the first dog and $18 for each dog thereafter for Lake County residents; $120 for the first dog and $56 thereafter for nonresidents. Dogs who want to visit just for the day can drop cash—$5 for county residents, $10 for nonresidents—in an envelope in a marked box at one of the entrances (don't forget to separate and hang the car tag from your mirror), so there's no need to go to a separate office first, as is the case with some other municipal beaches and parks that require permits.

PICK OF THE LITTER—LAKE COUNTY

BEST DOG PARKS
Lakewood, Wauconda (page 158)
Prairie Wolf, Lake Forest (page 161)
Jaycee Memorial Park, Deerfield (page 162)

BEST BEACHES
Independence Grove, Libertyville (page 156)
Sunrise Beach, Lake Bluff (page 159)

BEST PLACES TO EAT
Park Street, Mundelein (page 158)
South Gate Café, Lake Forest (page 162)
Cafe Central, Highland Park (page 167)

BEST EVENT
Camp Dogwood, Ingleside (page 155)

Lake County had the fewest number of changes of any in the Chicago metro area since the first edition of this book was published, perhaps because its dog policies were already so well established.

Twice a month, April–October, the forest preserves' dog areas open at 11 A.M. instead of 6:30 A.M., so they can mow and conduct other maintenance without worrying about dogs underfoot. At press time, the maintenance days were the first and third Wednesdays or Thursdays of the month, but check with the Lake County Forest Preserves office for updated schedules. Except on maintenance days, the dog areas are open 6:30 A.M.–sunset.

As the forest preserve properties often cross several suburban boundaries, I've listed each forest preserve area and municipal park in this chapter under the suburb where its entrance is most easily found. As in the other county chapters, nearby suburbs are grouped geographically to highlight clusters of dog-friendly features and to help you best plan a day's outing.

There are plenty of places to run, eat, and sleep in Lake County outside of the forest preserves. The local lawns, pooches, and people tend to be among the area's best manicured. Self-conscious dogs might want to run a brush through the fur before hopping in the car. Lake County runs from Lake Cook Road on the south to the Illinois–Wisconsin border on the north, and from Lake Michigan to the McHenry County line, 40-plus miles to the west. The area closest to the lake is also referred to as the "North Shore," a tony region that also includes some of Cook County's elite lakeside suburbs.

Lindenhurst and Lake Villa

If you didn't know you were less than an hour from the Chicago city limits, it would be easy to believe that you were in farm country. Peppered with small lakes, these suburbs are a place where a dog can be a dog—in other words, run fast, roll in smelly stuff, and chase small animals. Be sure to fill up the tank: It's easy to put 40 miles or more on the odometer just going from one park to another here.

PARKS, BEACHES, AND RECREATION AREAS

1 Duck Farm

🐾🐾🐾🦮 (See Lake County map on page 148)

Two wide-open, hilly meadows with a wetland area in between, Duck Farm just says "run" to dogs who make the drive out here. There are 48 full acres of space, much of them with nothing to stop your dog from running ahead at full speed. Except in the small, scenic wetlands (with good-smelling footbridges) that link the two areas, it's easy to keep an eye on your dog, even if she's several paces ahead. There are mown trails for a leisurely loop, or fields of prairie grass for a more exploratory jaunt. Near the entrance, there's an enclosed training area for obedience or agility practice.

Less secluded than the other Lake County Forest Preserve dog areas, Duck Farm does not offer the pensive getaway from the city that the other, more wooded parks do. Traffic from Route 132 is visible even from the park's farthest corners. There are many benches inside the Duck Farm area, so you can take a rest if you're worn out from all the romping. But none of the picnic tables are in shady areas, so bring sunscreen and extra treats (rawhide chews and other food, however, are prohibited inside the dog exercise areas). You're sure to make friends. The entrance to the small parking lot is on the west side of Route 132. The park is east of Route 83 on Grand Avenue/Route 132 in Lindenhurst.

PLACES TO EAT

Wolfe's Resort and DarBar: This lakeside joint invites you and your dog to "be part of the pack," meaning leashed dogs can join customers sitting outside at this lakeside bar. Route 132, just south of the dog exercise area, Lake Villa; 847/356-0070.

Waukegan and Gurnee

Just 40 miles north of Chicago and 60 miles south of Milwaukee, Waukegan is one of Lake County's more urban suburbs, with 87,000 residents. Unlike the quaint, cobblestoned towns of neighboring Lake Forest and Lake Bluff, Waukegan is a harbor town. Named for the Pottawatomie word for "fort" or "trading post," Waukegan's harbor is used by both commercial and leisure sailors. As a result, Waukegan's Lake Michigan shores aren't the interrupted doggy paradise of its neighbors to the south. But leashed dogs are warmly welcomed in this suburb's 38 parks and walking trails.

Nearby Gurnee is home to the Six Flags Great America amusement park and Gurnee Mills outlet mall (by some counts, Illinois' most-frequented tourist stop), but not much for dogs, except some pet-friendly motels.

PARKS, BEACHES, AND RECREATION AREAS

2 Waukegan Savanna Forest Preserve

🐾🐾🐾 (See Lake County map on page 148)

This area is not for every dog…Natasha thinks there's just something wrong with dogs who choose to harness themselves to sleds and pull their people through the snow. But many breeds think this looks like fun. Instead of practicing by pulling baby strollers and little red wagons through the city, as many urban dogs do, they can try mushing the right way in this dedicated dogsledding area.

One of only two parks in the Chicago area where dogs can learn to mush (pull sleds), the Waukegan Savanna has a wide, two-mile, exterior loop trail, which connects to an interior loop. Dogs must be on a harness or leash at all times. There is a limit of six dogs per sled and two dogs per *skijorer* (a cross-country skier pulled by pups). When there is no snow on the ground, dogs can learn the art of mushing with wheeled carts on these mown trails surrounded by high prairie grasses. Hikers and skiers are also allowed to use these wide trails, but they must yield to the dogsledding teams. An annual permit, separate from the one needed at the forest preserves' other dog exercise areas, is required for dogsledding. Fees are $50 per team for Lake County residents; $100 per team for nonresidents.

The entrance and parking lot are on the north side of Yorkhouse Road, west of Delany Road. Delany Road is east of U.S. Highway 41 in Waukegan.

3 Callahan-Franklin Dog Exercise Area

🐾🐾🐾 (See Lake County map on page 148)

Part of the Waukegan Park District's Larsen Nature Preserve, this fenced-in two-acre area is larger than the typical city or suburban park, but smaller than the vast playlands of the nearby forest preserves. It is an open, J-shaped

expanse of grass, unlike the hard-topped urban dog runs. There are trees and tall prairie grasses around the perimeter, but no shade anywhere in the middle. Cooper, with his fear of all things two-wheeled, appreciates the fact that bicycles are prohibited.

The fences here, like at many of the suburban dog parks, are low. Cooper could easily have cleared them had he wanted to. Perhaps that's the secret: With space to run inside, dogs don't want to jump the fence. There are no benches to rest on here, but there are trash cans and baggies within the park. Unfortunately, owners don't pick up here as frequently as in other parks, so a towel or wipe of the paws on the pavement is a wise idea before getting back into the car. Leashed dogs are welcome in the remainder of the 34-acre Larsen Nature Preserve. The jogging trail, which extends south of the dog exercise area, is popular with local pooches and their people. The parks are open until sunset.

There are no fees to use the park, but dogs must be up-to-date on their shots and at least four months old. The park is west of Sheridan Road and north of Glen Flora Avenue. From Sheridan Road, drive west on Glen Flora to Western, then turn north. The entrance to the park is on the west side of Western Avenue at Keith Street, south of Greenwood. There's a small parking lot at the entrance. Waukegan Park District; 847/360-4700; www.waukeganparks.org.

PLACES TO STAY

Budget Inn: "Medium-sized" dogs are welcome at this modest motel, for the equally modest fee of $15 per stay. People rates start at $60. 31 N. Green Bay Rd.; 847/336-9000.

La Quinta Inn & Suites, Gurnee: This 102-room hotel has a hot tub, sauna, and indoor swimming pool. Breakfast is included, and there are no fees for bringing pets. The hotel is near the amusement park. Rates average $100. 5688 N. Ridge Dr., Gurnee; 847/662-7600.

Residence Inn Waukegan: This 126-room hotel is meant for travelers planning on longer stays in an area saturated with motel and hotel chains. One- and two-bedroom apartments have kitchens with refrigerators, microwaves, and coffeemakers. Complimentary breakfast is included. Rates range from $99–$149. There's a $75 fee for a pet. 1440 S. White Oak Dr.; 847/689-9240; www.marriott.com.

Round Lake, Ingleside, and Grayslake

There are more than 37 parks in Round Lake alone, many of them with little lakes and ponds and the requisite anglers. These are not typical municipal parks, but full-fledged recreation areas with camping and fishing. Better yet, on-leash dogs are accepted as part of any outdoor adventure here.

Both Ingleside and Grayslake are more than 40 miles from the city of Chicago, 10-plus miles from Lake Michigan, and worlds away from the commotion.

PARKS, BEACHES, AND RECREATION AREAS

4 Cedar Valley Park

 (See Lake County map on page 148)

This is a popular, often crowded 70-acre park, with many trees, benches, and a play lot for kids. Summer afternoons, there's a likelihood of meeting some other furry friends, but it's also possible that there won't be a lot of room to frolic, depending on how many local residents are here. But there's a pond down the steep bank at Cedar Valley, and dogs are permitted to swim here, as long as they aren't bothering anyone and remain leashed to and from the pond. The park is located on Cedar Lake Road, which is west of Route 83. The park is bordered by Cedar Crest Court and Lakewood Terrace in Round Lake. 847/546-8558.

5 Hart's Hill and Hart's Woods Park

 (See Lake County map on page 148)

It's the sledding hill that's the attraction here. Actually, two hills, in case the bigger one wears out you or your basset-size pup. A warming house/concession building (an increasingly common perk at parks in this area) gives a place to warm toes and paws. The hill is lit for nighttime use, which is a welcome amenity when short days make going outside in the dead of winter a dark, dreary experience. Even if your snow dog appreciates the cold more than you do, you'll likely catch some of the enjoyment from watching—or participating in—this good, old-fashioned, infectious fun.

When there's no snow on the ground, there's still plenty of fun at Hart's Hill. The grass-covered hill is the perfect place for an energetic, leashed run

DOG-EAR YOUR CALENDAR

Imagine 180 acres of woods where your dog can run off-leash, jump off a dock into a lake for a swim, and practice agility moves; and the only folks he'll run into are other dogs and dog lovers. This pet planet actually exists, albeit just for a few four-day weekends per year. Held in May and October, **Camp Dogwood** is summer camp for dogs. In addition to the swimming and playing, there's pet massage (a pro teaches you how to do this at home), tracking, flyball, Frisbee, and even campfires, talent shows, ghost stories, and arts and crafts. Camp Henry Horner, a state facility, turns itself over to the dogs for as much frolic as little legs can stand. A canteen sells dog treats, T-shirts, books, training toys, copies of the group photos, and other souvenirs for home.

Dogs and the people who bring them to camp stay in tents, modest cabins, or lodges with running water. Day-only excursions to camp are also available. Fees range from $130 for day campers to $685 for spots in the deluxe lodge. Human meals—including Bug Juice (it tastes just like you remember it) and family-style dining—are included in the fees; dogs have to bring their own chow. Like at human camp, campers at Camp Dogwood make friendships that last after everyone goes home.

Camp Dogwood is held at the Camp Henry Horner Conference Facility, south of Fox Lake and west of Grayslake in Ingleside. The entrance to Camp Dogwood is located on West Nippersink Road at Camp Horner Road, west of the intersection of Nippersink Road and Wilson Road. To register, contact Camp Dogwood; 3501 N. Southport Ave., PMB 178, Chicago, IL 60657-1436; 312/458-9549; www.campdogwood.com.

(an excellent workout). If altitude isn't your thing, there are plenty of trees and ball fields, too. Hart's Hill is east of U.S. Highway 12. The hill and woods are separated by Hart Road, near the Route 134 intersection in Round Lake. 847/546-8558.

6 Fairfield Park

(See Lake County map on page 148)

To call this 44-acre recreation area a park is to shortchange a wildlife refuge, a forest, and a campground. Leashed dogs are welcome to camp, too, but reservations for both bipeds and quadrupeds must be made in advance. You should be adept at pitching a tent, because the winds can be strong here, even with the nearby oak trees. Fairfield Park is between Nippersink Road and Hart Road, south of Route 134, north of Route 120. Round Lake Area Park District; 814 Hart Rd., Round Lake; 847/546-8558.

7 Central Park

❀ (See Lake County map on page 148)

As befits its name, this park is the heart of Grayslake recreation. The 61-acre park is surrounded with tall, leafy, mature trees, and surfaced with well-kept green grass. Located in the middle of town, next to the railroad tracks and several schools, Central Park has a picnic area, playground, and soccer fields, as well as an entrance to Grayslake's impressive Greenway Corridor. The corridor's bike path runs through virtually all of the town, making getting anywhere in this suburb a pleasant afternoon's walk. (Bike trail maps can be downloaded at www.villageofgrayslake.com.) Connecting sections to complete the bike path are planned throughout town, including adding an underpass connection from Central Park to Grayslake Community High School and Grayslake Middle School. There is no parking lot at Central Park, but street spots are usually available. Parking overnight on city streets is prohibited. Central Park is on Lake Street, south of Washington Street, several blocks southwest of the College of Lake County. 847/223-8515.

Libertyville, Vernon Hills, and Mundelein

It might be hard to imagine now, but just a generation ago, these lake-dotted suburban communities 40 miles from the Loop were vacation destinations for Chicagoans who needed a getaway. The small lakes, with names like Loch Lomond, St. Mary's Lake, and Diamond Lake, are still there, of course. The country homes are still there, too, but now they're surrounded by houses of year-round residents, hotels, and businesses. Mundelein is home to one of the area's first dog daycare centers, **B. C. Dog Training, Grooming, and Pet Supply** (872 Tower Rd.; 847/566-1960; www.bcdogtraining.com).

PARKS, BEACHES, AND RECREATION AREAS

8 Independence Grove

❀❀❀❀ 🐕 (See Lake County map on page 148)

Having been raised a city dog, Natasha had no idea that nirvana was hidden in the suburbs. Yes, all of the Lake County Forest Preserve Dog Exercise Areas are impressive. But this 30-acre area is her paws-down favorite in this book. What makes her water-loving dog's heart race? A small lake/large pond (depending on your perspective), with multiple swimming holes, a beach-like open area at the front, and smaller shores all the way around the perimeter. Did you catch that? A lake with an off-leash trail all the way around its circumference. For people who tire of watching their dogs run circles around (and around) the lake, there are benches in both the sun and the shade, and trash

cans strategically placed along the length of the trail. Wooded areas surround the lake and trails, however, so owners must remain alert and be able to keep an eye on their dogs (and any droppings they leave behind).

Years ago, there was concern about a dog contracting blastomycosis, a fungal infection that can be lethal, at Independence Grove. The forest preserve people have tested the soil here repeatedly and found no evidence of the fungus, and concerns have abated. (For more information about blastomycosis, see the Introduction.)

The only downside to this dog heaven on earth is that you might miss it. The turnoff is hidden and poorly marked from Milwaukee Avenue/Route 21 (go slowly and look for the sign/entrance on the east), about a half-mile north of Buckley Road/Route 137. The fenced area is not double-gated, a bit of a concern since the entrance abuts a busy road. Dogs are not permitted on any other Independence Grove Forest Preserve land.

9 Butler Lake Park

😺😺 (See Lake County map on page 148)

Water-loving dogs like that they're generally permitted to swim at Butler Lake, which is part of this 60-acre village park. Dogs must be leashed elsewhere in the park, and while the lake is not an official off-leash area, officials don't bark if the dogs aren't disturbing anyone. The lake is shallow, which land managers have said may be impacting both native and exotic plants and the lake's fish population. If the lake is dredged and refilled to fix that, the dog swimming policy may change. Butler Lake Park has other amenities to seek out: seven baseball diamonds, two football fields, two picnic areas, and two bike paths, plus a warming house for cold winter days.

The park is west of Lakeside Cemetery, which is west of Milwaukee Avenue/Route 21. Lake Street runs through the park, just east of Stonegate Road in Libertyville. 847/918-PARK (847/918-7275).

PLACES TO EAT

Park Street: This American bistro serves up steaks, seafood, pastas, rack of lamb, and nightly specials. The neighborhood stop has a full wine list and a children's menu. Dogs are welcome guests at the popular tables out front. 14 East Park St., Mundelein; 847/949-1900; www.parkstreetdining.com.

PLACES TO STAY

Mundelein Super 8: This is one budget motel that has gotten dog-friendlier. The policy used to be small pets only, but now any size goes. Just tell the clerk in advance. There's a $6 fee per night, per dog. The motel is nothing fancy, as its rates, starting at $60, suggest. It's located at Route 45 and Route 60. 1950 S. Lake St., Mundelein; 847/949-8842.

Wauconda and Long Grove

Located on the far west side of Lake County, near McHenry County, Wauconda is centered around Bangs Lake, which is named after the town's founder. Bangs, and the lake-centric life here, is more for boating than bobbing for bones. But it is worth a special trip for the dog who likes to get some speed in his morning run, thanks to a forest preserve off-leash area. Long Grove, Wauconda's neighbor to the southeast, isn't known as much for its parks as for its folksy downtown. The antique- and festival-laden town admits leashed dogs to its many outdoor events.

PARKS, BEACHES, AND RECREATION AREAS

🔟 Lakewood

🐾🐾🐾🐾🐕 (See Lake County map on page 148)

Natasha's friend Milo is pretty much a homebody, and doesn't care for the cramped quarters of the dog-friendly areas in the city. But his demeanor immediately changed when he pulled up here. There may be more than 100 dogs romping here on any given weekend, but it can seem like you have the place to yourself. At 68 fenced acres, it's big enough for everyone, no matter how much space they need.

There are two training enclosures for obedience work or time-outs, two mown meadows for open romping and ball tossing, a mown trail, two fields of taller grass, and winding, forested paths for sniffing. While dogs love all the space, they also like to congregate near the front of the park, which makes for good human socializing. The wooded trails extend far back toward the fence.

It can be hard to keep an eye on an enthusiastic dog here, making it both difficult to clean up after him and to convince him that it's time to go home.

There's no running water here, for water fountains or in the campground-style human pit stops, but at least there are latrines, which are not a universal amenity in the forest preserves. The trash cans, unfortunately, are only at the entrance, not along the trails. The area is easy to see from Route 176; entrance to this park is on the east of Fairfield Road, just north of Route 176 in Wauconda.

Lake Bluff and Lake Forest

Just four square miles big, Lake Bluff has some of the North Shore's most spectacular views, both of the area's impressive historic homes and from the lakefront beach. Lake Forest, better known and bigger than little Lake Bluff, still retains much of that same small-town charm, especially around the town square near the train station. Lake Bluff is home to **The Down Town Dog** (57 E. Scranton; 847/295-2275), a specialty gift shop with canine cashmere sweaters, dog beds, collars, and a pastry case of dog treats. (The Down Town Dog also has a Chicago outpost in Macy's department store on State Street.)

PARKS, BEACHES, AND RECREATION AREAS

🔟 Sunrise Beach

🐾🐾🐾🐕 (See Lake County map on page 148)

Officially, Sunrise Beach's policy is much like that of Moraine Beach in Highland Park (see below). While there is no fee for residents and their dogs to use the off-leash area to their doggy hearts' content, nonresidents must shell out $150 for a dog pass and $50 for a human beach pass ($60 if issued after May 15). Guards stand atop the long stairs to the beach and don't admit anyone, no matter how floppy her ears or how sad her eyes, without a pass. On the way to and from the dog beach, dogs must be on a leash six feet or shorter. Residents and nonresidents alike must complete a Dog Responsibilities Contract before being permitted to use the beach.

The difference is, at Sunrise Beach the guards check for passes exclusively during the beach season, and even the park district administrators say they don't care who uses the area in the winter, as long as they pick up after their dogs, stay in the designated areas, and keep dogs leashed outside of the areas. That changes things! The aptly named Lake Bluff features a steep walk down several flights of stairs to the beach, which is at the far north end of Sunrise Beach. Natasha liked the scenic walk down, with leafy trees and plenty to sniff. Once on the sandy expanse, she ran with abandon inside the non-fenced, but clearly marked, dog area. Even when the lake is frozen solid during the winter, there's plenty of fun to be had here, along with pickup bags and

DOG-EAR YOUR CALENDAR

Dog Day: As part of its effort to get the word to dog lovers that many of its 750 acres are dog-friendly, Lake Forest Open Lands Association hosts an annual fundraiser each June, with a dog show (Lake Forest is home to many unusual breeds, confides one local), dog parade, tricks, and, of course, food. Lake Forest Open Lands Association; 272 E. Deerpath, Lake Forest, IL 60045; 847/234-3880.

Save-A-Pet Adoption Center: This is one of Lake County's most active no-kill shelters, with more than 40 different community events held during the year, ranging from garage sales and bake sales to a kitty tea. Dogs like September's **Pet-Athalon** best, a seven-mile race that starts in the Old School Forest Preserve, off St. Mary's Road near Route 176. Save-A-Pet Adoption Center; 31664 N. Fairfield Rd., Grayslake; 847/740-7788.

trash cans, so owners don't have to make the trek back up with their hands full. The beach is open until 10 P.M.

There's no parking at the beach level in Lake Bluff, which is a nice safety net for dogs who dart in front of cars, but makes beach access difficult for those who are disabled. In addition, parking is prohibited east of Moffat April–September. Take Center Street from U.S. Highway 41 or Green Bay Road to Moffat and walk the rest of the way east. Sunrise Beach is located at Sunrise and Scranton. Permits are issued in the Lake Bluff Park District office at 355 W. Washington Ave.; 847/234-4150; www.lakebluffparkdistrict.org.

12 Lake Forest Open Lands

🐾🐾🐾🦮 (See Lake County map on page 148)

The Lake Forest Open Lands Association describes itself as the local public television station of parks. This nonprofit, volunteer organization has acquired more than 700 acres of wetlands, woodlands, and ecologically significant prairie and savanna over the past three decades. All land is purchased by the group, so there's no danger of development, and it has all been restored, preserving both flora and fauna.

The association's six properties include walking and cross-country trails, wildflower meadows, and educational areas. Though the properties are open to the public, Lake Forest Open Lands prefers that users of the areas purchase memberships—ranging $65–1,000—to support the areas' conservation and upkeep. Memberships at the $100 level or higher (plus the submission of a dog registration form) gives you dog-walking privileges in five Open Lands preserves. Those five include: Derwen Mawr Preserve, Everett Fare Nature Preserve, Middlefork Farm Nature Preserve, Skokie River Nature Preserve, and West Skokie Nature Preserve. Dogs may be off-leash as long as they are under control and are put back on leash when in proximity of educational groups, other people, or other dogs. In addition, Open Lands holds an annual Dog Day event for Lake Forest and Lake Bluff residents and their dogs.

While the pricier dog membership might seem like a lot of red tape for going to the park, the effort is worth it, particularly for dogs and their owners who like to hike. While there's no shortage of scenic views and open spaces in Lake County, the Open Lands properties are some of the most pristine natural hiking and walking habitats around. And, unlike many conservancies that seem to believe dogs and nature don't go together, the Open Lands community welcomes leashed dogs and their ecologically appreciative owners.

The Open Lands are between Route 176 and Route 22, and the lake and the I-94 Expressway. Lake Forest Open Lands Association; 272 E. Deerpath, Lake Forest; 847/234-3880; www.lfola.org.

13 Prairie Wolf

🐾🐾🐾🐾🦮 (See Lake County map on page 148)

This is party central for pups in the Lake Forest area. Dogs and their people congregate here after work, and while there are 44 acres on which to romp, a lot of the action takes place near the entrance. There are two training enclosures at the front end of the park, near a large mown field. Designed for puppies and obedience training, these low, fenced pens are sometimes used as agility hurdles by energetic dogs who come to Prairie Wolf. There are several benches near the entrance, where a crowd of spectators gathers.

When you pull your dog away from all the excitement, there's still plenty more to be found, including several mown trails for easy exploring, tallgrass fields for tracking the scent of little critters, and a swimming pond toward the east end of the fenced facility.

The entrance to Prairie Wolf is on the east side of Waukegan Road/Route 43, which means you can hear the traffic whizzing by, as well as the rumble of the Metra train from the nearby tracks. This doesn't faze many—if any—dogs, but it can distract some people from the pleasantries at hand. There is parking off Route 43, but the entrance to the off-leash area is not double-gated, which could be a little dangerous, since the parking lot is frequently crowded and close to a busy road. All the Lake County Forest Preserve amenities—trash cans, doggy baggies, and daily permit box—are here. There are no latrines. The entrance to the dog exercise area is on Route 43, just south of Old Mill Road and north of Half Day Road/Route 22, in Lake Forest.

PLACES TO EAT

Bank Lane Bakery: Baking pans substitute for water bowls at this neighborhood bakery, which is owned by Down Town Dog's Maggie Ross. Sidewalk

tables are open to both people and their pets. 670 Bank Lane, Lake Forest; 847/234-8801.

South Gate Café: This restaurant has cut back on its previously over-the-top dog-friendly atmosphere. Now pups must be tied outside the fence of the outdoor patio, but it is still a nice respite after a day in the park. The restaurant is also owned by Maggie Ross, whose business card reads "Top Dog." Natasha wonders how her dog Roxie feels about that. 655 Forest Ave., Lake Forest; 847/234-8800.

Deerfield and Lincolnshire

The suburb of Deerfield was created in 1850 and named for Deerfield, Massachusetts, as well as for the deer found in this area. Today, you might see one of Bambi's kin on a quiet day in the park, but you're much more likely to see the bustling business district that Deerfield has become. Home to many nationally known companies, including Walgreens and Baxter International, Deerfield now holds many pond-filled office complexes and hotels and resorts that accommodate all travelers—both two- and four-legged.

Those pretty ponds also make homes for gaggles of geese. Natasha's been too busy researching the area to take on a second job, but some border collies she knows are paid to chase the large number of geese away from the office buildings and walkways in Deerfield and other suburbs (such as **Knox Swan & Dog Rental;** 847/304-1230; www.canadiangoosecontrol.com). The goose droppings are slippery on sidewalks and can be a hazard. So far, Natasha has remained sure-pawed.

PARKS, BEACHES, AND RECREATION AREAS

14 Jaycee Memorial Park

🐾🐾🐾🐾 🐕 (See Lake County map on page 148)

The dog park in Deerfield's Jaycee Memorial Park isn't huge, but what it lacks in size (compared to nearby suburban forest preserve dog exercise areas, not to the city's dog-friendly areas), it makes up for with toys. Bright, clean tires to jump through, hurdles to clear, and planks to walk are among the agility equipment that's free for the playing. Gravel and wood chips cover the ground, large trees line the fence, a path makes a loop, and water fountains are accessible to dogs who are panting from all the fun. There are a few benches with shade covering for those hot summer days, and there is easy access to trash cans for disposing of waste.

Dogs are not allowed on the playground equipment next to the fenced-in dog run, but there's no reason they'd want to be there, with all there is to entertain them in the dog park. The dog area is double-gated for safety. Another nice touch is a "dog house," naming community members who have donated to the upkeep of this clean park.

Entrance to the park is from the west side of Wilmot Road, which is several blocks east of the I-90/I-94 Expressway. The park is north of Deerfield Road, south of Greenwood Avenue. The dog area is in the southwest corner of the park. Ample parking is available. 1050 Wilmot Rd.; 847/945-0650.

15 James Mitchell Park

☙ (See Lake County map on page 148)

This small community park is family-focused: There are two swimming pools, basketball courts, a sand volleyball court, and a playground. Mitchell is just down the street from Jaycee Memorial Park's official dog park. So, there aren't a lot of reasons for a dog to stop here for a run or even a pit stop. But the large grassy area adjacent to Mitchell's playground is home to Deerfield's popular summer concert series, and on Sunday nights at 5 P.M., dogs are often here with their whole families, enjoying the sounds of summer. The small parking lot fills quickly, but street parking is available on Appletree Lane, just west of the park. The park is north of Deerfield Road, south of Hazel Road, and east of Wilmot Road. 847/945-0650.

16 Maplewood Park

☙ (See Lake County map on page 148)

This park has a little something for everyone who lives in this family-friendly suburb: a play lot with three separate areas to accommodate children of different ages, cross-country skiing, and picnic areas, including a gazebo with picnic tables, grills, and bathrooms. The bulk of the large grassy area here is taken up by two softball fields, perfect for romps in the off-season, but not the place to try to toss a ball when a game's on.

The bike path that loops around Maplewood is a good place for a stroll, particularly if you're with kids who want to entertain themselves in other ways at the park. But the park, which is not fenced, backs up against busy Deerfield Road. If you're making a special trip to Deerfield, Jaycee Memorial Park would be the first stop.

Take Hazel to Clay Court and then drive south to dead-end into the ample parking lots on the northern side of the park. Maplewood is north of Deerfield Road, west of the railroad tracks. 847/945-0650.

PLACES TO STAY

Marriott's Lincolnshire Resort: A 390-room hotel on 170 wooded acres is music to the ears of any size dog. Just don't try to swim in the pond. Self-service laundry is available, a nice option after a few muddy romps in the forest preserves. This resort is located in Lincolnshire, Deerfield's neighbor to the north, which does not permit dogs in any of its town parks. A $75 pet fee covers the entire stay. Rates start at $119. Parking is free. The resort is on Route 45, north of Deerfield Road. 10 Marriott Dr., Lincolnshire; 847/634-0100; www.marriott.com.

Residence Inn Chicago, Deerfield: Designed for stays of five days or more, the 128 rooms in this hotel come with kitchens and living rooms. Rates start at $89, with a $75 pet fee. Up to two dogs, 60 pounds and under, are allowed per room. 530 Lake Cook Rd., Deerfield; 847/940-4644; www.marriott.com.

Highland Park and Highwood

It's nothing personal, of course, but the pretty town of Highland Park would prefer that nonresident dogs not make the trip to use their breathtaking dog beach. This lakeside suburb is one of the most affluent in the area. But unlike its tinier neighbor, Lake Bluff, Highland Park is home to a number of attractions for non–Highland Parkers, such as interesting shopping, restaurants, and the Ravinia open-air music pavilion (Cooper howls in his Alpo every time he thinks about that outdoor concert venue being off-limits to dogs). As a result, Highland Park also has traffic, parking restrictions, and high fees for dogs who are just visiting. The town has a quaint appeal, and there are a number of pedestrian- and dog-friendly businesses in the area, a draw not necessarily found in other, more auto-dependent suburbs.

Tiny Highwood (population 5,500) is nestled between Lake Forest and Highland Park.

PARKS, BEACHES, AND RECREATION AREAS

17 Golf Learning Center

🐾 🦮 (See Lake County map on page 148)

A nice idea, anyway. That's what's behind this winter-only off-leash dog run on what is normally the driving range of Highland Park's Golf Learning Center. Locals (and well-heeled visitors) who pay the $35 annual permit ($250 for non-residents) to swim at Moraine Dog Beach (see below) can let their dogs run here November–March. There's nothing wrong with the space here; its grass is well

FETCHING NECESSITIES

Even in lovely Lake County, sometimes a dog and his owner need the basics. Here are some shops where you're welcome to stop, leash in hand.

The Dog House: Clothes, collars, backpacks, and canine accoutrements of all kinds. Pets can even try on the costumes and sweaters in-store to get the perfect fit. 405 Robert Parker Coffin Rd., Long Grove; 847/634-3060.

The Down Town Dog: Indulgent treats, even a pastry case, for dogs with discriminating tastes. 57 E. Scranton Ave., Lake Bluff; 847/295-BARK (847/295-2275); www.shopthedog.com.

Kaehler's Luggage: High-end leather goods and luggage. 654 Central Ave., Highland Park; 847/433-6500.

PETCO: Have a photo of your pooch taken here while you stock her pantry. 787 West Main St., Lake Zurich; 847/550-6760; www.petco.com.

Pet's General Store: Upscale treats and high-end pet food. 432 Peterson Rd., Libertyville; 847/247-1525.

PetSmart: This location of the national chain has a grooming center and obedience classes, as well as the essentials. 701 N. Milwaukee Ave., Vernon Hills; 847/816-3009; www.petsmart.com.

Très Bone Bakery & Boutique: Treats are made daily at this gourmet shop, which also stocks collars, leashes, and toys. Give your dog a taste of the barbecued ribs treats. 508 N. Seymour Ave., Mundelein; 847/837-8901; www.thepetgourmet.com.

Uncle Dan's: Backpacks, travel bowls, energy bars, and other gear for active pooches (and people). Check out the Granite Gear Flyer, a Frisbee that doubles as a seat cushion for when you need a rest after a day in the wilds. 1847 Second St., Highland Park; 847/266-8600; www.udans.com.

Village Antique Mall: Dogs are welcome inside, just watch the wagging tails around the breakables. 131 E. Maple Ave., Mundelein; 847/566-2363.

tended the rest of the year, and the Highland Park District adds a few benches, trash cans, snow fences, and Mutt Mitt dispensers for the winter. And it's better than this space going unused all season. But the space isn't very big—probably no bigger than many dogs have in their mansion-style backyards in Highland Park. There's no compelling reason to come here, unless you already have the permit for the summer season and are in the mood for a ball toss or a quick pit stop.

Permits are issued at the Heller Nature Center (2821 Ridge Rd.; 847/681-2189; www.pdhp.org). Proof of vaccinations is required. The entrance to the

Golf Learning Center is on the east end of Edens Highway/U.S. Highway 41/Skokie Valley Road, north of Park Avenue, next to the Target store. There's plenty of parking at the entrance to the dog run, which is clearly marked in giant red letters. 2205 Skokie Valley Rd.

18 Moraine Beach

🐾🐾🐾 🐕 (See Lake County map on page 148)

Everything that the Highland Park winter off-leash area isn't, Moraine Beach is. This fenced, off-leash beach is open April–November, dawn–dusk, and allows dogs to run and swim at the base of a beautiful bluff, while people get to gasp and understand why it is Highland Parkers work so hard to protect what they have. The walk down from the park—a pretty 12-acre space in its own right—is steep; some people are winded from the effort. But dogs, of course, are raring to go when they see the welcoming tides and smooth sand.

The picture permit card required to swim here is $40 (plus current Highland Park dog license) for residents and $120 (with rabies vaccination paperwork) for nonresidents. Given the parking restrictions for nonresidents in this area, it's hard to justify paying the $120 for seven months if you don't live here, which is probably the objective. If you think you and your dog will be in the area enough to justify it, permits are issued at the Heller Nature Center (2821 Ridge Rd.; 847/681-2189; www.pdhp.org). You must have your dog with you when you apply for the permit. Fees for frolicking without a permit are $500.

Moraine Beach is below Moraine Park at Sheridan Road. From Green Bay Road, take Moraine Road east. You must park west of Sheridan Road if you don't have a resident beach parking sticker (an extra $62). 2501 Sheridan Rd.

 Larry Fink Memorial Park

🐾🐾 (See Lake County map on page 148)

If you're in the area and want to play but can't afford the off-leash permits in Highland Park, this 71-acre park is a doggone-good compromise. There's a goose-filled pond fed by the Chicago River, which delights the heart of any bird dog. But because the river weaves its way through this grassy park, there's also a chance you might see an owl, deer, or other wildlife. Picnickers flock here in the summer, as do tennis players.

The park is open dawn–dusk. Larry Fink Memorial Park is on Clavey Road, between the Edens Expressway/U.S. Highway 41 to the west and Green Bay Road to the east, next to the Northmoor Country Club. 701 Deer Creek Pkwy.; 847/831-3810.

PLACES TO EAT

Cafe Central: This Highland Park bistro is run by Debbie Nieto, wife of Carlos Nieto (*the* Carlos of Chicago restaurant fame), and her son Adam. Debbie makes everyone who dines here feel like a regular, and that includes dogs at the restaurant's 12 outside tables. Open for lunch and dinner, Cafe Central is not a budget meal, but it's worth the price. 455 Central Ave.; 847/266-7878; www.cafecentral.net.

Java City: This coffeehouse near the Ravinia concert park offers sidewalk tables, water bowls, dog biscuits, and, of course, a good cup of joe. 723 St. John Ave.; 847/266-0728.

Michael's Chicago Style Red Hots: With 50 outdoor tables (both front and back), Michael's is one of the largest dog-friendly restaurants on the North Shore. Owner Michael Hoffman provides water bowls for the pups, and plenty of pet owners are seen sharing these classic hot dogs with their own dogs. 1879 Second St.; 847/432-3338.

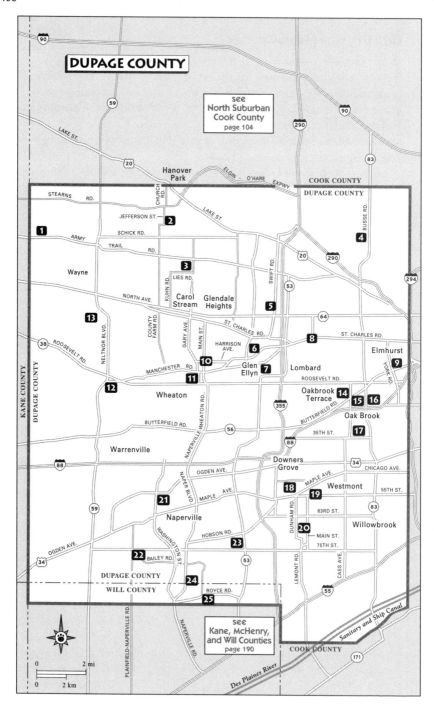

DUPAGE COUNTY

see
North Suburban
Cook County
page 104

Hanover Park

COOK COUNTY
DUPAGE COUNTY

1

STEARNS RD.
JEFFERSON ST.
ARMY
SCHICK RD.
TRAIL RD.
CHURCH RD.
LAKE ST.
BUSSE RD.
JEFFERSON ST. **2**
4

Wayne

3

LIES RD.
KUHN RD.
NORTH AVE.

Carol Stream
Glendale Heights
5

13

NELTNOR BLVD.
COUNTY FARM RD.
GARY AVE.
MAIN ST.
ST. CHARLES RD.
SWIFT RD.
53
64
8
ST. CHARLES RD.
Elmhurst
9

ROOSEVELT RD.
38
HARRISON AVE.
6
10
MANCHESTER RD.
Glen Ellyn **7**
Lombard
ROOSEVELT RD.
YORK RD.

12
11
Wheaton
Oakbrook Terrace **14**
15 **16**
355
Oak Brook

BUTTERFIELD RD.
NAPERVILLE-WHEATON RD.
BUTTERFIELD RD.
17
56
35TH ST.
Warrenville
88
Downers Grove
34
CHICAGO AVE.
88

NAPER BLVD.
OGDEN AVE.
MAPLE AVE.
18
19 Westmont
55TH ST.
21
59
DUNHAM RD.
63RD ST.
83
Naperville
20
MAIN ST.
75TH ST.
Willowbrook
HOBSON RD.
23
53
OGDEN AVE.
34
22 BAILEY RD.
WASHINGTON ST.
LEMONT RD.
CASS AVE.
DUPAGE COUNTY
WILL COUNTY
24
ROYCE RD.
55
25

KANE COUNTY
DUPAGE COUNTY

see
Kane, McHenry,
and Will Counties
page 190

Sanitary and Ship Canal

COOK COUNTY
171

Des Plaines River

0   2 mi
0   2 km

PLAINFIELD-NAPERVILLE RD.
NAPERVILLE RD.

90
59
LAKE ST.
20
ELGIN - O'HARE EXPWY
290
90
83
294

ARROOOOOOOOOOO

CHAPTER 7

DuPage County

Without the prestige of Lake County or the proximity of Cook County, DuPage County is sometimes overlooked. But with the number of places that he can roam here, your dog won't let you make that mistake.

While Cooper and Natasha explored many nice suburban parks in DuPage County, from a dog's-eye view, the real attraction is the Forest Preserve District of DuPage County. The forest preserve has seven off-leash training and exercise areas and one area set aside for dogsledding. That's one new area since the first edition of this book, plus a $350,000 renovation of another (more on that below). The forest preserves open one hour after sunrise and close one hour after sunset. Elsewhere in the forest preserves, dogs are permitted on 10-foot leashes, but they must stay off the nature preserve areas and other people's picnics. There's a $75 fine for having a dog off-leash in a non-designated area (and for not picking up after your dog). As the number of off-leash dog areas has increased—and, by extension, the number of dogs using the preserves—so, too, has enforcement in DuPage County. Since the first edition of this book, the forest preserve added required fees and permits

PICK OF THE LITTER—DUPAGE COUNTY

BEST CITY PARKS
Terrace View Park, Oakbrook Terrace (page 181)
McCollum Park, Downers Grove (page 184)
Riverwalk, Naperville (page 185)

BEST DOG PARKS
Mallard Lake Forest Preserve, Hanover Park (page 172)
Whalon Lake Dog Park, Naperville (page 188)

for use of its dog areas. Annual permits for county residents are $35 for the first dog, $5 for each additional dog. Nonresidents pay $150 per year for the first dog and $20 for each additional dog. Daily permits are $5 for residents, $15 for nonresidents. Applications are available online (www.dupageforest .com) and at visitors service centers. You are limited to bringing three dogs to a preserve at any one time. Considering how happy your dog will be to see ponds to swim in and fields to run through, three dogs is probably the maximum you can keep your eye on anyway.

Most forest preserve entrances have kiosks with maps, notices, and brochures that indicate the preserve's dos and don'ts regarding dogs. As noted in the individual park listings, some of these dog areas are not fenced. Although the Forest Preserve District is working to change this, caution should be used if your canine friend doesn't have a strong "come" command.

Keep in mind that DuPage County's forest preserves can be muddy, swampy, and slushy. That's all in a dog's day of fun, but it doesn't hurt to have a towel with you for the ride home.

Not every park, forest preserve, or green patch in the county is included in this chapter, just the ones that seem most worth a trip out from the city, including several new municipal off-leash areas. Most village halls have maps to their areas with other parks listed, and the Forest Preserve District of DuPage County has excellent trail maps available for those who want to explore.

This chapter covers the relatively small, comma-shaped area of DuPage County from east of Route 59 to the I-294 Expressway, and from the northern county limits near O'Hare International Airport to the southern county line near the I-355 and I-55 Expressway intersection.

Wayne

Unlike Naperville, Glen Ellyn, or Wheaton (all described later in the chapter), Wayne does not have a quaint downtown with pedestrian traffic and cute little shops. It has wide-open spaces, from farms to forest preserves. And dogs like it that way. Wayne straddles the border of Kane and DuPage Counties, but is included in this chapter only.

PARKS, BEACHES, AND RECREATION AREAS

1 Pratt's Wayne Woods

🐾🐾🐾🐕 (See DuPage County map on page 168)

By far the forest preserve's largest area, Pratt's Wayne Woods spans more than 3,400 acres, with a lake, grassland, marsh, and almost six miles of trails. Despite its name, however, there are no woodlands here, which makes for very little shade in the hot summer sun. Dogs who can take the heat like to join horseback riders and others on the many trails, which include a portion of the Illinois Prairie Path.

While just a small fraction of the space here is allotted for dogs, pooches gravitate toward the off-leash area at the east end of the park. The triangular space has several mown trails for both long and short walks (or runs, depending on your energy level). Bring a bottle of water and cool down by watching the model-airplane flying that also goes on here. If, like Natasha, your dog is afraid of horses, use caution getting from the parking lot to the off-leash area, which is only three-quarters fenced. Many equestrians frequent these trails.

Pratt's Wayne Woods is one mile north of Army Trail Road on the east side of Powis Road. The dog exercise area is south of the parking lot. Forest Preserve District of DuPage County; 630/933-7200; www.dupageforest.com.

Hanover Park, Wood Dale, and Carol Stream

Former farmland, Hanover Park is now home to more than 180 acres of parks and bike paths. Parts of Hanover Park cross over into Cook County, but it's included in this chapter only. The city of Wood Dale is surrounded by three golf courses, making a trip to the links a pastime for many who live here. Natasha came here ready to wade in a stream named Carol. To her dismay, Carol Stream is named after a real person, the daughter of Jay Stream, the man who developed the suburb 30 miles west of Downtown. While probably appreciative of the gesture, Ms. Stream left the area for a warmer climate in Arizona.

PARKS, BEACHES, AND RECREATION AREAS

❷ Mallard Lake Forest Preserve

🐾🐾🐾🐾🐕 (See DuPage County map on page 168)

You know when your dog runs in his sleep, having those little doggy dreams, and you sit on the couch wondering what's making his legs churn? Well, he could be dreaming of Mallard Lake.

Mallard Lake rates at least three paws on its non-dog merits, too. This is one of DuPage County's prettiest forest preserve areas, with little footbridges to take you from open meadows to small islands for fishing, hiking, or walking. All forest preserves have a way of quickly transporting you to a different time and place, which is sort of the point of preserving the forests. Less than 20 minutes after you arrive, it's hard to remember that you live in a crowded apartment building or have to fight to find a parking spot at the neighborhood Jewel. This

transition happens even more quickly at Mallard Lake, which covers 945 acres. Mown meadows create pathways among tall cattails (again, Natasha sighs, no sign of cats), connecting two looping trails, about one mile long in total.

The entrance to Mallard Lake on Lawrence Road is a little tricky to find, which may contribute to its idyllic ambiance. While it is north of Schick Road, the best way to enter is to turn west from Gary Avenue. Lawrence Road will turn into the parking lot of the forest preserve. The area is between Thorn Road and County Farm Road, and the dog area is south of the parking lot. Forest Preserve District of DuPage County; 630/933-7200; www.dupageforest.com.

Hampe Park

 (See DuPage County map on page 168)

This 20-acre community park has space—and that's a good thing, because it also has more than enough people and pooches to fill it. You'll find five soccer fields, three basketball courts, one roller-hockey court, two sand volleyball courts, a wheelchair-accessible playground, and a separate teen play area. If you come here on even a mildly warm day, you'll be greeted by many kids from the local schools, ready to play the sport of the season. The best bet for dogs is to let your paws hit the pavement and take to the walking and bicycle paths that weave through the park. There are picnic areas, restrooms, and benches if you need to take a break, or you could use these paths to connect to some of the area's other parks.

Natasha can't get too excited about Hampe (although she spent some time searching in the grass for the extra *e* she's sure should be on the end of the park's name). Carol Stream dogs seem perfectly happy here, and if you're in this neck of the suburban woods, there's no reason not to take a stroll. There are two separate parking lots at Hampe, with enough spots for 150 cars. Hampe is in the northwest corner of the suburb, west of Gary Avenue and south of Army Trail Road on Lies Road. Carol Stream Park District; 391 Illini Dr.; 630/784-6100; www.csparks.org.

■ Dog Park at White Oaks Park

 (See DuPage County map on page 168)

Most of the real exploration at the White Oaks Nature Trail at White Oaks Park is done by people, although you are welcome to bring your leashed dog along on your trail adventures. Though the dog park at White Oaks may have been added after the trail, it doesn't seem like an afterthought. Cooper thinks the Wildlife Feeding Station at the nearby Cabin Nature Center boosts the number of squirrels and birds to chase at the dog park, and that alone is worth baying at, in his opinion. The park is filled with trees in which the little critters can hide from Cooper's enthusiastic vocalizations, and the park is stocked with agility equipment, which he'd use if he could take his mind off the wildlife for a few minutes.

White Oaks Dog Park, at the corner of Wood Dale Road and Montrose Avenue, is open dawn–dusk. There are no fees, permits, or requirements to use the dog park, other than the standard vaccinations and pick-up-after-your-pet admonishments. 111 S. Wood Dale Rd.; 630/595-9333; www.wooddale parkdistrict.org.

Glendale Heights and Glen Ellyn

Called "the New England of the Midwest" by some, Glen Ellyn, 25 miles from the Loop, rolls out the red carpet for both visitors and their pups. Dogs are not allowed in Glendale Heights' 26 nearby city parks, which makes the suburb's forest preserve spots even more popular with pooches.

PARKS, BEACHES, AND RECREATION AREAS

🗲 East Branch Forest Preserve

🐾🐾🐾 🐕 (See DuPage County map on page 168)

Natasha calls this dog training area "Lab Planet," because of the overwhelming predominance here of that particular breed. Designed more than 25 years ago to train dogs for hunting and other outdoor sports, it's no surprise that East Branch, which even has a pond for water training, would attract a lot of retrievers.

What is a surprise is how nice this off-leash area is, both for hunting dogs and for those who have the gene, but do not have owners with the inclination to hunt. A lot of old-fashioned play goes on here, with an exceedingly friendly group of dog lovers and their faithful friends. There are several hills, pathways, and a pond where swimming is permitted (at least swimming by dogs—it's too muddy for people). Still, if your dog will be startled by the sounds of blank rounds, visit one of the dog exercise areas instead.

The downside is that East Branch is not fenced, and the only thing separating Swift Road from dogs running free is the parking lot. While Swift Road is not an expressway, it isn't a side street either, and cars do drive by swiftly. There's no fenced enclosure at all here, and floodplain and wetland conditions prevented the forest preserve from adding fences as part of a $350,000 renovation of the area in 2006. When she first worked on this book, Natasha saw more dogs jump out of their cars untethered here than at any other park she visited. The parking lot was small and at a lower grade than the preserve, which meant water and snow pooled at the bottom, creating an icy effect. The renovation project, which required the area to be closed for a good part of 2006, should take care of that once and for all. Improvements include a 100-car asphalt parking lot, three wetland-detention basins, a 20-foot-long pedestrian boardwalk that spans wetlands adjacent to the parking lot, and other amenities. Potable water was not in the budget but is the next item on the East Branch wish list.

Driving south on Swift Road from Army Trail Road, you'll pass the huge Pampered Chef headquarters building. The dog area is one mile north of North Avenue on the west side of Swift Road, west of the I-355 Expressway. Forest Preserve District of DuPage County; 630/933-7200; www.dupageforest.com.

6 Lake Ellyn Park

😺😺 (See DuPage County map on page 168)

Glen Ellyn natives are quite proud of Lake Ellyn Park. At just 11 acres, it's large for a city park, but barely holds a blade of grass to the nearby forest preserves, nature areas, and bicycle trails. But it is among the most popular local spots for weddings. There's an open play area, drinking fountains, a wooded picnic area, fishing pier, and public restrooms, but it's the pathways around the large, quaint lake that draw dog owners here. Despite being close to the suburb's main roads, this is a tranquil place, especially from which to watch the sunset reflected in the water. Your dog can watch the reflections of the geese in the water, and everyone will be happy.

Lake Ellyn Park, which is open sunrise–10 P.M., is right in the center of town, north of the railroad tracks, south of St. Charles Road, on Hawthorne Street at Lenox Road. Glen Ellyn Park District; 185 Spring Ave.; 630/858-2462; www.gepark.org.

7 Spring Avenue Recreation Center Dog Run

😺🐕 (See DuPage County map on page 168)

What a good idea. Dogs in Glen Ellyn could hop in the car for a short ride to the DuPage County Forest Preserve off-leash areas, but they didn't used to have one in their own backyard. So, the Glen Ellyn Park District put one in. Literally. In the park district's own backyard at the Spring Avenue Recreation Center (SARC).

When the nearby East Branch Forest Preserve (see above) closed for renovations, the SARC dog run got some of the dog run-off, and as a result, some dog overcrowding. The experience has made Glen Ellyn Park District officials hesitant to be known as dog-friendly. Any visiting pups should be on their best behavior so that they don't jeopardize the dog run for the locals.

A chain-link fence surrounds the dog run behind the Glen Ellyn Park District offices. The run is at the northeast corner of the property and is visible from Route 53, where many people traveling to and from work see dogs romping morning, afternoon, and night. Because the run is also visible from inside the park district offices, people behave well, pick up after their pets, and observe all the standard dog-park rules. Even on a cold winter day, there may be as many as 20 local dogs ripping up the turf. The area is open sunrise–10 P.M. The run is north of Route 53, west of the I-355 Expressway. Glen Ellyn Park District; 185 Spring Ave.; 630/858-2462; www.gepark.org.

Elmhurst and Lombard

The Pottawatomie Indian tribe (remember them from the North Side chapter?) first settled along Salt Creek centuries ago. The towns—now 20 miles from the Loop—remained largely farming communities until the 1930s. Lombard's claim to animal fame is that Morris, the 9Lives spokescat, was rescued from an animal shelter here and was buried here after his demise.

PARKS, BEACHES, AND RECREATION AREAS

🔟 Lombard Common

😺 😺 (See DuPage County map on page 168)

The suburban village of Lombard considers this its most inclusive park. Fortunately for Fido, that includes dogs. At 50 acres, Lombard Common has five softball and baseball fields, three basketball courts, a community building, six soccer and football fields, a horticultural park, ice skating, two playgrounds, sheltered picnic areas, restrooms, sand volleyball, a sledding hill, tennis courts, and walking paths.

That's all well and good. But any energetic dog worth his kibble will tell you that Lombard Common is Frisbee central. Not only is there almost always a human Ultimate Frisbee game going on, but there's also a Frisbee golf course, and many canine Frisbee fanatics practice here, thanks to the wide-open space and lack of tall trees to get in the way.

The Moran Water Park, with its waterslides, is a convenient landmark for finding Lombard Common, which is located at Grace Street and St. Charles Road. Lombard is north of Route 38 and west of Route 53. Lombard Park District; 227 W. Parkside; 630/627-1281; www.lombardparks.com.

🔟 Illinois Prairie Path

😺 😺 🐾 (See DuPage County map on page 168)

Part of a statewide rails-to-trails initiative to convert abandoned railroad routes to usable outdoor lands, the Illinois Prairie Path is one of the longest, most interesting walks you and your dog can take. Dogs like the high prairie grasses, and newcomers like the labels that identify plants they'll see along the way. The 62-mile, multi-use limestone trail runs through Cook, DuPage, and Kane Counties, about 25 miles west of the city. All along the path, there are trail maps, mile markers, and benches. Unless you've adopted a greyhound, neither of you are probably up for the whole 62-mile trek at one time. But that's okay, because one of the best things about IPP (as it's called) is that there are so many good stops along the way, often at local city parks or county forest preserves with parking, restrooms, and other amenities.

It's included here in the Elmhurst section because there aren't many other places for a dog to go in Elmhurst. Other highlights of the IPP are included in other sections of this chapter and in the Kane, McHenry, and Will Counties chapter.

Though use of the IPP is free, memberships range $20–1,000 and help support trail maintenance. Members receive detailed maps and newsletters. Non-members may also order maps by mail for $6 each. In Elmhurst, park east of York Road at Vallette Street, north of Butterfield Road/Route 56. Illinois Prairie Path, P.O. Box 1086, Wheaton, IL 60187; 630/752-0120; www.ipp.org.

PLACES TO STAY

TownePlace Suites Chicago: This all-suites hotel will offer you and your canine traveling companion plenty of room to stretch out inside, plus nearby walking paths and jogging trails for early morning exercise. In case you get muddy on your DuPage County adventures (very likely), self-service laundry is available in this 127-room hotel. There is a $75 pet fee, and rates average $139. 455 E. 22nd St., Lombard; 630/932-4400; www.marriott.com.

Warrenville, West Chicago, and Wheaton

Warrenville is home to Cantera, a former gravel quarry that's now a 650-acre office park, shopping mall, and new residential community. Those things may not get your companion's tail wagging, but access to the Illinois Prairie Path and the DuPage River will.

If you and your pup are in Wheaton on a summer Saturday, get up early enough to walk through the Wheaton French Market. Ensconced by the Metra train tracks at Main and Liberty Streets, you'll find fresh flowers and produce, crafts, jewelry, baked goods, and books. In France, you wouldn't see a booth man selling Ronco-type knives ("it slices, it dices"), but this is French American-style. You can stop for alfresco food for yourself at one of several kiosks at the market, then take your health-minded hound to the **Natural Pet Market** (263 Rice Lake Sq., Wheaton; 630/682-4522; www.naturalpetmarket.com) for its toys and treats.

PARKS, BEACHES, AND RECREATION AREAS

🔟 Adams Park

🐾 🐕 (See DuPage County map on page 168)

This centrally located site was previously the home of John Quincy Adams (related to, but not *the* John Quincy Adams), a member of the Chicago Board of Trade and a benefactor of Wheaton College. It's one square block of a big, manicured park with fountains, gazebos, and benches. There's not a lot of room to play, what with workers from local businesses and students coming

DIVERSIONS

Say cheese-filled marrow bone! You love nothing more than to stare at that little cold nose, right? Well, as they say, take a picture—it lasts longer. Here are a few area photographers who specialize in getting pets on film. Most make dog house calls.

Bonnie Boton: This Riverwoods photographer focuses on the friendship between you and Fido. 847/267-1442.

Marc Hauser: Black-and-white studio shots. 1810 W. Cortland St., Chicago; 773/486-4381; www.marchauser.com.

Randi Heimert Photography: Black-and-white studio shots with you and your pooch in the frame. 847/367-9929.

Renny Mills Photography: Mills is a Camp Dogwood photographer who has mastered both the studio pose and the action shot. She also offers silkscreens of photographs. 1914 W. North Ave., Chicago; 312/243-0716; www.rennymillsphoto.com.

Jill Norton: Black-and-white candid photographs. 725 Washington St., Suite 109, Evanston; 312/403-1222; www.jillnorton.com.

PawPrints by Jennifer: Jennifer Mordini zooms in on the bond between human and pet. She specializes in black-and-white in her Highland Park studio, but will do color outdoors. 847/579-WOOF (847/579-9663).

Petraits Pet Photography: Owner Sheri Berliner specializes in color and black-and-white portraits of your pup in your home. She can put your pup on bookmarks, mugs, and keychains, in case you want to give gifts. 773/777-2891; www.petraits.com.

Sam & Willy's: Okay, this is a neighborhood store. But there's an old-fashioned photo booth in the back, so if you can get your pup in the frame, you can have some cheap wallet-sized images of the two of you together. 3405 N. Paulina St., Chicago; 773/404-0400; www.samandwillys.com.

Shermy Cards, Inc.: Jeanne Warsaw is a pet photographer, but what gets people coming back each year is the way she puts canine faces on cards you can send to everyone you know. 2334 W. Farwell Ave., #2W, Chicago; 773/764-1159; www.shermycards.com.

Sutton Studios: *Forbes* magazine called David Sutton the best pet photographer in America. His black-and-white portraits are typically taken in his Evanston studio, with Sutton making cat-like noises to grab your pup's attention. 3417 Church St., Evanston; 847/679-8090; www.suttonstudios.com.

Heidi Thomsen: Thomsen's style captures pensive looks and close-ups of wet noses. 847/567-4686; www.heidithomsen.com.

Karen Woodburn Photography: "Abrasion Toning" adds hand detailing to black-and-white images. 122 First St., Batavia; 630/406-1151; www.kwoodburnstudios.com.

here to enjoy the pretty grounds, flower garden, and restored fountain. It is a good place to take a shady, serene break after a long day, or to meet up with friends before embarking on a more ambitious trip to some of the suburb's environs. There are drinking fountains all over the place in Wheaton, but Natasha gets a big kick out of the ones here. They're designed to look like tree stumps.

Adams Park is located on Main Street in downtown Wheaton, between Wesley and Seminary Streets. Wheaton Park District; 666 S. Main St., Wheaton; 630/665-4710; www.wheatonparkdistrict.com.

11 Lincoln Marsh Natural Area

🐾 🐾 (See DuPage County map on page 168)

This is one area of undeveloped nature that might actually get bigger. The City of Wheaton and the DuPage County Forest Preserve put together 100 different parcels of land to create 135 acres of prairie, woodlands, and savannas, and they hope to acquire more land around the perimeter. Sporting breed or no, there are few dogs who won't like looking for more than 300 species of prairie and wetland plants and animals on these wood-chip paths. White-tailed deer, red fox, mink, owls, bats, muskrats, bluebirds, and ducks have all been sighted by observant mutts.

Lincoln Marsh is another good place to hop on the Illinois Prairie Path (described in the Elmhurst section), with ample parking available. In addition to the ponds and wetlands area, Lincoln Marsh has more traditional park amenities, including drinking fountains, a picnic shelter, and an ice rink.

Lincoln Marsh is north of Route 38, west of Gary Avenue, and east of County Farm Road at Harrison Street. Wheaton Park District; 666 S. Main St., Wheaton; 630/665-4710.

12 Blackwell Forest Preserve

🐾 🐾 🐕 (See DuPage County map on page 168)

The eight miles of trails that link McKee Marsh and Silver Lake are well used. Cross-country skiers, bicyclists, equestrians, and others flock here in all seasons. Winter is no exception because dogsledding is permitted on the multipurpose trails, making this one of only two parks in the Chicago area where dogs can learn to mush (pull sleds). (The other is in the Lake County chapter.) While on the sledding trails, dogs must be leashed or attached to a harness. The limestone, mown turf, and asphalt trails, whether covered in snow or not, are often crowded. This is not the place to get away from society, even if many of the areas along the DuPage River are serene.

In addition to the draw of mushing, Blackwell's 1,300 acres offer latrines and even camping areas, making it an overnight option for those pups who know how to pitch a tent. There's a decent off-leash dog exercise area south of the parking lot, with mown turf, taller prairie grasses, and space to run. Since the printing of the first edition of this book, the area has been fully fenced. A strong recall is still a good idea, but it isn't as essential as it once was in order to unclip the leash in this popular preserve.

The Blackwell Forest Preserve is a quarter-mile east of Route 59 on the north side of Mack Road. There's a parking lot on the south side Mack Road near McKee Marsh, a quarter-mile east of Route 59. Forest Preserve District of DuPage County; 630/933-7200; www.dupageforest.com.

13 Reed-Keppler Dog Park

🐾 🐕 (See DuPage County map on page 168)

This suburb's new dog park is smack dab in the middle of the park district, in Reed-Keppler Park near the Dyer Nature Sanctuary. The fenced-in area is off-limits to kids under 10, but open to dogs with the proper paperwork. Each dog in Reed-Keppler Dog Park must be registered with a picture ID with the West Chicago Park District. Fees are $35 for the first dog for West Chicago residents, $20 for each additional dog. Nonresidents pay $70 for the first dog, $40 for each additional dog. Visitors are limited to three dogs in any one visit. The park is open sunrise–sunset, except on Mondays, when the dog park opens at 10 A.M. Given the price for nonresidents, and the plethora of other options in the area, this is a good bet for locals, but not worth an extra trip for visitors. The park is south of Hawthorne Lane, west of Arbor Avenue. West Chicago Park District, 630/231-9474; www.we-goparks.org.

Oak Brook, Oakbrook Terrace, and Willowbrook

These western suburbs are best known for shopping malls and office parks, but dogs know the real dirt: They're among the most welcoming in the area to pooches and their people. Take tiny Oakbrook Terrace (population 2,300), for example. A city ordinance states that dogs must be leashed or "under the effective voice control of a responsible person." Natasha finds this way of thinking most reasonable indeed. Fines for not having control (voice or otherwise) of your pup are $25 for the first offense and not less than $25 or more than $1,200 for the second offense.

PARKS, BEACHES, AND RECREATION AREAS

14 Heritage Center

🐾 🐾 🐕 (See DuPage County map on page 168)

Headquarters of the Oakbrook Terrace Park District offices and indoor facilities, Heritage Center is a gathering place for local pooches who like the leash-free look they can sport in Oakbrook Terrace. Heritage Park's eight acres house a softball field, sand volleyball courts, a pavilion, picnic areas, a playground, and lighted tennis courts. When a softball game isn't going on, you'll find a plethora of tennis balls being chased by retrievers, unobstructed by trees or shrubs. As at Dorothy Drennon (see next listing), dogs here (off-leash or otherwise) should be good with children.

Heritage Center is south of 14th Street, north of Butterfield Road/Route 56, and west of Summit Avenue. Oakbrook Terrace Park District; 1 South 325 Ardmore Ave., Oakbrook Terrace; 630/627-6100; www.obtpd.org.

15 Dorothy Drennon

🐾 🐾 🐕 (See DuPage County map on page 168)

This small six-acre park wouldn't be much to bark home about if it weren't for Oakbrook Terrace's leash law. There are sand volleyball courts and flower gardens (in which dogs are not allowed to play), as well as picnic tables, a gazebo, and ample grass. If your pup is the tennis ball–chasing sort, you'll have a good time here. Please, though, make sure any off-leash pups are kid-friendly. Dorothy Drennon is named after a schoolteacher and is a draw for local families.

Dorothy Drennon is south of Butterfield Road/Route 56 and north of Eisenhower Road on Nimitz Road. Oakbrook Terrace Park District; 1 South 325 Ardmore Ave., Oakbrook Terrace; 630/627-6100; www.obtpd.org.

16 Terrace View Park

🐾 🐾 🐾 🐕 (See DuPage County map on page 168)

Natasha has been told that Oakbrook Terrace dogs like Terrace View Park because its lighted softball field and wide-open spaces are conducive to running in circles and playing fetch. That's great, but given the choice between an off-leash swim and, well, just about anything else, she's headed for the shore. Dogs are allowed to swim in the small lake, provided that they don't disturb the many rods and reels of those trying to catch fish, upset the rented paddleboats, or hop up on the floating stage during one of the many summer concerts that take place here. Avoiding the fountains is a good idea as well.

If your dog isn't as single-minded, you might enjoy the walking trail that circles the lake, with views of different interesting nature areas, the gazebo and picnic tables, and the activity in the lighted inline-skating rink. Terrace View Park is west of Kingery Highway/Route 83, north of 22nd Street. Oakbrook Terrace Park District; 1 South 325 Ardmore Ave., Oakbrook Terrace; 630/627-6100; www.obtpd.org.

17 Mayslake Dog Exercise Area

🐾 🐾 🐾 🐕 (See DuPage County map on page 168)

Oak Brook...where the streets are paved with hamburgers. At least, that's what Watson was expecting when he heard he was driving to this southwest Chicago suburb that houses the headquarters of fast-food king McDonald's.

He quickly forgot about the lack of Big Macs when he saw the super-size dog run at Oak Brook's Mayslake Forest Preserve, dozens of times larger than the Chicago dog-friendly areas he normally frequents.

Mayslake has its good points: It offers more than a football field of fully fenced running space shaped suspiciously like the burger giant's Grimace character, ringed by a walking path, and dotted with picnic tables (including two permanent structures with roofs for rainy or excessively sunny days). The drawbacks: It's fairly barren (most trees are still too young to provide much shade, and dogs have taken their toll on the once-lush grass, now turned to mulch); the sound of traffic zipping by on the adjacent Kingery Highway/Route 83 doesn't exactly lend itself to serene thoughts; and the lake is outside the fenced-in dog area—off-limits to water-loving retrievers and labs.

Still, the locals (and Watson) sing the praises of Mayslake and flock to the area in the summer like the Hamburglar to a Happy Meal. The parking lot has just 28 spaces (two handicapped), which usually means cars are illegally parked on the roadside on warm-weather weekends (and liberally ticketed, says one local). Latrines for humans are located near the parking lot, and bags are available to clean up after your dog. There is a strictly enforced $75 fine for having dogs off-leash outside the fenced-in area.

To get to the lot, enter St. Pascal Drive at 31st Street from the north or 35th Street from the south, just west of Route 83. The entrance is located about halfway between 31st and 35th Streets. Forest Preserve District of DuPage County; 630/933-7200; www.dupageforest.com.

PLACES TO EAT

Einstein Bros. Bagels: Dogs look forward to a bagel (coated in carob) to call their own here. 17 W. 432 22nd St., Oakbrook Terrace; 630/617-9888.

PLACES TO STAY

La Quinta Inn–Oakbrook Terrace: This clean, no-frills hotel accepts dogs up to 50 pounds without an additional fee or deposit. You must be present when housekeeping enters the room to clean if your pup is not crated. Rates range $70–120. 1 S. 666 Midwest Rd., Oakbrook Terrace; 800/531-5900; www.lq.com.

La Quinta Inn–Willowbrook: Breakfast and local phone calls are included in room rates at this basic but serviceable all-suites hotel. Dogs must stay in a smoking room on the first floor, but there are no fees or deposits. Rates start at $101. 855 79th St., Willowbrook; 630/654-0077; www.lq.com.

Westmont and Downers Grove

Locals here call their home "Downers," but they don't mean that as a put-down. Dogs also tend to be pretty up on Downers Grove, so named because of the natural grove of trees that grew here when the suburb was founded. The area is still dotted with a fair amount of foliage, which dogs are allowed to explore in neighborhood parks. But they are not allowed on the athletic fields in Downers parks. Recent talk has included the possibility of establishing an off-leash dog park at Sterling Park. The city sponsors both a summer "Dog Day Afternoon" event and a holiday "Santa Paws" party at Lincoln Center (936 Maple Ave., Downers Grove; 630/963-1300; www.dgparks.org).

Westmont is home to **Doggie Wash** (98 W. 63rd St.; 630/455-0100), one of the favorite do-it-yourself dog washes of those who frequent the marshy forest preserves.

PARKS, BEACHES, AND RECREATION AREAS

18 Maple Grove Forest Preserve

 (See DuPage County map on page 168)

This 82-acre area feels small for forest preserve land, and it's oddly located—not adjacent to other forest preserves, the Illinois Prairie Path, or other amenities. Still, leashed dogs are allowed on this mile-long trail, which is popular for those in the Downers Grove area who want something a little more rural than the nearby suburban parks. The woodlands give ample shade on the walking path, with interpretive trails (signs provide information about what you're seeing) woven throughout. A picnic area provides a place to rest.

This forest preserve is located on the north side of Maple Avenue, which is what Naperville Road is called in Downers Grove. The area is east of the I-355 Expressway. There's a small parking lot with room for 15 vehicles. Forest Preserve District of DuPage County; 630/933-7200; www.dupageforest.com.

19 Patriots Park

(See DuPage County map on page 168)

Barth Pond, located in the middle of Patriots Park, is intended not for swimming but for "waterfowl observation." Natasha's friend Sandy has observed geese, ducks, and the occasional swan as she's frolicked here. Patriots Park is a nice, 28-acre park with a walking trail around the perimeter, mature trees, 16 picnic tables, drinking fountains, and a playground. Patriots' path is a popular dog-walking destination for those who live in Downers.

There are parking lots on the south side of 55th Street, as well as the east and west sides of the park. Patriots Park is open sunrise–dusk. The park is south of 55th Street, between Fairmont and Blodgett Avenues; 630/963-1300; www.dgparks.org.

DOG-EAR YOUR CALENDAR

Every church with a steeple, and many without, now have **Blessings of the Animals** in order to give furry friends a little pat from a higher power. Many Catholic churches have the ceremony on the Feast of St. Francis of Assisi, the first Sunday in October. Others use the appeal of floppy-eared congregants to get folks into the pews in the summer months. Natasha doesn't want to preach to anyone. All she knows is that after months of hogging her couch, Roger finally found a permanent home after he was blessed by Pastor Matt at **Epiphany UCC** (2008 West Bradley Pl., Chicago; 773/281-4144; www.epiphany-ucc.org). The following are a few other area options for hounds looking to get holy:

All Saints' Episcopal Church Chicago, 4550 N. Hermitage Ave., Chicago; 773/561-0111; www.allsaintschicago.org.

Church of Holy Apostles, 5211 W. Bull Valley Rd., McHenry; 815/385-5673; www.thechurchofholyapostles.com.

Holy Innocents Episcopal Church, 425 Illinois Blvd., Hoffman Estates; 847/885-7900.

Marytown, Our Lady of Fatima Friary, 1600 W. Park Ave., Libertyville; 847/367-7800.

Notre Dame Church, 64 Norfolk Ave., Clarendon Hills; 630/654-3365.

South Suburban Humane Society holds its annual blessing during the December holidays. Donations for less fortunate dogs and cats are welcome. 1103 West End Ave., Chicago Heights; 708/755-7387; www.sshspets.org.   **St. Elizabeth Seton,** 2220 Lisson Rd., Naperville; 630/416-3325.

St. Linus Church, 103rd Street & Lawler Ave., Oak Lawn; 708/422-2400.

St. Patrick Parish, 406 Walnut St., Yorkville; 630/553-6671.

20 McCollum Park

🐾🐾🐾 (See DuPage County map on page 168)

Sandy lives just a block from McCollum, the most popular park in Downers Grove. The main attraction is the 1.2-mile walking trail that includes a fitness trail, which is peppered with people and pups trying to get fit in the summer. Many families, kids, and dogs use this trail. Bicyclists are supposed to ride in the opposite direction so that there's never a chance of paws accidentally getting run over. Dogs are not permitted on the lighted soccer fields, sand volleyball courts, baseball fields, mini-golf course, horseshoe pit, or playground, but Sandy hasn't found those restrictions limiting. The 50-acre park includes

34 picnic tables, restrooms, drinking fountains, and a barbecue area. No word on whether or not Sandy finds leftovers there, but Natasha suspects she may be keeping that to herself. When you've had your fill of fun here, there are shady trees under which you can unwind.

Parking is available in two lots on the east side of Main Street; the larger one is by the water tower. You must pick up after your pet. Open sunrise–dusk. 6801 S. Main St.; 630/963-1300; www.dgparks.org.

Naperville

Despite having no off-leash areas of its own, Naperville gets two paws up from Cooper. Its city parks and trails are open to leashed dogs and provide bags for picking up waste; it's home to two of the DuPage County Forest Preserve off-leash areas and one of the Forest Preserve District of Will County off-leash areas; and all of its tourism materials mention dogs in some way, highlighting dog-friendly hotels and other businesses. The suburb's downtown features pedestrian-friendly cafés, stores, and shady places to rest. **A.D.O.P.T.** pet shelter (630/355-2299; www.adoptpetshelter.org) in Naperville has a walk-athon fundraiser each spring. Parts of Naperville extend into Will County, but it is included in this chapter only.

PARKS, BEACHES, AND RECREATION AREAS

🖽 Riverwalk

🐾🐾 (See DuPage County map on page 168)

These five miles of paths are lined with bricks and dotted with plastic-bag dispensers. Weaving along the banks of the DuPage River, the Riverwalk offers plenty of little corners in which you can sit and enjoy the fresh air. You'll also

DIVERSION

Even if your pup spent every day going from park to park, there still might be a day his wet nose was out-of-joint. Treat his blues with **Energy Healing for Pets** from Ruby Room Boutique Spa. Ruby Room healers come to your house or apartment, city or suburbs, and clear the negative energy in your house and in your canine's psyche. (You are still responsible for the pet hair.) Fees are $175, which includes 15 minutes on your house, 30 on your pup, and 30 minutes for you (healthy master, healthy pup and all that). Ruby Room Boutique Spa; 1743 W. Division St., Chicago; 773/235-2323; www.rubyroom.com.

find covered bridges, gazebos, benches, and plenty of dog-loving kids who'll want to give your furry one a hug.

Because the Riverwalk connects downtown Naperville to many of the city's parks, it's rarely empty, and you and your dog will feel safe walking here evenings any time of the year. The covered bridges give the walk some scenic winter panoramas when covered with snow, and the fall colors here are remarkable.

Naperville's Riverwalk extends through downtown, south of Jackson Avenue. The closest free parking is on the north side of Aurora Avenue, but there are more than 2,200 free parking spots in downtown Naperville. Naperville Park District; 320 W. Jackson Ave., Naperville; 630/848-5000; www.naperville parks.org.

🐾 Springbrook Prairie Dog Exercise Area

🐾🐾🐾🐕 (See DuPage County map on page 168)

When heading out to Springbrook Prairie, emphasize the "prairie" part of the name in your mind. The area—on-leash and off-leash portions—totals more than 1,700 acres of grasslands, restored prairie, and wetlands. It's home to owls, foxes, coyote, and even garter snakes and skunks, in part because much of the portion of then forest preserve in which it is located is undeveloped. There's a short 1.8-mile trail, which will be expanded into a looped, limestone-based trail in the near future, and Springbrook Creek, in which dogs are not supposed to wade (or pee).

The dog exercise area is northwest of the parking lot on 83rd Street west of Book Road and includes mown meadows for running and fetching and small paths for walks and hikes. Since the first edition of this book was published, the entire dog exercise area at Springbrook has been fenced and now has a double- gate entry. In addition to the dog exercise area, Springbrook has a model-aircraft field located on the west side of the preserve.

Springbrook Prairie is a quarter-mile south of 75th Street on the east side of Naperville/Plainfield Road, between Route 59 and Modaff Road in Naperville. Forest Preserve District of DuPage County; 630/933-7200; www.dupageforest.com.

23 Greene Valley Forest Preserve

🐾🐾🐕 (See DuPage County map on page 168)

The county's newest off-leash dog park is nestled in 1,414 serene acres of forest preserve that has flora not often found in the rest of the forest preserve system. There are 10 miles of trails on which you and your leashed pup can explore aged oak woodland, savanna, and wetland. Bicyclists, horseback riders, and cross-country skiers are frequent users of the trails, while the 190-foot Greene Valley hill is the go-to spot for sledders, model-airplane fans, and those who want to see a great view of the Chicago city skyline. Greene Valley has the added bonus of being one of the most accessible forest preserve areas around for people with disabilities, with both barrier-free restrooms and entrances to the trail system.

Of course, the protected plants aren't under paw in the new the dog run area, which is south of the parking lot. As one of the few fully fenced, double-gated off-leash areas in the DuPage County Forest Preserve system, this is a better choice for dogs who are still perfecting their "come" commands than some of the others in the area.

Greene Valley is on the east side of Greene Road south of Hobson Road and one-third mile north of 75th Street. Forest Preserve District of DuPage County; 630/933-7200; www.dupageforest.com.

24 DuPage River Park

🐾🐾 (See DuPage County map on page 168)

There's something for everyone in this 272-acre park. There are picnic shelters, two horseshoe pits, restrooms, and a pond (in which dogs are not allowed to swim). There are athletic fields, on which dogs are not allowed to play, but still enough wide-open space for many afternoon games of Frisbee at the northwest end of the park. Natasha figures she can always play Frisbee in the city, but she can't always walk along river trails, so that's what she opts to do here, checking out some pretty striking waterfalls, finding unusual plants, and scaring off raccoons and other wildlife along a half-mile stretch. Another kind of wildlife—teenagers—takes over certain areas of River Park in the summer, in the form of YMCA camps, but the park is so big, you can always sniff out some pooch-friendly space.

DuPage River Park is on the southeast side of town and crosses over into part of Will County, south of Royce Road, between Route 53 and Naperville Road. There's parking for 100 cars. Across Naperville Road is Knoch Knolls Park. 808 Royce Rd. Naperville Park District; 320 W. Jackson Ave., Naperville; 630/848-5000; www.napervilleparks.org.

25 Whalon Lake Dog Park

🐾🐾🐾🐾 (See DuPage County map on page 168)

Though technically in Will County, Whalon Lake is nestled in Naperville and is a quick drive from other dog-friendly destinations in the suburb. This forest preserve is undergoing big renovations, including an 80-acre fishing lake being built in an abandoned quarry. The lake will be stocked with largemouth bass, bluegill, and channel catfish. Hiking and biking trails are also being added.

For those with four feet, the real appeal of the Whalon Lake dog run is that its off-leash, fenced acres are divided in two sections. A 2.5-acre portion is separately fenced and reserved for small dogs. Pooches under 35 pounds can romp and play without fear of being overtaken by well-meaning bigger pups. (At 37 pounds to Natasha's 65, Cooper appreciates the concern, but he still prefers to play with the big boys.) Whalon Lake is perfect for summer days, with a shade structure and drinking water. Unfortunately for Natasha, the lake is on the leashes-only portion of the preserve.

Permits are required for use of the off-leash acreage at Whalon Lake (and are also valid for use at Hammel Woods Dog Park). Annual fees are $25 for Will County residents and $50 for nonresidents. An owner can register up to three dogs; proof of rabies vaccinations is required. Permits can be obtained by mail or at the Forest Preserve District Office in Joliet, the Plum Creek Nature Center in Beecher, the Isle à la Cache Museum in Romeoville, or at the Monee Reservoir. Registrants will receive a permit and vehicle tag. Permit holders are entitled to register for reasonably priced agility classes offered at the park. (Hammel Woods Dog Park, the other dog park of the Forest Preserve of Will County, is properly classified in the Will County chapter.)

Whalon Lake Dog Park is open 8 A.M.–5 P.M. November–March and 8 A.M.–8 P.M. April–October. The park is about a mile west of Route 53 on Royce Road. It is north of I-55 and west of Bolingbrook Drive. Forest Preserve District of Will County; 815/727-8700; www.fpdwc.org.

PLACES TO EAT

El Centro: Locals like this independently owned Mexican restaurant because it is moderately priced, open until the wee hours, and delivers. Visiting pups prefer it for the few outdoor tables with umbrellas for shade and the tasty steak tacos. 1015 E. Ogden Ave.; 630/355-8888; www.elcentronaperville.com.

Timpano: This Cuban joint turns off some with its loud music and smoky interior. Which is just another reason why it's best to visit *con perro* and sit at the plentiful outdoor tables. If your dog wants to sing to the beat or bang on the conga drum, no one here will mind, just as long as he's tied to the outside of the wrought iron fence. Try some of the Argentine wines. 22 E. Chicago Ave.; 630/753-0985.

PLACES TO STAY

BridgeStreet: Not a hotel, per se, BridgeStreet fulfills temporary housing needs of business travelers and their four-legged friends. This is decent corporate housing—ranging from studio, one-, two-, and three-bedroom fully furnished apartments, to condominiums and town houses. You and your pup can rent by the week, month, or longer. BridgeStreet has locations throughout the city and suburbs, but Naperville is one of the largest and has one of the most liberal dog policies, with no size restrictions. Pet-friendly locations have walk areas and grassy common areas for leashed dogs. Treats and toys are available for pet guests upon arrival, as well as lists of local dog walkers, groomers, pet parks, agility courses, and, Cooper hopes, a copy of this book. 847/564-3000 or 800/278-7338; www.bridgestreet.com.

TownePlace Suites Naperville: Dogs under 80 pounds can stay in these suites with a $75 nonrefundable fee, but don't let them swim in the large pond out front. Rates start at $120. 1843 W. Diehl Rd., Naperville; 630/548-0881; www.marriott.com.

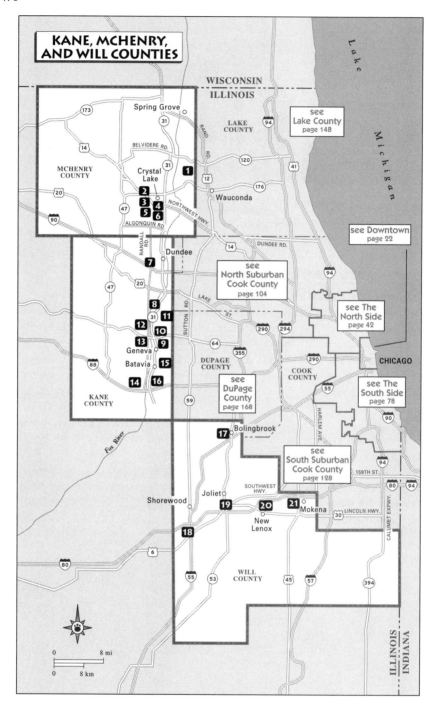

CHAPTER 8

KANE, MCHENRY, AND WILL COUNTIES

see Lake County page 148

see Downtown page 22

see North Suburban Cook County page 104

see The North Side page 42

see The South Side page 78

see DuPage County page 168

see South Suburban Cook County page 128

WISCONSIN
ILLINOIS

Lake Michigan

MCHENRY COUNTY

Spring Grove

BELVIDERE RD.

Crystal Lake

NORTHWEST HWY.

ALGONQUIN RD.

LAKE COUNTY

Wauconda

Dundee

DUNDEE RD.

RANDALL RD.

SUTTON RD.

LAKE ST.

DUPAGE COUNTY

COOK COUNTY

CHICAGO

Geneva

Batavia

KANE COUNTY

Fox River

Bolingbrook

HARLEM AVE.

159TH ST.

Shorewood

Joliet

SOUTHWEST HWY.

New Lenox

Mokena

LINCOLN HWY.

CALUMET EXPWY.

WILL COUNTY

ILLINOIS
INDIANA

0   8 mi
0   8 km

Kane, McHenry, and Will Counties

These three so-called collar counties complete the six that are generally referred to as "Chicagoland." Each has its own charms and character, with a combination of quaint small towns and large, amenity-packed suburbs. But they share one common denominator: open space. In addition to the forest preserves and city parks with which you've already become familiar in the area, these counties are the gateway to some of the prettiest (and dog-friendliest) state parks in Illinois. The convenience of these state sanctuaries cannot be overstated. You can come for the day, or bring a tent (and a reservation) and camp out for a weekend. When traffic's light, you can get to the great outdoors faster than residents of other metro areas can get their cars out of their parking garages.

This chapter is geographically organized by county, and then by suburb, again to help you and your collared companion plan your outings. These three

PICK OF THE LITTER—KANE, MCHENRY, AND WILL COUNTIES

BEST DOG PARKS
Lippold Park/Hound Town, Crystal Lake (page 194)
Fermilab Dog Training Area, Batavia (page 204)

BEST PLACE TO EAT
Dockside Inn, Wonder Lake (page 194)

BEST EVENT
Poochapalooza, Batavia (page 198)

counties run from the McHenry–Wisconsin border on the north, running west of Lake and DuPage Counties and south of Cook County. (Several parks are in towns, such as Tinley Park and Naperville, that stride county lines. Those parks appear in the chapter with the town with which they are most frequently associated.)

If your dog is looking for more organized action, check out the events of the **Fox Valley Dog Training Club** (www.fvdtc.org/events). Agility instruction, flyball classes, and Frisbee demonstrations are offered both for old pros and dogs looking to learn some new tricks at parks throughout the area. For more detailed trail maps along the 86-mile Fox River Trail, look for a copy of *Hiking and Biking in the Fox River Valley* (Roots & Wings, 1997) by Jim Hochgesang.

McHenry and Wonder Lake, McHenry County

People do live and work here year-round. But most city residents think of this area as a resort close to home. Even if you aren't lucky enough to own a boat (or have a dog-loving friend who does), you and your pooch won't be disappointed by a trip here.

If you're looking for recreation outside of the state parks, your options are more limited, however. The McHenry Parks and Recreation Department does not permit dogs in its parks, although it has developed preliminary plans for a fenced, off-leash dog park. Cooper is chomping at the bit to explore it for the next edition of this book.

PARKS, BEACHES, AND RECREATION AREAS

1 Moraine Hills State Park

🐾🐾🐾 (See Kane, McHenry, and Will Counties map on page 190)

Dogs and their owners like this Illinois state park and the 48-acre lake near its center because it is one of the few glacial lakes in Illinois that has remained largely undeveloped.

One option for enjoying this pristine landscape is a romp at Pike Marsh, a 115-acre area in the southeast corner of the park. The state park authority lists Ohio goldenrod, Kalm's lobelia, dwarf birch, white cattails (no, white cattails are not attached to white cats), among the rare plants you might find. Pike Marsh is also home to pitcher plants, much admired by Natasha for their ability to attract, trap, and digest insects.

Another option is the 120-acre Leatherleaf Bog, which a textbook example of a moraine—a collection of rock left by a glacier. In addition to more great plants, you may sniff out some red fox, coyote, white-tailed deer, eastern cottontails, mink, opossum, and raccoons, which all call Moraine Hills home. Great blue herons, ducks, and geese are the birds most frequently sighted by dogs and their masters.

More than 10 miles of limestone-paved trails are the best way to start hiking, biking, or skiing through the area. To explore Moraine Hills, hop on a two-mile stretch of the Fox River Trail (the whole thing is 86 miles), the three-mile Leatherleaf Bog Trail, or the four-mile Lake Defiance Trail, all of which have color coding to keep you from getting lost (in case you don't happen to be hiking with a bloodhound).

To get to Moraine Hills, take Route 12 north to Route 176. Turn west on Route 176 to River Road. The entrance is two miles north of River Road. For information on camping at Moraine Hills, write to the Illinois Department of Natural Resources, Office of Public Services; 1 Natural Resources Way, Springfield, IL 62702-1271; 217/782-7454. 1510 S. River Rd., McHenry; 815/385-1624.

PLACES TO EAT

Dockside Inn: The outdoor patio of this otherwise ordinary bar and grill becomes pup central when Camp Dogwood (see the DuPage County chapter) is in session. But you don't need your counselor's permission. You and your pooch can come any time the patio's open. 4106 E. Lakeshore Dr., Wonder Lake; 815/653-7300.

Crystal Lake, McHenry County

Crystal Lake is one of a dozen or so small towns northwest of Chicago that have boomed with development as city-goers seek bigger home lots for the buck. And yes, there is an actual body of water called Crystal Lake. Sadly for dogs, the town prohibits canines at both public-access beaches, Main and West, because of a county health code. But don't let that bit of legislation make you think Crystal Lake is not dog-friendly. Among other things, the park district hosts an annual Howl-O-Ween pet costume party and a dog parade for kids and their pets. If you need supplies while in town, check out **Huggable Hounds** (6211 Northwest Hwy.; 815/479-8625).

PARKS, BEACHES, AND RECREATION AREAS

2 Lippold Park/Hound Town

🐾🐾🐾🐾 🐕 (See Kane, McHenry, and Will Counties map on page 190)

In June 2003, the village of Crystal Lake opened its first official dog-friendly area (DFA) at this flat, sprawling 309-acre complex that includes soccer and football fields, baseball and softball diamonds, a Frisbee golf course, and other recreational amenities.

Watson thinks this is just about the best DFA story he's heard. The dog park was built thanks to the efforts of students from Great Expectations, an alternative school operated by the McHenry County Regional Office of Education. The Great Expectations program, which targets youths in grades 6–10 who have demonstrated long-term behavioral problems at their original schools, includes community service as part of its curriculum. In 2003, that service went to the dogs.

"We had been getting requests for a dog-friendly area a couple times a year, but the project had been on the back burner for quite a while," says

FETCHING NECESSITIES

You've already loaded the dog into the car, so you might as well get some errands done together. Or buy him a treat. If he could drive, here's where he'd go.

Cats 'N' Dogs: Offering unique gifts and necessities, Cats 'N' Dogs is a long-time favorite of area residents. 215 W. State St., Geneva; 630/232-0001; www.woofwoofmeow.com.

Le Doggie Divine: The area's most elite pet spa and boutique. 315 W. State St., Geneva; 630/208-4992.

Lucky Dog: A good stop for natural pet food and treats. 105 W. Main St., St. Charles; 630/444-1557.

PETCO: All the basics, plus plenty of parking spaces. 230 S. Virginia St., Crystal Lake; 815/356-7387; www.petco.com.

PetSmart: In addition to being able to pet adoptable dogs, you'll find obedience class registration, an on-site veterinarian, and, of course, pet food. 2775 Plainfield Rd., Joliet; 815/439-7100; www.petsmart.com.

Scoo-B-Do's: Do-it-yourself dog wash. 9 Jackson St., East Dundee; 847/426-2284.

Wet Nose: Stocks Planet Dog and other must-have toys and treats. 1308 Commons Dr., Geneva; 630/232-7000; www.wetnose.com.

Park Planner Ann Viger. "Then a group of students came forward and got a $42,000 federal grant from the No Child Left Behind Program to do a community project, and this is what they chose."

The park district identified a two-acre location on the eastern edge of Lippold, just south of the softball fields, and, working with the students, had nearly finished the DFA's design halfway through the school year. (Watson would like to point out that it takes city officials in some areas twice that amount of time to do the same job.) Hound Town is a grassy, 40-foot-by-100-foot area, ringed by a gravel walking path and a chain-link fence. The DFA has a kiosk, picnic tables, benches, and limestone paths, not to mention access to restrooms, plenty of plastic bags and trash cans, and drinking water.

Lippold bustles with activity on weekends, as dogs and their families come out in force to bark and cheer, respectively, at their kids' soccer games. The place can be a madhouse, and unless your boy or girl is playing, it's not a great destination in and of itself, unless you're headed to Hound Town.

Kids under six are not permitted in the off-leash area. Kids ages 6–12 must be accompanied by a grown-up. Crystal Lake residents pay $30 for the first dog and $6 for each additional dog for a key to Hound Town that is valid through the end of the year; nonresidents pay $60 for the first dog and $10 for each additional dog. For those watching their wallets, there are also weekly rates available, and fees are half-price after Labor Day. Hound Town is open dawn–dusk.

Lippold is west of the intersection of Routes 176 and 14, with ample parking available at the Route 176 park entrance. Crystal Lake Park District; 815/459-0680.

🖾 McHenry County Prairie Trail
🐾🐾🐾 (See Kane, McHenry, and Will Counties map on page 190)
The 29.5-mile McHenry County Prairie Trail runs through Sterne's Woods and Fen and Veteran Acres along what was once a Chicago and Northwestern rail line. The trail stretches from Algonquin (south of Crystal Lake) to the Wisconsin state line and is accessible from Sterne's Woods and Fen, Veteran Acres, and numerous other parks along the way, including Glacial Park. You and your pooch can put paw to pavement and sniff out other interesting side trips along the way. This is a paved trail frequented by bicyclists and in-line skaters, but dogs are allowed on-leash. Crystal Lake Park District; 815/459-0680.

🖾 Sterne's Woods and Fen
🐾🐾🐾 (See Kane, McHenry, and Will Counties map on page 190)
This 185-acre plot of woodlands was added to Illinois' list of nature preserves in 1994 and offers miles of wooded, winding paths, nice hilly terrain, and much more seclusion than Lippold Park (see above)—you don't have to compete with crowds of soccer parents. A plethora of good scents (deer and otherwise) will keep any pooch's nose twitching. Fido will likely plead to be let off-leash, but resist his fervent glances—park rangers patrol the trails and ticket hikers who flout leash laws.

Enter the parking lot for Sterne's Woods from East Hillside Road, north of Route 176 and east of Walkup Avenue. Crystal Lake Park District; 815/459-0680.

🖾 Veteran Acres
🐾🐾🐾 (See Kane, McHenry, and Will Counties map on page 190)
The southwest edge of Sterne's Woods touches Veteran Acres, a 140-acre park and nature preserve that melds the tennis courts, baseball and softball fields, and picnic shelters of Lippold with the wooded splendor of Sterne's. Veteran's landscape was carved by a glacier, which left behind a pond and hills (used for sledding in the winter). A walking path circles the pond, with wooden bridges that cross over wetland areas, and there are plenty of hiking trails as well. The sports and picnic areas are near the park entrances and draw families on the weekends. (You'll be stopped for a petting break many a time by rollicking youngsters.) To get to the trails, you have to go down into the "bowl" formed

by the glacier (that's where the pond is), and then come back up on the other side, where the landscape shifts from prairie to coniferous forest and a few things in between. (A special bonus for people is the Nature Center, which has loads of cool stuff, including small animals and a new butterfly garden. Though dogs would love to get up close and personal with a raccoon in the confines of the center, animals of the domesticated kind are understandably not allowed.)

You can park in a lot off Walkup Avenue just north of Route 176, or turn north on Main Street from Route 176 just east of Walkup and park in the lot near the Nature Center. The Nature Center lot provides easier access to the hiking paths. (Insider tip: A third, secluded lot about two blocks east of the Nature Center butts right up to some of the trailheads.) Crystal Lake Park District; 815/459-0680.

Lake in the Hills, McHenry County

What dog wouldn't love a town with a name like Lake in the Hills? Unfortunately, the town's four lakes—Woods Creek Lake, Goose Lake, Willow Lake, and Lake Scott—are all off-limits to off-leash dogs. Furthermore, the village has a "one leash, one person" rule. So, Cooper and Natasha can't go for a leashed stroll in town unless they bring along a second human for leash control.

PARKS, BEACHES, AND RECREATION AREAS

6 Bark Park
🐾🐾🐕 (See Kane, McHenry, and Will Counties map on page 190)

Bark Park is the exception that makes Lake in the Hills worth a dog's time. This fenced-in park has ample amounts of shade and sun-dappled grass, with 3.5 acres on which to romp. Fresh drinking water is available on-site, although dogs are expected to bring their own water bowls. (Cooper's not sure where to carry his; he doesn't have any pockets.) There are ample plastic bags supplied, and thanks to regular community cleanup sessions, the park is usually in good shape. And the locals don't just get together for do-gooder events. A local activities group hosts pet blessings, Halloween costume parties, and photos with Santa.

There is a rule of two dogs per human in Bark Park. Kids under six are not permitted in the off-leash area. Kids ages 6–12 must be accompanied by a grown-up. Lake in the Hills residents pay $40 for the first dog and $6 for each additional dog for a key and ID tag to enter Bark Park; nonresidents pay $60 for the first dog and $10 for each additional dog. You must buy your tag in person at the Village Hall, 600 Harvest Gate, during regular business hours (8:30 A.M.–5 P.M., Monday–Friday. Thursdays the office is open until 7:30 P.M.). The park is open dawn–9 P.M.

DIVERSIONS

A coat of fur and 100-degree temps are enough to make almost any canine want to go for a cool dip by summer's end. Add water-dog genes like Natasha's, and the desire can be almost unbearable. Several park districts feel Natasha's pain. The weekend before they drain the community swimming hole (or close the beach) for the summer, they give it over to the dogs.

Dog Day Afternoon: Prairie Oaks Family Aquatic Center in the West Chicago Park District picks the Friday after Labor Day as its dog day. 129 W. National St., West Chicago; 630/231-9474; www.we-goparks.org.

Doggie Dip: The first Saturday after Labor Day is the day to head to the Family Aquatic Center in the Vernon Hills Park District. 635 N. Aspen Dr., Vernon Hills; 847/996-6800; www.vhparkdistrict.org.

Poochapalooza: Harold Hall Quarry Beach is open to canine swimmers on the Saturday after the beach closes to the public. Nonresident dogs pay $14 for the morning or afternoon swim. The fee includes a complimentary bandana. 400 S. Water St., Batavia; 630/879-5235; www.bataviaparks.org.

Puppy Paddle: The Tuesday after Labor Day is the designated swim at the Family Aquatic Center in the Palatine Park District. 340 E. Palatine Rd., Palatine; 847/991-0333; www.palatineparkdistrict.com.

Schaumburg Park District: This suburb has a number of pools, one of which hosts a pup pool event in the fall. Call for details. 235 E. Beech Dr., Schaumburg; 847/985-2115; www.parkfun.com.

Bark Park is northwest of Sunset Park, just north of the skate park. Parking is rarely a problem. 9027 Haligus Rd., Lake in the Hills; 847/960-7400; www.lith.org.

Dundee Township, Kane County

Dundee Township, on Kane County's east side, oversees parks in several suburbs, including Carpentersville, East Dundee, West Dundee, and Sleepy Hollow, and leashed dogs are permitted to play in all of them. Discussion over Dundee Township (the city, not the park district) plans to build an off-leash dog park near the town of Sleepy Hollow continue. The proposed area is part of a wetlands restoration project on 1,000 acres north of Boncosky Road. Natasha says not to worry: She's never seen a headless horseman in *this* Sleepy Hollow.

PARKS, BEACHES, AND RECREATION AREAS

7 South End Park and Island

🐾🐾 (See Kane, McHenry, and Will Counties map on page 190)

An 11-acre park in West Dundee, South End was undergoing significant renovations at press time, which stand to make it an even more dog-worthy destination. Locals like the playground, ball diamonds, lighted basketball court, and picnic area, which are all packed in the summer. Dog lovers and others on the go like that the park connects to the Fox River Bike Trail that winds through this area. Pups are generally permitted to dog-paddle in the river here, as long as they don't disturb kids (or adults) who come to feed the ducks.

South End Park is open dawn–dusk. The park is at the intersection of Riverview Street and First Street on the Fox River. 847/428-7131.

Elgin, St. Charles, and Geneva, Kane County

Along with Batavia, Geneva and St. Charles make up Chicago's Tri-Cities, strung like beads along the Fox River. Both have expensive new upscale shopping malls, as well as older riverside shopping districts, lined with antique stores, boutiques, and little restaurants in distinctive quarters. Movie buffs might recognize Geneva's downtown from its cameo in the film *Road to Perdition*. Many city-dwellers know Kane County because of the Kane County Flea Market, a monthly event at the fairgrounds to which dogs are not invited (although most of Natasha and Cooper's furniture was purchased there).

However, there are plenty of pooch-friendly events held there throughout the year. The real attraction of St. Charles and Geneva is their vacation-town appeal, a mere 40 miles from Chicago. You and your dog can stroll around these towns and find plenty to do. Geneva is home to the **Kane County Cougars,** the Class A minor league farm team for the Oakland Athletics. Once a year the Cougars have an annual bring-the-dogs-to-the-ballpark event. Cooper assures you, no real cougars will be in attendance. Call for dates (34W002 Cherry Ln., Geneva; 630/232-8811; www.kccougars.com).

Nearby Elgin is the major city to Geneva and St. Charles's small towns, providing such necessities as chain hotels that accommodate pets.

PARKS, BEACHES, AND RECREATION AREAS

8 Pottawatomie Park

🐾 🐾 (See Kane, McHenry, and Will Counties map on page 190)

Pottawatomie Park takes its name from one of the tribes that lived in the area before white settlers moved in. The park, on the Fox River just north of St. Charles's downtown, features golf and mini-golf, a swimming pool, and playgrounds. It has grassy areas, suitable for walking, picnicking, running, an on-leash ball toss, or just lounging in the shade of grand old oaks. Benches along the waterfront are a great place to rest and watch the paddleboats slowly go by, but pups ought not to try to join them for a dip in the water. Natasha's Corgi friend Mikey likes to climb the old stone steps, where he can see the whole park and beyond. Natasha is more partial to the wooden pavilion, which is a replica of the original one built here in 1892.

The 47 acres include walking trails, drinking fountains, and restrooms, as well as a good chunk of St. Charles's population (27,000) on a nice summer day. Pottawatomie Park is half a mile north of Main Street on North Second Avenue. Parking is always free for residents and free most of the year for nonresidents; between Memorial Day and Labor Day nonresidents pay $5 per car. 630/443-4636; www.st-charlesparks.org.

9 Wheeler Park

🐾 (See Kane, McHenry, and Will Counties map on page 190)

The still-steep southwest entrance is a throwback to the days when a quarry once stood on this site in Geneva. The slope is a dramatic entrance to the 57-acre park. Ignore the people-friendly amenities (mini-golf course, concession stand, baseball diamond, tennis courts, and the best playground in town) and head straight for the path that winds around hill and dale and past bountiful flower gardens. This is where Mikey prefers to have his canine portraits shot.

The park is open dawn–dusk. From Route 38 (State Street), turn north on Route 31, left on North Street, and the park entrance is on the right. 630/232-4542; www.genevaparks.org.

🔟 Blackhawk Forest Preserve

🐾🐾🐾 (See Kane, McHenry, and Will Counties map on page 190)

At the historical site of the burial of unknown soldiers of General Winfield Scott's army, you'll know you're in the right place when you see the large carved-wood statue of Blackhawk near the entrance. Blackhawk Forest Preserve has more than 284 acres, including 81 acres of wetland and 35 acres of wooded areas. Pups and their people love the Fox River, rock ledges, and an eight-foot-high waterfall they can see here. Neither species is supposed to swim in the river, but the walks through the area are remote, isolated, and relaxing. Botanists can point out two unusual kinds of cactus in the sand here, as well as the very rare prairie grape fern. Natasha doesn't know what that looks like, but she knows that she's supposed to stay on the trails to avoid trampling it. The natural waterfall cascades into the creek near the center of the preserve.

Like other suburban forest preserve districts covered in this book, Kane County forest preserves are designed to protect plant and animal life. Dogs are not allowed to run free, nor is hunting permitted. There are areas set aside for picnicking, hiking, fishing, boating, and camping, and, since the first edition of this book was published, two off-leash facilities have been added (see Fox River Bluff Forest Preserve and Aurora West Forest Preserve). The preserves are open daily 8 A.M.–sunset. There is no access fee.

Blackhawk is located on Route 31 in South Elgin, one mile north of McLean Boulevard. Kane County Forest Preserve; 630/232-5980; www .co.kane.il.us/forest.

1️⃣1️⃣ Fox River Bluff Forest Preserve

🐾🐕 (See Kane, McHenry, and Will Counties map on page 190)

The good news is that the Kane County Forest Preserve added two off-leash dog parks in the past four years. Neither of them requires permits or fees in order to be enjoyed by resident or nonresident dogs. The bad news is, neither of them are fenced. This is of particular concern at Fox River Bluff. The park offers a sweeping view of the Fox River and its eastern bank, which isn't to be discounted. But the area is across the street—a busy street—from St. Charles North High School, and speeding teenagers are a fact of life. Mikey has witnessed many a dog owner dashing into traffic after his distracted, off-leash dog. Dogs permitted to be off-leash here should have remarkable mastery of the "come" command.

Like all of the Kane County forest preserves, Fox River Bluff is open daily 8 A.M.–sunset. There is no fee to access the area. 5N860 Weber Dr., St. Charles; 630/232-5980; www.co.kane.il.us/forest.

12 Leroy Oakes Forest Preserve

🐾🐾🐾 (See Kane, McHenry, and Will Counties map on page 190)

While Mikey was gracious in showing city dogs around his neck of the Chicagoland woods, he was reluctant to take others to Leroy Oakes. Despite the fact that he must stay on leash, he thinks this is the best forest preserve site for dogs in the area. He chases butterflies, stalks the ducks by the ponds, and wades in the creek. There are 352 acres of trails that allow him to meander up and down hills, through woods, and down to Ferson Creek. As Natasha is afraid of horses and Cooper is afraid of bicycles, they don't like sharing the trails with horseback riders and bicyclers, but Mikey knows how to mind his manners.

Leroy Oakes, which is named for a man, not a tree, and therefore is the most-misspelled preserve around, is west of Randall Road. 37W370 Dean St., St. Charles; 630/232-5980; www.co.kane.il.us/forest.

13 Campton Hills Dog Park

🐾🐾🐕 (See Kane, McHenry, and Will Counties map on page 190)

Mikey can't quite figure out why this dog park at the far western edge of Campton Hills Park is always so crowded. Sure, if he lived in the heart of the city, he'd understand why more than two dozen canines regularly hightail it over here. After all, this is a free off-leash park, with a small obstacle course, a few small trees, and a double gate for safety.

But, this isn't the city, and a small corner of a 348-acre park pales in comparison to the off-leash forest preserves in the area. This is essentially a temporary park, and in a few years it may grow into a destination of its own. For now, save it for when you're in the neighborhood and need a safe place to play. No permits are required, but dogs must wear proof of vaccination. The dog park is open dawn–9 P.M. Campton Hills Park is located west of Randall Road at the intersection of Campton Hills and Peck Roads. Park off of the Campton Hills entrance. It's a long (leashed) walk from the Peck Road entrance to the dog park. St. Charles Park District, 630/587-3373; www.st-charlesparks.org.

PLACES TO EAT

Krispy Kreme Doughnuts: Few things make people drool like a dog, but a Krispy Kreme doughnut is one of them. Both you and your dog are welcome to drive through to get "hot doughnuts now" and eat at a few outside tables. Most visitors just wolf them down in the car. Your dog won't be quite as excited about it as you are, but you probably don't care much for pigs' ears, so fair is fair. 922 S. Randall Rd., St. Charles; 630/443-1000.

Town House Books & Café: Mikey likes the bricked patio of this outdoor café, where he can watch all the girls go by. Because it is connected to a bookstore, he can make sure he has an updated copy of this book for his next big adventures. People tend to be more attracted by the menu of apricot chicken, avocado tuna melt, and tuna salad sandwiches. 105 N. Second Ave., St. Charles; 630/584-8603; www.townhousebooks.com.

PLACES TO STAY

Days Inn Chicago-Elgin: This modest, unassuming hotel accommodates dogs with a charge of $10 per pet, per night. Rates range $55–68. 1585 Dundee Ave., Elgin; 847/695-2100; www.daysinn.com.

Oscar Swan Country Inn: Well-behaved dogs are welcomed into this 1900s estate, which includes the Swan mansion, barn, gardens, and swimming pool (though pups are excluded from the latter). The inn is just a 10-minute walk to Geneva's shopping district. The bed-and-breakfast has eight rooms and rates range $99–169 a night. 1800 W. State St., Geneva; 630/232-0173; www.oscarswan.com.

Pheasant Run Resort & Spa: The name is a little bit distracting. Cooper didn't see any pheasants on the grounds, and the building looks less like a resort and more like a hotel. Nonetheless, dogs weighing less than 25 pounds may stay in courtyard rooms, which open to a grassy area, and that's nothing to turn up your wet nose at. The complex is just three miles from downtown St. Charles. Room rates are $119–149, plus a $100, non-refundable pet fee. 4051 E. Main St., St. Charles; 630/584-6300; www.pheasantrun.com.

Quality Inn, Elgin: Free local phone calls, newspapers, and other amenities help to make you feel at home in this serviceable chain. Dogs of any size pay a $10 nightly fee. Rates start at $65. 500 Toll Gate Rd., Elgin; 847/931-4800; www.qualityinn.com.

Batavia and Aurora, Kane County

Batavia is one of the few far-flung suburbs that is actually pedestrian-friendly. Straddling the Fox River, Batavia is the southernmost of the Tri-Cities; to the north are sister cities Geneva and St. Charles. About 45 miles directly west of Downtown, Batavia is just about as far outside the city as a place can get and still be called a suburb. Nicknamed "the Windmill City," this eminently walkable town earned its moniker by becoming the world's No. 1 windmill manufacturer by 1890. Batavia hosts several annual canine events, including a pet parade and a hike-the-trails day.

Powered in part by hydraulic energy from the Fox River, the windmill industry boomed until the 1930s, and then went bust during World War II. Much has changed since then, but some of the old windmill-production buildings still stand on the river's banks—including what is now the beautiful government center and police station. The limestone structure also highlights another key aspect of Batavia's past: quarrying.

The city has expanded in recent years, but the heart of community life is

DIVERSION

Agility classes are so 1990s. If you're tired of getting your dog to jump through hoops—literally—you now have another option for organized exercise. Mare (pronounced like "Mary") Potts's **Flydogs** teaches Frisbee tricks, flyball, and other fetching exercises to dogs and their owners in the city and suburbs. The non-competitive classes have the advantage of allowing people to practice at home with their pets without a lot of space or expensive equipment ("All you need is a $1.50 Frisbee," Potts says). If you want to check out Potts's tricks in action, check out a pregame show at one of the Kane County Cougars' baseball game infield shows. In addition to performing at special events, Potts will teach your pooch in her own backyard. Aurora; 630/820-1703; www.flydogs.ws.

still in the old downtown area, where the Fox River cuts the city in two and the Wilson Street bridge connects east to west.

PARKS, BEACHES, AND RECREATION AREAS

14 Aurora West Forest Preserve

🐾🐾🐕 (See Kane, McHenry, and Will Counties map on page 190)

This 496-acre preserve has a three-mile mowed grass trail that meanders through fields, in addition to plenty of woods for a curious dog to explore. You can sniff out oak trees, as well as lots of native grasses, clover, and some red pine. Because the preserve doubles as the flying field for a local model-airplane club, this is not the place for dogs who are afraid of noisy objects (like Cooper). Because the off-leash area is not fenced, the forest preserve emphasizes that the area is intended for trained dogs.

Aurora West is a former farm field on Hankes Road, between Galena Boulevard and Highway 56. Ignore the signs at the entrance that contradict each other; one says "off-leash" and the other says "on-leash." Open 8 A.M.–sunset. Aurora; 630/232-5980; www.co.kane.il.us/forest.

15 Fermilab Dog Training Area

🐾🐾🐾🐾🐕 (See Kane, McHenry, and Will Counties map on page 190)

For those not into physics research, the Fermi National Accelerator Laboratory remains a mystery. Natasha's human friend Cat (yes, she has a friend named Cat) grew up in Batavia. While she can tell you all about the physics landmarks, like the discoveries of the bottom and top quarks and the tau neutrino (Natasha has no idea what that is), that occurred inside the Fermilab buildings, she also recommends the grounds as a destination for outdoor enthusiasts and dog lovers.

The 6,800-acre site offers the public more outdoor activities than you can shake a subatomic particle at. Bike paths and horse trails meander across the site on beautiful scenic routes. In warm weather, the ponds draw many anglers, the paths have countless leashed dogs, and bird-watchers keep close tabs on avian action. Picnics are popular, too, especially with the ducks and geese that swim on the pools in front of the main building, the architecturally distinct Wilson Hall (which looks like a big upside-down Y). Wintertime sees cross-country skiers gliding across the grounds and ice skaters turning figure-eights on the ponds. Volunteers and lab staff have worked over the years to restore hundreds of acres at Fermilab to a native tallgrass prairie ecosystem, similar to what settlers would have seen. The spring brings with it a beautiful barrage of prairie flora and fauna, too, when new calves are born in the buffalo herd.

That's right. Buffalo. Fermilab's famous herd of North American buffalo is perhaps the site's biggest attraction and can be viewed year-round. The lab's first director, Robert Wilson, established the herd as a symbol of Fermilab's pioneering work on the frontiers of physics. Now about 50 strong, the herd's big shaggy animals spend their days lumbering around their large pasture. Two wire fences separate onlookers from the buffalo, which often graze close to the edges. Most buffalo-viewing folks park along the roadside near the pasture—the walk from the main lot is a long one, even for an enthusiastic dog.

As if all that weren't enough, Fermilab is also home to a one-mile-square off-leash dog exercise area. The area is not fenced, but it's remote, not frequently used, and is as clean and pristine as the rest of Fermilab's wilds. Dogs, however, are not permitted in Lake Law, the small pond near the off-leash exercise area.

The downside—and there had to be one at a place this good—is that due to the nature of its work, the 40-year-old Fermilab is subject to closures based on national security alerts. During the reporting and writing of this book, public access was restricted and reopened several times. Before planning a day at Fermilab—and it is worth a full day—call or check the website for an update. Entry is free, and the grounds are open dawn–dusk.

From the I-88 Expressway, exit at Farnsworth heading north. Farnsworth becomes Kirk Road. Follow Kirk Road to Pine Street. Turn right at Pine Street, which is Fermilab's main entrance. 630/840-3351; www.fnal.gov.

16 Riverwalk

🐾🐾 (See Kane, McHenry, and Will Counties map on page 190)

Near the police building in downtown Batavia is the city's new Riverwalk, funded by donations and built by volunteers. More than 50 locals, who call themselves "The Plain Dirt Gardeners," till community soil here. Your pup is welcome to take a peek, but ask him to keep his paws off. Pride in the city's past has led to the ongoing restoration, preservation, and outdoor exhibition of seven Batavia-made windmills that you and your dog can explore along this riverside boardwalk. The city's official nickname was actually changed many years ago to "the City of Energy," in honor of Fermilab. In spite of the name change, each summer Batavia celebrates Windmill City Days, an outdoor festival.

Dogs, walkers, and bikers alike appreciate the paved paths that parallel both banks of the Fox River on this 12-acre peninsula. On your walk, you may pass the Depot Museum, a relocated railroad depot that houses historical curiosities such as the bed and dresser Mary Todd Lincoln used during her 1875 stay at Batavia's Bellevue sanitarium. Riverwalk runs through downtown Batavia, which is east of Route 31. Batavia Park District; 327 W. Wilson St., Batavia; 630/879-5235; www.bataviaparks.org.

Bolingbrook, Will County

Once called "Westbury," Bolingbrook was created by young families who bought up new homes along the old Route 66 in the 1960s, lured by decent home prices and sizeable backyards (not to mention the catchy song). Few then had trees, lawns, or even paved streets. Now the suburb of 55,000 people has many leafy additions for your and your hound to explore.

PARKS, BEACHES, AND RECREATION AREAS

🐾7 DuPage River Greenway

🐾 🐾 (See Kane, McHenry, and Will Counties map on page 190)

This 1.5-mile linear path traverses 38 acres of woodlands, prairies, and wetlands from Royce Road near Route 53 to Hidden Lakes Historic Trout Farm, running along Bolingbrook's northern edge parallel to the East Branch of the DuPage River.

More than 25 communities, park districts, and forest preserve districts are involved in the regional bikeway plan for the DuPage River. Ultimately, 42 miles from Glendale Heights to Shorewood will be linked up to Bolingbrook by the Greenway. Plans are to expand the length of the Greenway to 2.5 miles within the next three years. The path is 10 feet wide, so there's plenty of room for bicyclists, cross-country skiers, dog walkers, in-line skaters, and others.

Parking and restrooms are available at Hidden Lakes Historic Trout Farm. A concession stand and a nature museum are open during the summer, but pups, of course, are not permitted inside the museum. The Greenway entrance is on Royce Road, west of Route 53, south of the county line. Bolingbrook Park District; 201 Recreation Dr.; 630/739-0272; www.bolingbrookparks.org.

Joliet, Will County

With 94,000 people, Joliet is more a city unto itself than a suburb. Because this is the site of one of the area's largest correctional facilities, the phrase, "He was sent to Joliet," does not mean what Natasha thinks it means. You may remember John Belushi's *Blues Brothers* character "Joliet" Jake, who had, of course, done a little time. (Fox's TV show *Prison Break* is filmed here.) Colloquial expressions aside, Joliet is a nice place for dog lovers to visit. Just don't break the leash laws.

PARKS, BEACHES, AND RECREATION AREAS

🐾8 Hammel Woods

🐾🐾🐾🐾 🐕 (See Kane, McHenry, and Will Counties map on page 190)

Like those in other suburban counties, the Forest Preserve District of Will County offers virgin forests and fields for pups (and their people) to appreciate. Dogs are allowed in all but nature conservation areas (clearly marked) on leashes of 10 feet or less. The 300-acre Hammel Woods in Joliet is one of the best places to enjoy Will County's miles of hiking trails, meandering through a mature forest and along a ridge overlooking the scenic DuPage River. The Route 59 access has a 1.5-mile loop trail with limestone and natural surfaces suitable for hiking and biking. While pawing along on this trail, rest your weary tail at the Grinton Grove observation deck. Outdoors enthusiasts visit

the DuPage River access point on Black Road, where they enjoy fly-fishing, canoeing, and camping. The Crumby Recreation Area on Black Road offers visitors a picnic pavilion and a half-mile loop trail with a spur that connects to longer trails crisscrossing Hammel Woods.

Permits are required for use of the seven off-leash acres at Hammel Woods Dog Park (and are also good for use at Whalon Lake Dog Park). Annual fees are $25 for county residents and $50 for nonresidents. An owner can register up to three dogs, and proof of rabies vaccinations is required. Permits can be obtained by mail or purchased at the Forest Preserve District Office in Joliet, the Plum Creek Nature Center in Beecher, the Isle à la Cache Museum in Romeoville, or the Monee Reservoir. Registrants will receive a permit and vehicle tag. Permit holders are entitled to register for reasonably priced agility classes offered at the park. (The second dog park of the Forest Preserve District of Will County is in the DuPage County chapter because it is located in Naperville.)

Hammel Woods Dog Park hours are 8 A.M.–5 P.M. November–March and 8 A.M.–8 P.M. April–October. The dog park is located at the Hammel Woods DuPage River access, on Black Road between the I-55 Expressway overpass and Route 59 in Joliet. Forest Preserve District of Will County; 815/727-8700; www.fpdwc.org.

19 Pilcher Park

🐾🐾 (See Kane, McHenry, and Will Counties map on page 190)

This 640-acre park and nature center is one of Joliet's favorite garden gems. From family picnics to Audubon Society meetings, almost everyone who enjoys the outdoors in this city stops by Pilcher Park. And dogs are no exception. The trails and paths that run through this huge area are of varying degrees of difficulty, so no matter how out of shape you are (or your pooch is), you'll find a path you ought to take.

Natasha is intrigued by the artesian well, called Flowing Well, that many locals flock to as if it were the Fountain of Youth. Active dogs like being able to go for a run here alongside their masters, who hike, bike, and cross-country ski. Despite its popularity, Pilcher Park is so large that it's easy to get some alone time for you and your pup. Some bicyclists have reported some loitering and pick-pocketing after dark, but the park is officially only open 9 A.M.–4 P.M., so that shouldn't be a concern anyway.

The park is located at Gougher Road north of Route 30/Lincoln Highway. From the I-80 Expressway, exit on Route 30 heading west. Gougher Road is the first stoplight. 2501 Highland Park Dr., Joliet; 815/741-7277.

PLACES TO STAY

Comfort Inn–Joliet South: All dogs welcome, no size limit, no fees or deposits. Rates range $70–99. 135 S. Larkin Ave., Joliet; 815/744-1770; www .comfortinn.com.

Plainfield and New Lenox, Will County

Like neighboring Mokena, Plainfield and New Lenox were railroad communities built in an area that was once a favorite hunting ground of Native Americans, with abundant timber and water from the Des Plaines, DuPage, and Kankakee Rivers. Indian burial mounds for more than 4,000 people still exist in the area today. Neighboring University Park, home to Governors State University, has a lovely sculpture garden, though dogs aren't allowed to lift their legs near the art.

PARKS, BEACHES, AND RECREATION AREAS

20 Old Plank Road Trail

🐾 (See Kane, McHenry, and Will Counties map on page 190)

This paved running, biking, and walking trail was once an abandoned 1850s railroad line that now links many south suburban communities with a continuous greenway. Outdoors enthusiasts of all stripes like the smooth surfaces, gentle slopes, and uninterrupted space of the paths. The 21-mile Old Plank Road Trail stretches to Cook County and is covered in the South Suburban Cook County chapter as well. On some sunny weekends, it may be too crowded to take a pup on a solitary walk, but it's great for a dog who wants to run (and an owner who can keep up with her). With a good wet nose, be prepared to sniff out mink, beaver, fox, and deer.

A parking lot and restrooms make New Lenox a good place to access the trail. Old Plank Road Trail runs just south of, and parallel to, old U.S. Route 30 and can be entered from any cross street.

21 Van Horne Woods

🐾🐾🐾 🐕 (See Kane, McHenry, and Will Counties map on page 190)

It can be confusing that there are two similarly-named parks in this area. There's the Van Horne Woods Forest Preserve, but what you and your pooch want is the Van Horne Woods. This one-acre off-leash area is fully fenced and free of charge. In addition, it's rarely crowded and offers ample parking for those who are already in this neck of Chicago's woods.

The dog park entrance to Van Horne Woods is on Frontage Road near Caton Farm Road, just off of the I-55 Expressway. Plainfield Park District; 100 W. Ottawa St., Plainfield; 815/436-8812; www.plainfieldparkdistrict.com.

GRRRRR

CHAPTER 9

Beyond the Windy City

If you've explored the preceding parks, forest preserves, hotels, and restaurants as carefully as a flea stalking through a Husky's coat, you and your pup may be dog tired. Perhaps what you need to recharge is a little vacation. A number of great getaway destinations lie less than a day's drive from Chicago, many with relaxing beaches, interesting riverbanks, and dog-friendly bed-and-breakfasts and campgrounds. Included in this chapter are just a few favorites in Illinois, Michigan, and Wisconsin.

Galena, Illinois

The greater Galena area of northwestern Illinois (which includes Stockton, Elizabeth, Apple River, and Hanover) is a favorite weekend respite for both Chicagoans and Iowans, particularly for history buffs. More than 85 percent of the city is part of the Galena Historic District, including the Ulysses S. Grant Home, on the National Register of Historic Places,. As you might expect in a locale with all this history, Galena is an antiquer's paradise, and many shops have outdoor displays in warm weather, making it easy for dogs to tag along.

PICK OF THE LITTER—
BEYOND THE WINDY CITY

BEST STATE PARKS
Starved Rock State Park, Utica, Illinois (page 214)
Governor Nelson State Park, Waunakee, Wisconsin (page 219)

BEST DOG PARKS
Prairie Moraine Parkway, Madison, Wisconsin (page 220)
Granville Dog Park, Milwaukee, Wisconsin (page 223)

BEST PLACES TO STAY
TierraLinda, Galena, Illinois (page 214)
Sweethaven, Union Pier, Michigan (page 225)

If you and your dog grow weary of walking through the quaint streets, of enjoying good food at the many restaurants with cozy patios, and of roaming through antique stores, you can hop in the car and quickly arrive at some of Illinois' most interesting state parks. Galena/Jo Daviess County Convention and Visitors Bureau; 101 Bouthillier St., Galena; 877/464-2536; www.galena.org.

PARKS, BEACHES, AND RECREATION AREAS

Apple River Canyon State Park

This 300-acre park is, as its name suggests, a canyon formed by the Apple River. As you hike through it, you'll see deep ravines, springs, and dramatic cuts through limestone bluffs that seem more characteristic of the western United States than the prairie states. Maybe that's because this area was once part of a seabed that stretched from the Alleghenies to the Rockies.

Dog lovers can take five different winding trails through the canyons, fish in the river, chow down at four different picnic areas, or just run, walk, and hike. Dogs must be leashed in all state parks. There are 47 campsites available by advance reservation.

Apple River Canyon State Park is more than two hours west of the Loop. From Highway 20 (near Rockford), drive for approximately 50 miles to Route 78. Take Route 78 north to Canyon Road. 8763 E. Canyon Rd., Apple River; 815/745-3302.

Blanding Landing Recreation Area

Located on the Mississippi River between Hanover and Galena, this summery 18-acre spot offers picnic tables, barbecue grills, a playground, restrooms, showers, a boat landing, and even fish-cleaning tables. Camping with fishing and boating access, flush toilets, showers, and potable water is available, but advance reservations are needed, and on weekends there is a minimum stay of two nights. Blanding Landing is on South River Road in Hanover, west of Route 84/Blackjack Road. 815/591-2326.

Grant City Park

Less rustic than the open wilderness of the state parks listed here, Grant City Park is Galena's prime green space, complete with picnic tables, surrounding the Ulysses S. Grant Home. This isn't the type of place where you and your dog can run like the wind, thanks in part to the many tourists who stop here to view the president and Civil War general's brick abode. But it is a great place for a leisurely walk before heading back to your bed-and-breakfast. To aid in your R&R efforts, the grounds feature a drinking fountain, pavilion, decorative fountain, gazebo, and flower gardens. The park is north of Highway 20 on the east bank of the Galena River. If on paw, walk over the footbridge from the Main Street Historic District.

Mississippi Palisades State Park

You've probably heard of Pacific Palisades, but likely never really thought about what the word "palisades" meant. You'll get a textbook answer when you see the cliffs along a river at Mississippi Palisades. Here you'll find caves formed by limestone sinkholes as well as cool rock formations and foliage such as ferns and other colorful plants. Look for two favorite rock shapes, one called Indian Head and another called Twin Sisters, on top of the bluffs. You and your dog can check out these works of nature by taking to the 13-mile trail system. According to the state park authority, in general, the five trails in the northern part of the park provide a more gentle workout. The five in the south, which are much closer to the bluff, are, as you might expect, more demanding. There are four overlooks designed for those who aren't serious hikers but who like the views nonetheless.

The trails are open all year, and if you're hardy enough to weather the park in January and February, you might see eagles. Wisconsin's favorite animal, the badger, appears throughout the year. The only exception to the park's schedule is its three-day closure during the firearm deer season. The park is three miles north of Savanna in Carroll County. 16327A Route 84, Savanna; 815/273-2731.

PLACES TO STAY

Best Western Quiet House & Suites: Two of the rooms in this small hotel welcome dogs of any size, as long as they aren't left alone, with a $15 additional fee per night. Most rooms have refrigerators and microwaves. Rates range $150–205. Hwy. 20 E., Galena; 815/777-2577; www.quiethouse.com.

Cloran Mansion: Dogs of all sizes are permitted in the cedar-sided cottage next to this restored Victorian home. You can sit in your private whirlpool while your dog rests in front of the three-sided fireplace. The property is 1.5 acres, so there's no lack of places to go for a walk. Dog lovers pay a one-time $25 fee, no matter the length of stay. Rates range $189–225. 1237 Franklin St., Galena; 815/777-0583; www.cloranmansion.com.

Galena Rentals: One of this company's rental homes is pet-friendly, and it's a gem: It sleeps six humans and has its own wooded area and garage, plus plenty of amenities. No fees, deposits, or weight limit—just treat the place like you'd treat your own home. Small dogs and their people also have the option of another rental home that sleeps four; dogs must weigh less than 20 pounds. Rates range $130–250. 773/631-5253; www.galenarentals.com.

TierraLinda: Five miles south of Galena, this bed-and-breakfast, whose name means "beautiful earth" in Spanish, lives up to its moniker. You can barely see the farmhouse from the road, and once you're there you'll want to explore the surrounding landscape. Cooper is amused by the unusual twist of a hotel that welcomes all dogs, but no children under the age of seven. Rooms are $125, plus an additional $20 per dog. 826 S. Rocky Hill Rd., Galena; 815/777-1234; www.beautifulearth.com.

Peoria and LaSalle, Illinois

Peoria's the butt of many jokes about downstaters. But if you're passing by on the way to Starved Rock in nearby LaSalle, or just driving through the state to get to St. Louis, Peoria's the best place for a pit stop. Cooper doesn't know much about its dog-worthiness, but he knows the most interesting places for you to bury your bone while on the road. Peoria Area Convention and Visitors Bureau; 800/747-0302; www.peoria.org.

PARKS, BEACHES, AND RECREATION AREAS

Starved Rock State Park

This state park is named after its grim history: in the late 1700s, a band from the Illiniwek tribe was trapped on this sandstone butte by allies of the Ottawa tribe and eventually starved to death. Steps to the top of the rock and a small trail lead to a plateau where you and your dog can look out in all directions over the Illinois River. After you've paid homage, you can take to 15 miles

DOG-EAR YOUR CALENDAR

Dog Days of Wisconsin: Since 1995, Wisconsin has gone to the dogs every August. That's when Pam Paulsen started Dog Days of Wisconsin, her summer camp for pups and their people. Just like human camp, there are scheduled periods of organized activities. The high-energy activities include lure coursing, tracking, agility, and swimming in Pickerel Lake. If your pup has developed a love of agility training, you can learn to make agility equipment (think of it as practical arts and crafts). Other useful skills you can take home include pet first-aid, treat cooking, and massage.

The fun takes place at the 200-acre Camp Helen Brachman, located in central Wisconsin near Steven's Point, about 140 miles from Milwaukee. 5780 W. Hemlock St., Milwaukee, WI; 414/353-9260 or 800/CAMP-4-DOGS (800/226-7436); www.dogcamp.com.

Illinois Basset Waddle: While the highlight is a primo spot in the Village of Dwight's Harvest Days parade, this is a weekend-long celebration of basset hounds. The costumed canines and their owners come together each September for contests only a basset could win: longest ears, lowest clearance to the ground, and best howler, as well as a parade and a night-before party. Sponsored by Guardian Angel Basset Rescue in Dwight (in Livingston County, 80 miles southwest of Chicago), more than 700 dogs join in the efforts that attract fans of the breed from all over the United States and Canada. For more than eight years, they've raised more than $50,000 annually for homeless Hush Puppies. Guardian Angel Basset Rescue; 108 E. Main St., Dwight, IL; 708/758-7455; www.bassetrescue.org.

of hiking trails that wander through wooded forests, beside steep cliffs, and alongside remarkable waterfalls. In the winter, the waterfalls freeze, which is a sight to see if your dog has the furry coat to handle the cold.

Starved Rock is about two hours southwest of Chicago along the Illinois River. The only camping here is car camping in the lot-style campground. 2568 E. 950th Rd., Oglesby; 815/667-4726. (While the park is generally recognized as being in Utica, the Department of Natural Resources recommends entering the Oglesby address in online map services in order to get the best directions to Starved Rock.)

PLACES TO STAY

LaSalle Peru KOA Kampground: Just north of Starved Rock State Park, this campground has a fishing creek and many oak trees. The campground is open April–October. Rates range $26–40. 756 N. 3150th Rd., Utica; 815/667-4988; www.koa.com.

Marcia's Bed and Breakfast: This three-room home with a separate cottage permits pets, and pups love it, thanks to lakefront property and tons of trees. There is a $10 additional fee for dogs. Rates range $95–125. 3003 Rte. 71, Ottawa; 815/434-5217.

Door County, Wisconsin

Illuminated by lighthouses, this peninsula has 250 miles of shoreline, five state parks, 17 county parks, and too many beaches and quaint little villages to count. Maybe that's why so many Chicagoans flock here each summer. The area juts into Lake Michigan about 230 miles north of Chicago, and the roads north are filled with Illinois-license-plate-holders planning to shop, swim, and sail. In addition to the peninsula, nearby Washington Island is another draw for swimming and sightseeing, and dogs are allowed on the Washington Island Car Ferry (800/223-2094; www.wisferry.com), as long as they remain in a vehicle or on the lower deck with a leash. Even better, dogs ride for free. The Door County Chamber of Commerce website lists more accommodations that allow pets (www.doorcounty.com/stay/pets.aspx).

PARKS, BEACHES, AND RECREATION AREAS

Newport State Park
🐾 🐾 🐾

These 2,400 acres of wilderness are open year-round for hiking, cross-country skiing, running, and snowshoeing. If you trek down all nine of the park's designated trails, you'll get a Newport State Park patch to affix to your collar or hang in the doghouse. There are also picnic areas with grills. 475 County Hwy. NP, Ellison Bay; 920/854-2500; www.dcty.com/newport.

PLACES TO STAY

Applewood Cottage: This place looks just as its name suggests: a large farmhouse on 10 acres of open land, with access to many private hiking trails. Dogs are welcome guests with a $50 or $100 refundable fee, depending on the length of your stay. The cottage has DIRECTV and high-speed Internet for dog lovers who want to stay connected. Rates range $125–150. 8186 Elm Rd., Fish Creek; 920/868-9232; www.theapplewoodcottage.com.

Feathered Star Bed and Breakfast: There's a black and white spaniel pictured on this bed-and-breakfast's website, which is pretty much the only endorsement Natasha needs. There's no size limit for dogs here, but a $10 fee per night is required. The three-acre grounds provide plenty of room to play. Rates range $120–140. 6202 Hwy. 42, Egg Harbor; 877/743-4066; www.featheredstar.com.

Lake Geneva, Wisconsin

Most Chicagoans who make the 1.5-hour drive to Lake Geneva do so in search of golf or a spa. But there is entertainment aplenty for dogs and their owners in this cushy resort town. Lake Geneva is named after its body of water, which is the favorite of visiting pups. Lake Geneva Area Convention and Visitors Bureau; 800/345-1020; www.lakegenevawi.com.

PARKS, BEACHES, AND RECREATION AREAS

Big Foot Beach State Park

This 272-acre park has 2,200 feet of sandy beaches. But it's only open May–October, and in the prime summer months, the beaches are packed with people. Come early or late in the season if you want to walk your leashed pooch on the beach. Otherwise, turn to the five miles of hiking trails overlooking lagoons, wooded areas, open grass, and marshlands. Located on Highway 120, south of Lake Geneva. A state park sticker is required, and can be purchased on-site at any Wisconsin state park. 1452 Hwy. H, Lake Geneva; 262/248-2528.

PLACES TO STAY

Eleven Gables Inn: This mansion is surrounded by maple trees, verandas, and a 100-foot pier that extends into Lake Geneva. There are no fees for dogs of any size, but dogs are allowed only in rooms with private entrances

FETCHING NECESSITIES

For the most part, Cooper and Natasha think shopping is something they must tolerate in order to get to the next park. Better to go than to stay at home, but not something to which they look forward. Watson has convinced them that things are different at **Mounds Pet Food Warehouse.** To him, it's one of the best recreational activities in Madison. Mounds is the area's answer to PetSmart—only locally owned and operated with great deals on food, treats, and toys... and a free Mounds bar for every human who enters. All Mounds stores serve as daily Humane Society adoption centers, and the company works closely with other smaller local shelters as well.

In addition, come summertime Mounds throws the annual Dog Fest (the 2006 theme was Hawaii Fi-Do: A Dog's Day in Paradise; Watson looks smashing in a lei). Visit any of the three Madison-area locations at 2110 S. Stoughton Rd., Madison, 608/221-0210; 8311 University Ave., Middleton, 608/831-3000; or 5350 King James Way, Fitchburg, 608/271-1800.

and prior approval is required before you arrive with a four-legged guest. Rates range $109–179. 493 Wrigley Dr., Lake Geneva; 262/248-8393; www.lkgeneva.com.

The Nautical Inn of Lake Geneva: This 1900s-themed home sleeps 6–14 guests, and their pets, depending on which rooms you reserve. Rates, based on six people, range $200–595, with a two or three night minimum stay, depending on the season. 705 Wisconsin St., Lake Geneva; 262/949-9503; www.thenautical.biz.

Madison, Wisconsin

Watson enjoyed visiting Madison so much when he wrote the passages for the first edition of this book that he now lives there. But moving to the city—sometimes called "the Berkeley of the Midwest" because of its liberal, diverse, reform-minded population—isn't necessary to enjoy Madison's bounty of dog-friendly amenities and unique mixture of nature and culture. Situated on the isthmus between Lakes Mendota and Monona (Mendota's the bigger one to the north), Madison is both the capital of Wisconsin and home to the University of Wisconsin (UW). And it's only about a three-hour drive from Chicago.

Any visit to the city must include a stroll down State Street—an avenue of boutiques, coffeehouses, and restaurants that connects the state capitol building (see it lit up at night) with the campus. Madison restricts auto traffic on State, so it has a peaceful, small-town vibe, and makes for laid-back people- and dog-watching, shopping, and dining. Dogs are not usually

DIVERSION

If you have one of those dogs (like Boris was) who follows you wherever you go, or nips at your heels and rounds up the other dogs, but won't fetch if his life depends on it—call Shannon Wolfe. Owner of **Magic's Legacy Stock Dog Training,** Wolfe is one of the few people in the area who will teach dogs to herd, just for the fun of it. The dogs learn to work on the farm herding real live sheep. Natasha doesn't understand why a dog would pick this over, say, a dip in a cold lake, but to each her own. Wolfe will work with any breed of dog, but the real beauty here is seeing a dog who doesn't delight in the regular canine games embrace his true herding nature. 262/279-9917; www.magicslegacy.com.

allowed in stores, but there are plenty of trees and benches to which you can safely secure them while you run into **The Soap Opera** (319 State St.; 608/251-4051) for a bar of Bee & Flower Sandalwood Soap for washing up after picking up. Or, try **Shakti** (320 State St.; 608/255-5007) for some healing crystals for Lassie's arthritis.

Food vendors set up carts near the campus end of State, selling everything from falafel to fried rice. Grab some pad thai (with chicken for Watson), pick a spot of lawn on Library Mall and see how many tattoos, Birkenstocks, and piercings you can count.

One word of caution: Although the famous Madison farmers market that sets up on Saturdays around the capitol is must-see fun for humans, canine companions are frowned upon. Really, the crowds packed into the square make it virtually impossible for a dog to navigate without getting his paws stepped on.

The Greater Madison Convention and Visitors Bureau; 608/255-2537; www.visitmadison.com.

PARKS, BEACHES, AND RECREATION AREAS

Governor Nelson State Park

Not to be confused with three other state parks in Wisconsin named for governors, this park on 10,000-acre Lake Mendota has a designated "pet swimming area," although the only domestic animal Watson has ever seen here has been a dog. There are also leash-only trails along restored prairie and savanna, effigy mounds on the Woodland Trail, and a boat launch and ski trails. The park is just north of Madison off the I-90/I-94 Expressway. 5140 City Highway M, Waunakee; 608/831-3005.

Howard M. Temin Lakeshore Path
🐾🐾🐾

While downtown, be sure to visit the Memorial Union (800 Langdon St., 608/265-3000), the student union in the heart of the **UW campus.** Dogs are welcome on campus as long as they're leashed and picked up after.

The outdoor Union Terrace overlooking Lake Mendota fills up in the summer with alumni and tourists, and dogs often frolic in the water along the stone shores—albeit without official sanctioning. (Madison does have plenty of approved beaches for dogs to dip a paw in the lake; read on to locate two of the best.) Grab a beer and brat at the Terrace (pets are not permitted on the Terrace itself for safety reasons) and kick back at a picnic table by the waterfront, where Watson is welcome.

From the Terrace, walk west along the shore of Mendota out to Picnic Point. Sometimes Watson flashes his big brown eyes at students, hoping they'll drop a cheese curd or a badger (he doesn't really understand that the badger is their mascot, not an animal they eat). Picnic Point is more often used by human couples than those with dogs because it's so romantic: a narrow, heavily wooded finger of land that juts into Lake Mendota, accessible via a wide dirt path. The path connects to 300 acres along the lake, and, as is common on any good college campus, there's always someone playing Frisbee on the grass here.

Prairie Moraine Parkway
🐾🐾🐾🐕

For its population (about 210,000), Madison boasts a of wealth of off-leash dog parks—or, in keeping with the politically correct speak of the area, "pet exercise areas." One of the best (and, therefore, most crowded on spring and summer days) is the mega-size Prairie Moraine Parkway, also known as the Verona Dog Park. Located on Highway PB (or peanut butter, as Watson calls it, named after his favorite taste sensation) and Wesner Drive just south of Madison proper, Prairie Moraine makes an excellent stop on your way to or from Chicago. Despite its popularity with locals, Prairie Moraine feels like it's in the middle of nowhere. Depending on the day, there are points on the path, particularly during stretches that thread through woods, where you feel like you're alone in the wilderness. This 160-acre parcel of land connects to the Dane County portion of the Ice Age Trail, one of only eight national scenic trails in the United States (leashes required; see the Milwaukee section for more information on the Ice Age Trail). Watson particularly likes to go in the fall, when apple trees at the north end drop enough fruit to keep the vet away for days. Great place for a picnic, with one caveat: Bring your own water. Daily $3 honor system registration required on entering all Dane County and Madison off-leash areas ($20 for the year).

Yahara Heights County Park

Although smaller and not isolated like Prairie Moraine (you will hear traffic and an occasional plane from the Dane County Airport), Yahara offers an important feature not found at its larger sister: a lake. One side of the 20-acre park is bounded by Cherokee Marsh, the largest remaining wetland in Dane County. The shoreline features a dog exercise pier, giving water-loving Labs a chance to dive. (Watson prefers to use the ramp to walk into the water. He thinks it is more befitting a sophisticated canine like himself.) Yahara Heights is located at the intersection of Highway 113 and County M just north of Madison. To access the parking lot, drive north on 113 to River Road, make a right, then make another immediate right on Catfish Court. Continue on Catfish, ignoring the Dead End sign and keep going on the dirt road when the asphalt ends.

PLACES TO EAT

Afghan/Mediterranean Kabul Restaurant: This is one of a number of State Street restaurants that set out tables on the sidewalk. It is Watson's favorite, because it is the most dog-friendly, although most of its neighbors will allow you to tie Fido under the table. Look for water bowls to deduce the most welcoming. 541 State St.; 608/256-6322.

PLACES TO STAY

Crowne Plaza Madison: As Chicagoans divide their city into the north and south sides, Madisonians split their town into east and west, with the capitol building at the center. Much of the pet-friendly lodging is east of the capitol, easier to access from I-90/I-94. On the scale of pet friendliness, the Crowne Plaza rates on the higher side: On check-in, all dogs receive their own goody bags with treats and toys. Room rates vary with availability, but a king bed on a normal weekend runs about $129 plus a nightly $20 pet fee. 4402 E. Washington Ave.; 608/244-4703.

Days Inn Madison/Monona: This is a modest, serviceable hotel, as are most pet-friendly lodgings in Madison, plus it's only a short drive downtown. And as Watson says, because practically every hotel in Madison is just a stone's throw from a Culver's outlet, as this one is, they're all good. Culver's, home of the "butterburger" and thick, creamy Wisconsin frozen custard, is headquartered just north of Madison in Sauk City. A $50 returnable damage deposit is required, plus there is an additional $10 per night pet fee. Room rates start at $79 on weekdays, $85 on weekends. 4402 E. Broadway Service Rd.; 608/223-1800.

Milwaukee, Wisconsin

Natasha's human friend Jason calls Milwaukee "Chicago's best-kept secret." Milwaukeeans don't laugh too loudly at that, but he means it as a compliment. Just 1.5 hours from Chicago, Milwaukee offers much of what its bigger sister does—miles of lakefront—with half the traffic. A book could be written on all of Milwaukee's excellent parks. Until then, check out these highlights, head to the Historic Third Ward for a bite to eat, or, just as you would in Chicago, head east to the lake. Juneau Park and Veterans Park are the Lincoln Park equivalents along Lake Michigan. Dogs are not allowed on the city's beaches. A community group, Residents for Off-Leash Milwaukee Parks (www.milwaukeedogparks.org) offers tips on other dog parks within an easy drive of the Cream City (nicknamed such because of the color of the brick on many city buildings).

One final piece of advice: Please, don't bother with the *Laverne & Shirley* jokes—Milwaukeeans have heard them all. Twice. Visit Milwaukee. 800/554-1448; www.visitmilwaukee.org.

PARKS, BEACHES, AND RECREATION AREAS

City of Waukesha Dog Run

This off-leash dog park in suburban Waukesha is essentially just a half-mile long wooded trail. There's a small area for wrestling and playing fetch, but it is of more interest to neighborhood dogs than as a destination for visitors. The park is open dawn–dusk. Located at the intersection of Comanche and MacArthur Roads, east of Merrill Hills Road, Waukesha; www.waukeshadogparks.org.

Granville Dog Park

When locals set out to create Granville, their aim was to build Milwaukee's first public off-leash facility. Now, their modest aim is to turn it into "the best dog park in the world." The large, hilly park hosts an exceedingly friendly contingent of human and canine park users, most of whom follow the park's commonsense rules. As tempting as the nearby river and streams are to water dogs, they are not part of the off-leash area. The park is open sunrise–sunset, and is north of Good Hope Road and west of Highway 45; www.pipdogpark .com or www.milwaukeedogparks.org.

Havenwoods State Forest

Imagine this: a 237-acre island of nature in the heart of the city. Havenwoods offers grasslands, forest, wetland, a creek, and garden areas. If you are tired of hiking and walking through beautiful woods not knowing what it is you are looking at, get bird, butterfly, and wildflower lists from the Environmental Awareness Center. These trails are popular for hiking, biking, and cross-country skiing. Dogs must be on an eight-foot leash, and are allowed only on certain paths (the Environmental Awareness Center will tell you which ones are strictly paws off). 6141 N. Hopkins, Milwaukee; 414/527-0232.

Ice Age National Scenic Trail

One of only eight national scenic trails in the country, the Ice Age Trail will be a 1,000-mile walking/hiking trail in, and unique to, Wisconsin. At press time, about 600 miles of the trail were ready for you and your cold-nosed companion. The purpose of the Ice Age Trail is to tell the story of the ice age alongside scenes created by glaciers, but many people and their dogs just like being able to hike, bike, and snowshoe. The Ice Age Park & Trail Foundation accepts memberships and donations to support building the trail, which, when completed, while be half as long as the Appalachian Trail. Dogs are allowed on all parts of the trail with the exception of the 13-mile stretch in the city of Janesville May 15–September 15. Dogs are never permitted on Pike Lake State Forest's beach. 306 E. Wilson St., Madison; 800/227-0046; www.iceagetrail.org.

Runway Dog Exercise Area

Drive just 10 miles south of downtown to Oak Creek, turn down a gravel road, and you'll find the Cream City's newest place for dogs to roam off-leash.

Permits are required in order to explore the quarter-, half-, and three-quarter-mile-long trails, which are largely treeless (bring a sunhat in the summer). Fees are $5 per day or $20 for the year, with an additional $5 for each additional dog. Discounts are available for seniors and those with disabilities. Runway is open dawn–dusk. The park is southeast of the Cudahy Nature Preserve on East Rawson Avenue, accessible via 794 East from downtown. Turn east where the freeway ends at Layton Avenue. 1214 E. Rawson Ave., Milwaukee; 414/257- 7275; www.county.milwaukee.gov/display/router. asp?docid=11518 or www.milwaukeedogparks.org.

PLACES TO STAY

Executive Inn: Just west of Marquette University and convenient to downtown, this 40-room budget hotel will be happy to take you and your dog for a night. Maybe your pooch can't dial up, but thanks to free wireless Internet, you can. Free parking, too. Rates start at $69. 2301 W. Wisconsin Ave.; 414/342-8400; www.execinn.com.

Hotel Metro: Cooper loves the big art deco suites at this charming downtown hotel, but if he and Natasha both visit, they need to be approved by the manager, as do all dogs weighing more than 25 pounds. It's a quick walk to the lake, as well as two parks, from here. There is a $25 per day nonrefundable pet fee. Rates range $199–219. 411 E. Mason St.; 414/272-1937; www .hotelmetro.com.

La Quinta: Dogs like the outpost of this modest chain hotel because it is close to Little Menomonee River Parkway. If you pay by cash, you'll be asked for a $25 deposit in case your pup forgets his housetraining. Dogs must be in kennels while the room is cleaned, and, of course, on a leash at all other times. Average rate is $69. 5442 N. Lovers Lane Rd.; 414/535-1300; www.lq.com.

Harbor Country, Michigan

Chicagoans who don't head to Door County, Wisconsin, choose Harbor Country, Michigan, a trifecta of beach towns—Benton Harbor, Union Pier, and New Buffalo—in part because they're close to the Indiana border and therefore a short drive from home (less than two hours). Life here is all about swimming, sleeping in, and grabbing a milkshake after dinner. In other words, pretty dang good. If you can, rent a dog-friendly cabin on the beach for a week, and then sit and stay.

PARKS, BEACHES, AND RECREATION AREAS

Warren Dunes State Park

These sand dunes rise 240 feet above Lake Michigan, showing beautiful views of the coastline. Dogs aren't allowed to take a swim here, but they are allowed on the trails that wind through the first part of this 1,950-acre state park.

(Don't worry, the No Dogs signs are clear. You'll know where you're allowed and where you're not.) This area is now one of Michigan's most popular, meaning that June–August, you and your pooch will not be alone in the great outdoors. If you haven't visited sand dunes, it's worth the trip, as the scenery is remarkably different from Wisconsin's forests or Illinois' prairies. The entrance to "the Dunes," as they're called by locals, is just east of the I-94 Expressway, north of Route 12. 12032 Red Arrow Hwy., Sawyer; 616/426-4013.

PLACES TO STAY

Red Roof Inn: If you're staying in this area, you really want a cottage near the lake. But if you're just passing through, this motel will do, particularly because it's close to several city parks. Pets who weigh less than 80 pounds can stay without any extra fees. Average rate is $45. 1630 Mall Dr., Benton Harbor; 269/927-2484; www.redroof.com.

Sans Souci: Dogs are only permitted in the two cottages at this resort, but since they're lakeside with sunset or sunrise views, it's hardly being sent to the doghouse. Plus, there are 50 acres for playing. All pet visitors are up to the owners' discretion. Rates are $225 per night, $1,350 per week, for up to four people. 19265 Lakeside Rd., New Buffalo; 269/756-3141; www.sanssouci.com.

Sweethaven: A private deck, a well-equipped kitchen, a quick walk to the beach, and, get this, a dog to play with on about nine acres of land. The owner's sweet Lab, Buster, won't charge you or your dog any extra fees to stay here. There is a three pet maximum. Average nightly rate is $222; weekly rates are also available. 9517 Union Pier Rd., Union Pier; 269/469-0332; www.sweethavenresort.com.

Saugatuck and Douglas, Michigan

Farther north on Lake Michigan than Benton Harbor, Union Pier, and New Buffalo, Saugatuck and Douglas are the summer artists' resorts. In 1910, a group of Chicago artists established the Summer School of Painting on Ox-Bow Lagoon in Saugatuck, and the tone has been artsy ever since. More chic (and therefore more expensive) than the Union Pier area, Saugatuck and Douglas also offer more to do for those who get tired of swimming and lounging on the beach (not that Natasha ever does, of course). If you want to get out and about, just stroll down the boardwalk, and you'll find something to eat and furry friends with whom you can play.

Some call the area "the Fire Island of the Midwest," because it attracts a gay and lesbian population looking to beat the heat of the city (both Chicago and Detroit), but visitors who don't fall into that category feel welcome and have fun here as well. The Saugatuck/Douglas Convention & Visitors Bureau lists more accommodations that allow pets on its website (www.saugatuck.com).

PLACES TO STAY

Douglas Dunes Resort: This 20-acre resort is the first choice for gays and lesbians looking to vacation in an everyone's-welcome resort. Thankfully, the no-discrimination policies apply to dogs, too. There are no size limits, just a $10 fee per night. Rates range $35–290. Pack your dancing shoes. 333 Blue Star Hwy., Douglas; 269/857-1401; www.douglasdunes.com.

Ship-n-Shore Motel: Dogs aren't allowed between Memorial Day and Labor Day, but the rest of the year, there are no size limits, although they do charge a $20 additional fee for four-legged guests. There's immediate access to the water here, and rates are lower during the off-season. If you have to check in with the office while you're away, Ship-n-Shore offers free high-speed Internet access. Off-season rates range $60–119. 528 Water St., Saugatuck; 269/857-2194; www.shipnshoremotel.com.

RESOURCES

Public and Government Offices

Laws, operating hours, and regulations often change. If you have a question about your local agency, here's who you can ask.

CHICAGO

Chicago Park District: 541 N. Fairbanks; 312/742-PLAY (312/742-7529); fax 312/742-5391; www.chicagoparkdistrict.com.

Chicago Police Department: 311(non-emergency phone number); www.ci.chi.il.us/communitypolicing or http://12.17.79.6.

Coalition Against Dog Fighting: 312/944-6610 or 847/265-9995.

SUBURBS

Addison Park District: 120 E. Oak St., Addison; 630/833-0100; fax 630/833-6025; www.addisonparkdistrict.org.

Algonquin Recreation Department: 2200 Harnish Dr., Algonquin; 847/658-2700; fax 847/658-4564; www.algonquin.org.

Alsip Park District: 12521 S. Kostner Ave., Alsip; 708/389-1003; fax 708/389-1529; www.alsipparks.org.

Antioch Parks and Recreation Department: 806 Holbek Dr., Antioch; 847/395-2160; fax 847/838-4328; www.antioch.il.gov.

Arlington Heights Park District: 410 N. Arlington Heights Rd., Arlington Heights; 847/577-3000; www.ahpd.org.

Aurora Department of Parks and Recreation: 1000 Ray Moses Dr., Aurora; 630/978-4774; fax 630/978-1459; www.aurora-il.org.

Barrington Countryside Park District: P.O. Box 1393, Barrington; 847/783-6772; www.bc-pd.org.

Barrington Park District: 235 Lyons Dr., Barrington; 847/381-0687; fax 847/381-8794; www.barringtonparkdistrict.org.

Bartlett Park District: 696 W. Stearns Rd., Bartlett; 630/540-4800; fax 630/837-6608; www.bartlettparkdistrict.com.

Batavia Park District: 327 West Wilson St., Batavia; 630/879-5235; fax 630/879-9537; www.bataviaparks.org.

Bedford Park District: 6700 S. 78th Ave., Bedford Park; 708/458-2265; fax 708/458-2279.

Bensenville Park District: 1000 W. Wood St., Bensenville; 630/766-7015; fax 630/766-9280; www.bensenvilleparkdistrict.org.

Village of Bensenville, Redmond Recreational Complex: 735 E. Jefferson St., Bensenville; 630/594-1190; fax 630/594-1143; www.bensenville.il.us.

Berkeley Park District: 1200 Lind Ave., Berkeley; 708/544-1935; fax 708/449-6189.

Berwyn Park District: 3701 S. Scoville Avenue, Berwyn; 708/788-1701; fax 708/788-1345; www.berwynparks.org.

North Berwyn Park District, Community Center: 1619 South Wesley, Berwyn; 708/749-4900; fax 708/749-4966; www.nbpd4fun.org.

Bloomingdale Park District: 172 S. Circle Ave., Bloomingdale; 630/529-3650; fax 630/529-9184; www.bloomingdaleparks.org.

Blue Island Park District: 12804 Highland Ave., Blue Island; 708/385-3304; fax 708/385-3318; www.blueislandparks.org.

Bolingbrook Park District: 201 Recreation Dr., Bolingbrook; 630/739-0272; fax 630/739-1039; www.bolingbrookparks.org.

Bridgeview Park District: 8100 Beloit Ave., Bridgeview; 708/594-1818; fax 708/594-1735.

Broadview Park District Main Office, Schroeder Park: 2600 S. 13th Ave., Broadview; 708/343-5637; fax 708/681-0106; www.villageofbroadview.com.

Brookfield Recreation Department: 8820 Brookfield Ave., Brookfield; 708/485-7344; fax 708/485-3050; www.villageofbrookfield.com.

Buffalo Grove Park District: 530 Bernard Dr., Buffalo Grove; 847/850-2100; fax 847/459-5741; www.bgparkdistrict.org.

Burbank Park District: 8050 S. Newcastle Ave., Burbank; 708/599-2070; fax 708/599-2063; www.burbankparkdistrict.org.

Burr Ridge Park District: 10 S. 474 Madison St., Burr Ridge; 630/920-1969; fax 630/920-1973; www.brparks.org.

Burr Ridge, Pleasant Dale Park District: 7425 S. Wolf Rd., Burr Ridge; 630/662-6220; fax 630/662-9239; www.pleasantdaleparks.org.

Butterfield Park District: 21 W. 730 Butterfield Rd., Lombard; 630/858-2229; fax 630/858-2234; www.butterfieldpd.com.

Calumet Memorial Park District: 626 Wentworth Ave., Calumet City; 708/868-2530; fax 708/868-2536; www.calumetmemorialparkdistrict.com.

Village of Calumet Park Recreation Department: 12426 S. Loomis, Calumet Park; 708/597-3535; fax 708/597-1471.

Carol Stream Park District: 391 Illini Dr., Carol Stream; 630/784-6100; fax 630/665-9045; www.csparks.org.

Cary Park District: 255 Briargate Rd., Cary; 847/639-6100; fax 847/639-6290; www.carypark.com.

Channahon Park District: 24856 W. Eames St., Channahon; 815/467-7275; fax 815/467-5677; www.channahonpark.org.

Chicago Heights Park District: 1400 Chicago Rd., Chicago Heights; 708/755-1351; fax 708/755-0940; www.chparkdistrict.org.

Chicago Ridge Park District: 10736 S. Lombard Ave., Chicago Ridge; 708/857-2653; fax 708/636-5758; www.chicagoridgeparks.com.

Clarendon Hills Park District: 315 Chicago Ave., Clarendon Hills; 630/323-2626; fax 630/323-5362; www.clarendonhillsparkdistrict.org.

Clyde Park District: 1909 S. Laramie Ave., Cicero; 708/652-3545; fax 708/652-3549; www.clydeparkdistrct.com.

Forest Preserve District of Cook County: 536 N. Harlem Ave., River Forest; 800/870-3666; www.fpdcc.com.

Country Club Hills Park District: Civic Center/Administrative Center, 4200 W. 183rd St., Country Club Hills; 708/798-8497; fax 708/798-7352; www.cchparks.org.

Countryside Recreation Department: 5550 East Ave., Countryside; 708/482-3645, ext. 2595; www.countryside-il.org.

Crete Park District: 515 First St., Crete; 708/672-6969; fax 708/672-6945; www.cretepark.com.

Crystal Lake Park District: 1 E. Crystal Lake Ave., Crystal Lake; 815/459-0680; fax 815/477-5005; www.crystallakeparks.org.

Darien Park District: 133 Plainfield Rd., Darien; 630/655-6400; www.darienparks.com.

Deerfield Park District: 836 Jewett Park Dr., Deerfield; 847/945-0650; fax 847/945-0699; www.deerfieldparkdistrict.org.

Des Plaines Park District: 2222 Birch St., Des Plaines; 847/391-5700; fax 847/391-5707; www.desplainesparks.org.

Dolton Park District: 721 Engle St., Dolton; 708/841-2111; fax 708/841-2177.

Downers Grove Park District: 2455 Warrenville Rd., Downers Grove; 630/963-1304; fax 630/963-1543; www.dgparks.org.

Dundee Township Park District: 665 Barrington Ave., Carpentersville; 847/428-7131; fax 847/836-2380; www.dtpd.org.

DuPage County Forest Preserves: 3 S. 580 Naperville Rd., Wheaton; 630/933-7200; www.dupageforest.com.

Elgin Parks & Recreation Department: 100 Symphony Way, Elgin; 847/931-6120; fax 847/531-7020; www.cityofelgin.org.

Elk Grove Park District: 499 Biesterfield Rd., Elk Grove Village; 847/437-9494; fax 847/228-3508; www.elkgroveparks.org.

Elmhurst Park District: 225 Prospect Ave., Elmhurst; 630/993-8900; fax 630/993-8913; www.epd.org.

Elmwood Park Parks and Recreation: 11 Conti Pkwy., Elmwood Park; 708/452-7300; www.elmwoodpark.org.

Village of Elwood Park & Recreation Department: 201 E. Mississippi, Elwood; 815/423-6778; fax 815/423-6861.

City of Evanston Parks, Forestry and Recreation: 2100 Ridge Ave., Evanston; 847/866-2900; www.cityofevanston.org.

Evergreen Park Recreation Department: 3450 W. 97th St., Evergreen Park; 708/229-3373; fax 708/636-8686; www.evergreenpark-ill.com.

Park District of Forest Park: 7501 Harrison St., Forest Park; 708/366-7500; fax 708/366-1142; www.pdofp.org.

Fox Lake Parks and Recreation Department: 66 Thillen Dr., Fox Lake; 847/587-2151; fax 847/587-2237; www.foxlake.org.

Fox River Grove Recreational Council: P.O. Box 461, Fox River Grove; 847/516-0755; www.frgrc.org.

Fox Valley Park District: 712 S. River St., Aurora; 630/897-0516; fax 630/897-6896; www.foxvalleyparkdistrict.org.

Frankfort Park District: 140 Oak St., Frankfort; 815/469-9400; fax 815/469-9275; www.frankfortparks.org.

Frankfort Square Park District: 7540 West Braemar Lane, Frankfort; 815/469-3524; fax 815/469-8657; www.fspd.org.

Park District of Franklin Park: 9560 Franklin Ave., Franklin Park; 847/455-2852; fax 847/455-9053; www.fpparks.org.

Geneva Park District: 710 Western Ave., Geneva; 630/232-4542; fax 630/232-4569; www.genevaparks.org.

Glencoe Park District: 999 Green Bay Rd., Glencoe; 847/835-4648; fax 847/835-4942; www.glencoeparkdistrict.com.

Glendale Heights Park District: 250 Civic Center Plaza, Glendale Heights; 630/260-6060; fax 630/260-6733; www.glendaleheights.org.

Glenview Park District: 1930 Prairie St., Glenview; 847/657-3215; fax 847/724-8601; www.glenviewparkdist.org.

Godley Park District: 500 South Kankakee St., Godley; 815/458-6129; fax 815/458-6108.

Grayslake Park District: 151 Hawley St., Grayslake; 847/223-4404; fax 847/223-6386; www.glpd.com.

Gurnee Park District: 4374 Old Grand Ave., Gurnee; 847/623-7788; fax 847/623-8121; www.gurneeparkdistrict.com.

Hampshire Park District: 390 South Ave., Hampshire; 847/683-2690; fax 847/683-1741; www.hampshireparkdistrict.org.

Hanover Park District: 1919 Walnut, Hanover Park; 630/837-2468; fax 630/837-9720.

Harvard Parks and Recreation: 201 W. Front St., Harvard; 815/943-6468; fax 815/943-4556; www.cityofharvard.org.

Harvey Park District: 15335 Broadway Ave., Harvey; 708/331-3857; fax 708/331-8531; www.harveyparkdistrict.org.

Hazel Crest Park District: 2600 W. 171st St., Hazel Crest; 708/335-1500; fax 708/335-0355.

Hickory Hills Park District: 8047 W. 91st Pl., Hickory Hills; 708/598-1233; fax 708/598-0084; www.hhparkdistrict.org.

Park District of Highland Park: 636 Ridge Rd., Highland Park; 847/831-3810; fax 847/831-0818; www.pdhp.org.

Memorial Park District: 700 Speechley Blvd., Hillside; 708/547-3900; fax 708/547-3342; www.mempark.org.

Village of Hinsdale Park and Recreation Department: 19 East Chicago Ave., Hinsdale; 630/789-7090; fax 630/789-7016; www.villageofhinsdale .org/pr.

Hodgkins Park District: 8997 Lyons St., Hodgkins; 708/354-6563; fax 708/354-9269.

Hoffman Estates Park District: 1685 W. Higgins Rd., Hoffman Estates; 847/885-7500; www.heparks.org.

Homewood-Flossmoor Park District: 3301 Flossmoor Rd., Flossmoor; 708/957-0300; fax 708/957-8574; www.hfparks.com.

Huntley Park District: 11419 Rt. 47, Huntley; 847/669-3180; fax 847/669-2836; www.huntleyparks.org.

Inverness Park District: 300 Highland Rd., Inverness; 847/934-6300; fax 847/934-8867; www.invernessparkdistrict.com.

Island Lake Parks and Recreation Department: 3720 Greenleaf Ave., Island Lake; 847/526-4851; fax 847/526-1534; www.villageofislandlake.com.

Itasca Park District: 350 E. Irving Park Rd., Itasca; 630/773-2257; fax 630/773-4524; www.itascaparkdistrict.com.

Joliet Park District: 3000 W. Jefferson St., Joliet; 815/741-PARK; fax 815/741-7280; www.jolietpark.org.

Justice Park District: 7747 S. Oak Grove Ave., Justice; 708/458-1370; fax 708/458-1371.

Forest Preserve District of Kane County: 719 S. Batavia Ave., Building G, Geneva; 630/232-5980; fax 630/232-5924; www.co.kane.il.us/forest.

Village of Kenilworth Park District: 419 Richmond Rd., Kenilworth; 847/251-1691; fax 847/251-3908; www.villageofkenilworth.org.

Park District of LaGrange: 4903 Gilbert Ave., LaGrange; 708/352-1762; fax 708/352-8591; www.pdlg.org.

Community Park District of LaGrange Park: 920 Barnsdale Rd., LaGrange Park; 708/354-4580; fax 708/354-4577; www.communityparkdistrict.org.

Lake Bluff Park District: 355 W. Washington Ave.; 847/234-4150; www.lakebluffparks.org.

Lake County Forest Preserves: 2000 N. Milwaukee Ave., Libertyville; 847/367-6640; fax 847/367-6649; www.lcfpd.org.

Lake Forest Open Lands Association: 272 E. Deerpath Rd., Lake Forest; 847/234-3880; www.lfola.org.

Lake Forest Parks & Recreation Department: 400 Hastings Rd., Lake Forest; 847/234-2600; fax 847/615-4251; www.cityoflakeforest.com.

Lake in the Hills Parks and Recreation Department: 847/960-7460; fax 847/960-7465; www.lith.org.

Lakemoor Parks and Recreation Board: 234 W. Rand Rd., Lakemoor; 815/385-1117; www.lakemoor.net.

Lake Zurich Park and Recreation Department: 200 S. Rand Rd., Lake Zurich; 847/438-5146; fax 847/540-5081; www.volz.org.

Lemont Park District: 16028 127th St., Lemont; 630/257-6787; fax 630/257-6944; www.lemontparkdistrict.org.

Libertyville Parks and Recreation Department: 625 West Winchester Rd., Libertyville; 847/918-PARK (847/918-7275); fax 847/362-0815; www.libertyville.com.

Lincolnshire Park Board: 1 Old Half Day Rd., Lincolnshire; 847/883-8600; fax 847/883-8608; www.lincolnshire.recware.com.

Lincolnwood Parks & Recreation Department: 847/677-9740; www.lincolnwoodil.org.

Lindenhurst Park District: 22oo E. Grass Lake Rd., Lindenhurst; 847/356-6011; fax 847/356-6063; www.lindenhurstparks.org.

Lisle Park District: 1825 Short St., Lisle; 630/964-3410; fax 630/964-7448; www.lisleparkdistrict.org.

Lockport Township Park District: 1911 S. Lawrence Ave., Lockport; 815/838-1183; fax 815/838-4974; www.lockportpark.org.

Lombard Park District: 820 S. Finley Rd., Lombard; 630/627-1281; fax 630/627-1286; www.lombardparks.com.

Markham Park District: 16053 Richmond Ave., Markham; 708/596-3366; fax 708/596-3373.

Matteson Parks & Recreation Division: 4450 West Oakwood Ln., Matteson; 708/748-1080; fax 708/748-1423; www.vil.matteson.il.us.

Maywood Park District: 921 S. 9th Ave., Maywood; 708/344-4740; fax 708/344-1553.

McCook Park District: 4911 Riverside Ave., McCook; 708/447-7048; fax 708/447-7157.

McHenry County Conservation District: 18410 U.S. Highway 14, Woodstock; 815/338-MCCD (815/338-6223); fax 815/334-2877; www.mccdistrict.org.

McHenry Parks and Recreation Department: 333 S. Green St., McHenry; 815/363-2160; fax 815/363-3186; www.ci.mchenry.il.us.

Midlothian Park District: 4500 S. Kostner, Midlothian; 708/371-6191; fax 708/371-6375; www.midlothianparkdistrict.org.

Morton Grove Park District: 6834 W. Dempster, Morton Grove; 847/965-1200; fax 847/965-7484; www.mortongroveparks.com.

Mt. Prospect Park District: 1000 W. Central Rd., Mount Prospect; 847/255-5380; fax 847/255-1438; www.mppd.org.

Mundelein Park and Recreation District: 1401 N. Midlothian Rd., Mundelein; 847/566-0650; fax 847/566-8557; www.mundeleinparks.org.

Naperville Park District: 320 W. Jackson Ave., Naperville; 630/848-5000; fax 630/848-5001; www.napervilleparks.org.

New Lenox Community Park District: One West Manor Dr., New Lenox; 815/485-3584; fax 815/485-3589.

Niles Park District: 6676 W. Howard St., Niles; 847/967-6633; www.niles-parks.org.

Norridge Park District: 4631 N. Overhill Ave., Norridge; 708/457-1244; fax 708/457-8385; www.norridgepk.com.

North Barrington Parks and Recreation Commission: 111 Old Barrington Rd., North Barrington; 847/381-6000; fax 847/381-3303; www.northbarrington.org.

Northbrook Park District: 545 Academy Dr., Northbrook; 847/291-2960; www.nbparks.org.

Northfield Park District: 401 Wagner Rd., Northfield; 847/446-4428; fax 847/446-4431; www.nbparks.org.

North Riverside Parks and Recreation Department: 2401 S. DesPlaines Ave., North Riverside; 708/442-5515; fax 708/447-4292; www.northriverside-il.org.

Oak Brook Park District: 1450 Forest Gate Road, Oak Brook; 630/990-4233; fax 630/990-8379; www.obparks.org.

Oak Forest Park District: 15601 S. Central Ave., Oak Forest; 708/687-7270; fax 708/687-9937; www.oakforestparks.org.

Oak Lawn Park District: 9400 S. Kenton Ave., Oak Lawn; 708/857-1044; fax 708/636-9877; www.olparks.com.

Park District of Oak Park: 218 Madison St., Oak Park; 708/383-0002; fax 708/383-5702; www.oakparkparks.com.

Olympia Fields Park District: 20712 Western Ave., Olympia Fields; 708/481-7313; fax 708/481-8735; www.olympiafieldsparkdistrict.org.

Orland Hills Recreation Department: 16553 S. Haven Ave., Orland Hills; 708/349-7211; fax 708/349-3840; www.orlandhills.org.

Orland Park Village Recreation: Loebe Recreation Center, 14650 South Ravinia Ave., Orland Park; 708/403-7275; fax 708/403-6274; www.orland-park.il.us.

Oswegoland Park District: 313 E. Washington St., Oswego; 630/554-1010; fax 630/554-1577; www.oswegolandparkdistrict.org.

Palatine Park District: 250 E. Wood St., Palatine; 847/991-0333; fax 847/991-2127; www.palatineparks.org.

Palos Heights Recreation Department: 6601 W. 127th St., Palos Heights; 708/361-1807; fax 708/361-7679; www.palosheights.org.

Palos Park Recreation: 8901 W. 123rd St., Palos Park; 708/671-3760; fax 708/671-3767; www.palospark.org.

Park Forest Recreation and Parks: 350 Victory Dr., Park Forest; 708/748-2005; fax 708/503-8561; www.villageofparkforest.com.

Park Ridge Recreation and Park District: 2701 Sibley, Park Ridge; 847/692-5127; fax 847/692-6949; www.parkridgeparkdistrict.com.

Peotone Park District: 8 Blue Devil Dr., Peotone; 708/258-3343; fax 708/258-0562.

Prospect Heights Park District: 110 W. Camp McDonald Rd., Prospect Heights; 847/394-2848; fax 847/394-7799; www.phparkdist.org.

Richmond/Spring Grove Recreation Program: 5600 Hunter Dr., Richmond; 815/678-4040; www.richmond-il.com.

Richton Park Parks and Recreation: 4455 W. Sauk Trail, Richton; 708/481-8950; fax 708/481-8980; www.richtonpark.org.

Riverdale Park District: 151 W. 137th St., Riverdale; 708/841-0095.

River Forest Park District: 401 Thatcher Ave., River Forest; 708/366-6660; www.rfpd.com.

River Grove Recreation: 2621 Thatcher Ave., River Grove; 708/453-8000, ext 303; http://vorg.us.

Riverside Playground & Recreation Board: 10 Pine Ave., Riverside; 708/442-7025; fax 708/442-9161; http://riverside.il.us.

Rolling Meadows Park District: 3000 Central Rd., Rolling Meadows; 847/818-3220; fax 847/818-3224; www.rmparks.org.

Romeoville Recreation Department: 900 West Romeo Rd., Romeoville; 815/886-6222; fax 815/886-6245; www.romeoville.org.

Roselle Park District: 555 W. Bryn Mawr Ave., Roselle; 630/894-4200; fax 630/894-5610; www.roselleparkdistrict.com.

Rosemont Park District: 6140 N. Scott, Rosemont; 847/823-6685; fax 847/823-5798.

Round Lake Area Park District: 814 Hart Rd., Round Lake; 847/546-8558; fax 847/740-8180; www.rlapd.org.

Schaumburg Park District: 235 E. Beech Dr., Schaumburg; 847/985-2115; fax 847/985-2114; www.parkfun.com.

Village of Schiller Park Recreation Department: 9526 Irving Park Rd., Schiller Park; 847/678-2550; fax 847/671-3564; www.villageofschillerpark.com.

Shorewood Parks and Recreation Department: 903 W. Jefferson St., Shorewood; 815/725-2150; www.vil.shorewood.il.us.

Skokie Park District: 9300 Weber Park Pl., Skokie; 847/674-1500; fax 847/674-9201; www.skokieparkdistrict.org. South Elgin Parks and Recreation: 10 N. Water St., South Elgin; 847/622-0003; fax 847/622-0462; www.southelgin.com.

South Barrington Park District: 3 Tennis Club Ln., South Barrington; 847/381-7515; fax 847/381-2824; www.sbpd.net.

South Holland Parks and Recreation Department: 501 E. 170th St., South Holland; 708/331-2940; fax 708/331-3202; www.southholland.org.

St. Charles Park District: 8 North Ave., St. Charles; 630/584-1055; fax 630/584-9172; www.st-charlesparks.org.

Streamwood Park District: 777 Bartlett Rd., Streamwood; 630/372-PARK; www.streamwoodparkdistrict.org.

Sugar Grove Park District: 61 Main St., Sugar Grove; 630/466-7436; fax 630/466-8675; www.sgparks.org.

Summit Park District: 5700 S. Archer Rd., Summit; 708/496-1012; fax 708/496-7275.

Tinley Park District: 8125 W. 171st St., Tinley Park; 708/342-4200; fax 708/342-4291; www.tinleyparkdistrict.org.

University Park Parks and Recreation Department: 698 Burnham Dr., University Park; 708/534-6456; fax 708/534-4837; www.university-park-il.com.

Vernon Hills Park District: 294 Evergreen Dr., Vernon Hills; 847/996-6800; fax 847/996-6801; www.vhparkdistrict.org.

Villa Park Parks and Recreation: 320 E. Wildwood St., Villa Park; 630/834-8525; fax 630/834-8528; www.invillapark.com.

Warrenville Park District: 3 S. 260 Warren Ave., Warrenville; 630/393-7279; fax 630/393-7282; www.warrenvilleparks.org.

Wauconda Park District: 600 N. Main St., Wauconda; 847/526-3610; fax 847/526-3791; www.waucondaparks.com.

Waukegan Park District: 2000 Belvidere St., Waukegan; 847/360-4700; fax 847/244-8270; www.waukeganparks.org.

Westchester Park District: 10201 Bond St., Westchester; 708/865-8200; fax 708/865-8242; www.wpdparks.org.

West Chicago Park District: 157 W. Washington St., West Chicago; 630/231-9474; fax 630/231-2352; www.we-goparks.org.

Western Springs Parks: P.O. Box 35, Western Springs; 708/246-4225; www.wsparks.org.

Westmont Park District: 55 E. Richmond St., Westmont; 630/969-8080; fax 630/969-7923; www.wpd4fun.org.

Wheaton Park District: 666 S. Main St., Wheaton; 630/665-4710; fax 630/665-5880; www.wheatonparkdistrict.com.

Wheeling Park District: 333 W. Dundee Rd., Wheeling; 847/465-3333; fax 847/537-3481; www.wheelingparkdistrict.com.

Forest Preserve District of Will County: 17540 W. Laraway Rd., Joliet; 815/727-8700; fax 814/722-3608; www.fpdwc.org.

Willowbrook Parks and Recreation Department: 7760 Quincy St., Willowbrook; 630/323-8215; fax 630/323-0787; www.willowbrookil.org.

Wilmette Park District: 1200 Wilmette Ave., Wilmette; 847/256-6100; www.wilmettepark.org.

Winfield Park District: 0N020 County Farm Rd., Winfield; 630/653-3811; fax 630/653-3919; www.winfieldparkdistrict.com.

Winnetka Park District: 540 Hibbard Rd.; 847/501-2040; fax 847/501-5779; www.winpark.org.

Wood Dale Park District: 111 E. Foster Ave., Wood Dale; 630/595-9333; fax 630/595-9699; www.wooddaleparkdistrict.org.

Woodridge Park District: 2600 Center Dr., Woodridge; 630/353-3300; fax 630/353-3310; www.woodridgeparks.org.

Woodstock Recreation Department: 820 Lake Ave., Woodstock; 815/338-4363; fax 815/334-2279; www.woodstockil.gov.

Worth Park District: 11500 S. Beloit Ave., Worth; 708/448-7080; fax 708/448-4079; www.worthparkdistrict.org.

Zion Park District: 2400 Dowie Memorial Dr., Zion; 847/746-5500; fax 847/746-5506; www.zionparkdistrict.org.

Community Groups and Resources

There's no better way to improve the life of your pup than to get involved with those agencies that make the rules on dog parks, dogfighting, and other dog-related issues.

Beck Lake Dog Area Group: 8939A Robin Dr., Des Plaines; 847/635-7024; www.becklakedogs.org.

The Canine Clubhouse: Online and real-world community for dog lovers. www.thecanineclubhouse.com.

Chicago Canines: Listserv for local dog lovers. www.chicagocanine.com.

Chicagoland Tails: Bimonthly newspaper with local doggy event updates. www.chicagolandtails.com.

Dog Advisory Work Group (D.A.W.G.): 312/409-2169; www.dawgsite.org.

Friends of the Chicago River: 312/939-0490; www.chicagoriver.org.

Friends of the City of David R. Lee Animal Care Shelter: 312/747-1392.

Friends of the Forest Preserves: www.fotfp.org

Friends of the Parks: www.fotp.org.

Hamlin Dog Park Group: 773/525-8592.

Hollywoof Action Committee: Working toward a new DFA in Edgewater. www.hollywoof.org.

Hyde Bark D.O.G.: www.hydebarkdog.org.

Midway Plaisance Advisory Council: 1130 Midway Plaisance, Chicago; 312/745-2470; www.hydepark.org/parks/midway/midway.html.

MonDog: Montrose Harbor Dog Beach/Susan Kimmelman Off-Leash Dog Beach group. www.mondog.org.

Paws Park Advisory Group: Overseeing the DFA in River Park. 773/960-8494.

Puptown Dog Owners Group: 2422 W. Gunnison, #1, Chicago; 312/294-2500; www.puptown.org.

South Loop DogPAC: Overseeing Grant Bark. www.southloopdogs.com.

Veterinarians and Emergency Hospitals

Accidents happen. The following is a list of some of the area's emergency animal clinics (some are open 24 hours, but most are open nights and weekends only, when most veterinarians are closed), as well as a sample of full-service and specialty veterinarians. Here's hoping you won't need them, but better safe than sorry.

CHICAGO

Chicago Veterinary Emergency Services: Late-night and weekend veterinary care on the North Side. 3123 N. Clybourn Ave.; 773/281-7110.

Family Pet Animal Hospital: Full-service traditional and alternative veterinary care. 1401 W. Webster Ave.; 773/935-2311; www.familypetanimalhospital.com.

Handle with Care: Dr. Kimberly Curtis offers home veterinary services, acupuncture, and chiropractic treatment. 312/458-0969.

Paws Chicago Lurie Family Spay/Neuter Clinic: Low-cost spay and neuter facility. 3516 W. 26th St.; 773/521-SPAY (773/521-7729).

Portage Park Animal Hospital: Traditional veterinary services. 5419 W. Irving Park Rd.; 773/725-0260; www.portagepark.com.

The Royal Treatment Veterinary Spa: 1500 N. Wells St.; 312/440-9663; www.royaltreatmentvetspa.com.

Judith Swanson, DVM: Alternative pet medicine including acupuncture and homeopathy. 1465 W. Catalpa Ave.; 773/561-4526; www.4mfg.net/drswanson.

SUBURBS

Animal Emergency and Referral Center: 1810 Skokie Blvd., Northbrook; 847/564-5775.

Animal E.R. of Arlington Heights: 1195 E. Palatine Rd., Arlington Heights; 847/394-6049; www.pettrauma.com.

Animal 911: 3735 W. Dempster, Skokie; 847/328-9110.

Bramer Animal Hospital: 1021 Davis St., Evanston; 847/864-1700; www.brameranimalhospital.com.

Dundee Animal Hospital: 199 Penny Ave., Dundee; 847/428-6114.

TOPS Veterinary Rehabilitation: 1440 E. Belvidere Rd., Grayslake; 847/548-9470; www.tops-vet-rehab.com.

Veterinary Specialty Center, Emergency & Critical Care: 1515 Busch
Pkwy., Buffalo Grove; 847/459-7535; www.vetspecialty.com.

Groomers

A clean dog is a happy dog. OK, dogs don't care...a clean dog is a happy
dog owner.

CHICAGO

Animal Lovers Pet Salon: 2277 N. Clybourn Ave.; 773/296-9343.

Bark Bark Club: 5943 N. Broadway; 773/878-7233; www.barkbarkclub.com.

City Groomers: 1407 W. Irving Park Rd.; 773/832-4711.

Dog Day Afternoon: 6712 W. Belmont Ave.; 773/685-0404.

Doggy Dooz Pet Styling: 1111 W. Belmont Ave.; 773/472-9944.

Dog House of Beauty: 3806 W. Irving Park Rd.; 773/588-8586;
www.doghouseofbeauty.com.

The Dog Scene: 5637 N. Ashland Ave.; 773/334-2121.

Dogs Only Grooming Salon: 361 E. 69th St.; 773/224-3661.

Groomies: 22 E. Elm St.; 312/654-9555.

Grooming Gallery: 911 N. Damen Ave.; 773/252-7400.

Happy Tails: 3335 N. Broadway St.; 773/348-9625.

Paws-a-tively!: 109 W. North Ave.; 312/951-6547.

Pet Friendly: 2748 N. Southport Ave.; 773/472-8169.

Poodle Pampering: 4949 N. Damen; 773/561-8125; www.poodlepampering.com.

Ruby Room: Boutique people spa offers in-home energy healing for your
pooch. 1743 W. Division St.; 773/235-2323; www.rubyroom.com.

Ruff Haus Pets: 4652 N. Rockwell; 773/478-5100; www.ruffhauspets.com.

Scrub A Dub Dub: 1478 W. Summerdale Ave.; 773/275-PETS; www.scruba
dubdub.net.

Scrub Your Pup: 2935 N. Clark St; 773/348-6218; www.scrubyourpup.com.

Shear Critters: 5281 N. Elston Ave.; 773/205-7255.

Sit! Chicago: 2316 W. Leland Ave.; 773/784-2741; www.sitchicago.com.

Soggy Paws: Two locations for this self-service or grooming shop.
1148 W. Leland Ave.; 773/334-7663; and 1912 S. State St.; 312/808-0768;
www.soggypaws.com.

Spa Bark: Mobile grooming out of Bark Chicago Inc.; 773/486-BARK (773/486-2275); www.barkchicago.com.

Streeterville Pet Spa & Boutique: 401 E. Ontario; 312/787/7792; www.streetervillepet.com.

Three Pups in a Tub: 556 W. 37th St.; 773/268-WASH (773/268-8274).

Underdogg, Inc.: 1157 N. State St.; 312/482-8947.

SUBURBS

All My Dogs: 689 N. Cass, Westmont; 630/321-1088.

Animal Artistry: 600 Waukegan Rd., Glenview; 847/486-8300.

The Barker Shop: 1404 W. 55th St., LaGrange; 708/354-0400; www.thebarkershop.com.

Beauty in the Beast Professional Pet Grooming: 740 12th St., Kenilworth; 847/251-2288.

Cameo Pet Grooming: 220 W. Crystal Ave., Lombard; 630/268-8888; www.cameopetgrooming.com.

Canine Coiffure: Grooming with kennel service. 454 Green Bay Rd., Highwood; 847/432-0771.

The Clip Joint: 277 Green Bay Road, Wilmette; 847/256-5570; www.clipjoint.offthewallquest.com.

Cut and Dry Dog Grooming: 2958 Central St., Evanston; 847/328-6277.

Dede's Shear Magic: 3100 Grand Blvd., Brookfield; 708/387-0088; www.dedesltd.com.

The Dog Wash: 340 Linden Ave., Wilmette; 847/256-8440.

For Pet's Sake: Mobile grooming. 847/491-1057.

Fritz n' Al's Place: 6421 N. Cicero Ave., Lincolnwood; 847/329-9923.

Groomingayle's Pet Salon: 1719 Glenview Rd., Glenview; 847/998-9100.

Lil' Critter Dog Grooming: 731 E. Roosevelt Rd., Lombard; 630/627-5488.

Love on a Leash Grooming Salon: 570 S. York St., Elmhurst; 630/941-0589.

Pats Grooming Emporium: Boarding and play groups, too. 7638 Madison, Forest Park; 708/366-0430.

Paws Here: 502 Pennsylvania Ave., Glen Ellyn; 630/858-7052.

Pet Boutique: 1087 Conway Rd., Lake Forest; 847/615-9663.

Poochie Barber: 9707 Southwest Hwy., Oak Lawn; 708/422-0255.

Puttin' on the Ritz Pet Salon: 615 S. LaGrange Rd., LaGrange; 708/588-0700.

Rover's Place: Doggy daycare, boarding, and dog wash. 1238 Old Skokie Rd., Highland Park; 847/831-3784; www.roversplacechicago.com.

Scoo-B-Do's: 9 Jackson St., East Dundee; 847/426-2284.

Scrubbers: 404 Lake St., Oak Park; 708/358-0181.

Shaggy Dog Shop, Inc.: Offers pick-up and delivery. 1339 N. Western Ave., Lake Forest; 847/234-2383.

Shear Comfort: 433 Asbury Ave., Evanston; 847/328-1210.

Sun Dog Pet Supplies: 6120 S. Cass Ave., Westmont; 630/968-0799.

Yuppie Puppy Dog & Cat Grooming: 807 N. Harlem Ave., Oak Park; 708/358-2200.

Yuppy Puppy Inc.: Specializes in spa treatments for North Shore pooches. 970 N. Shore Dr., Lake Bluff; 847/234-6200; www.ayuppypuppy.com.

Animal Shelters

A friend in need is a friend indeed. If you're in the market for a furry friend, consider one of these shelters. In addition to adopting out needy animals, many host fun events throughout the year, and all are in constant need of donations and volunteers.

CHICAGO

Animal Adoption Associates: Former home to Natasha, Trouble, and Bella. 2046 W. Irving Park Rd.; 773/348-0042.

Anti-Cruelty Society: Boris and Milo's former home. 510 N. LaSalle St.; 312/644-8338; www.anticruelty.org.

Chicago Canine Rescue: 312/850-1254.

City of Chicago Animal Care and Control: Watson's previous address. 2741 S. Western Ave.; 312/744-5000; www.cityofchicago.org.

4 Legs: Pet supply store with an adoption resource center. 3809 N. Clark St; 773/472-5347.

Lake Shore Animal Shelter: 13 W. Lake St.; 312/409-1162; www.lakeshore animalshelter.org.

PAWS Chicago: Rescuer of Scully, Stella, and many others. 1997 N. Clybourn Ave.; 773/935-PAWS; www.pawschicago.org.

Red Door Animal Shelter: 2410 W. Lunt; 773/764-2242; www.reddoorshelter .org.

SUBURBS

Adopt-A-Pet: P.O. Box 408, Mt. Prospect; 847/870-8999; www.adoptapet-il.org.

Anderson Animal Shelter: 420 Industrial Dr., Naperville; 630/355-2299; www.adoptpetshelter.org.

Anderson Animal Shelter: 1000 S. La Fox Rd., South Elgin; 847/697-2881; www.andersonanimalshelter.org.

Animal Care League: 1013 Garfield St., Oak Park; 708/848-8155; www.animalcareleague.org.

Animal House Shelter: 13005 Ernesti Rd., Huntley; 847/977-2066; www.animalhouseshelter.com.

Animal Welfare League: 6224 S. Wabash, Chicago, and 10305 Southwest Highway, Chicago Ridge; 708/636-8586; www.animalwelfareleague.com.

A Caring Place Humane Society: P.O. Box 2481, Darien; 630/375-7976; www.acaringplacehs.org.

DuPage County Animal Care & Control: 120 N. County Farm Rd., Wheaton; 630/682-7197; www.dupageco.org/animalcontrol.

Evanston Animal Shelter, C.A.R.E: 2310 Oakton St., Evanston; 847/866-5080; www.care-evanston.org.

Fox Valley Animal Welfare League: 600 S. River St., Aurora; 630/892-9445; www.fvawl.org.

Helping Paws Animal Welfare Association: 257 King St., Crystal Lake; 815/459-2641; www.helpingpaws.net.

Hinsdale Humane Society: 22 N. Elm St., Hinsdale; 630/323-5630; hinsdalehumanesociety.org.

Humane Society of Plainfield: 14411 S. Route 59, Plainfield; 815/436-2700.

Joliet Township Animal Control: 2807 McDonough, Joliet; 815/725-0333.

Naperville Area Humane Society: 1620 W. Diehl Rd., Naperville; 630/420-8989; www.napervillehumanesociety.org.

Oak Park Animal Care League: 1013 Garfield, Oak Park; 708/848-8155; www.animalcareleague.org.

Orphans of the Storm: 2200 Riverwoods Rd., Riverwoods; 847/945-0235; www.orphansofthestorm.org.

Save-A-Pet: 31664 N. Fairfield Rd., Grayslake; 847/740-7788; www.save-a-pet-il.org.

Skokie Animal Control: 5127 W. Oakton, Skokie; 847/933-8484; www.skokie.org/health/animal.html.

Stray's Halfway House: P.O. Box 68811, Schaumburg; 630/351-3150; www.strayshh.org.

South Side Humane Society: 6363 Lincoln Highway, Matteson; 708/720-2440.

South Suburban Humane Society: 1103 W. End Ave., Chicago Heights; 708/755-7387; www.sshspets.org.

West Suburban Humane Society: 1901 W. Ogden Ave., Downers Grove; 630/960-9601; www.wshs-dg.org.

Will County Animal Control: 1200 S. Cedar Rd., New Lenox; 815/462-5633.

Will County Humane Society: 24109 W. Seil Rd., Shorewood; 815/741-0695; http://willcountyhumane.com.

Transportation and Pet Taxis

It's not quite as easy to get around town on four legs rather than two (you'd think the more legs, the better). Below are some pet taxi services that will take your dog to the vet or the groomer, as well as private firms that will shuttle you and your pup to the airport or wherever else you need.

Airport Express: Airport transport permits pets in kennels, price depends on destination. 888/2-THEVAN (888/284-3826); www.airportexpress.com.

Annie's Animals: 773/645-9970; www.anniesanimals.com.

Chicago Pet Chauffeurs: Door-to-door transportation will even take your dog on vet visits. 773/665-2327; www.chicagopetchauffeurs.com.

Duchman's Limousine: Airport transport permits pets with no additional charge. 708/895-6747.

Omega Airport Shuttle: Airport transport permits pets with a $7 fee. 773/483-6634; www.omegashuttle.com.

Out-U-Go: 6955 North Ave., Oak Park; 708/383-7905; www.outugo.com.

Paws Around Chicago: Pet taxi service in the city and suburbs, emergency service available late nights, weekends, and holidays. 773/418-2431.

Pet Domain: Pet taxi in the Loop and Gold Coast. 312/363-3013.

Smart Car: Airport and other transport permits pets in kennel, with a $15 fee. 800/871-7627.

312pets: Serving Downtown and the North Side. 312/923-9228 or 866/312-PETS (866/312-7387); www.312pets.com.

Dog Walkers and Doggy Daycare

It's a shame you can't take your pooch with you wherever you go, but these dog walkers and daycare providers offer an option for when you have to be away. Many dog walkers will visit your hotel room to keep your pup from disturbing the neighbors while you're out.

CHICAGO

A Bark in the Park: Also offers pet taxi services. 773/871-0124; www.a-bark .com.

All for Doggies: For the social dog, over five hours of playtime a day. Agility training, boarding, and grooming services available. 1760 N. Kilbourn; 773/395-0900; www.allfordoggies.com.

Bark Avenue Play Care: Daycare, boarding, training, and grooming. 1959 W. Fulton St.; 312/455-8582; www.barkavenueplaycare.com.

BARK Chicago Inc.: 2450 N. Western Ave.; 773/486-BARK (773/486-2285); 1804 W. Lake St; 312/850-BARK (312/850-2285); www.barkchicago.com.

The Barking Lot: Also offers grooming, pick-up and delivery services, and a retail store. A Webcam lets you watch your dog in the playrooms. 2442 W. Irving Park Rd.; 773/583-0065; www.barkinglotinc.com.

Bow Wow Lounge: Includes pick-up and drop-off services. 945 W. Dakin St.; 773/525-0277; www.bowwowlounge.com.

Canine Empire: Indoor swimming pool, 24/7 pick-up and drop-off at this club. 1765 N. Elston Ave.; 866/DOGS-RULE (866/364-7785); www.canineempire.com.

Chicago Dog Walkers: 2215 W. Cortland St.; 773/394-9961; www.chicago-dogwalkers.com.

Chicago Pet Care: Dog-walking specialty. 773/477-0136; www.chicagopet care.com.

Chicago Pet Sitting: 312/337-8474; www.chicagopetsitting.com.

Citizen Canine: A bed-and-breakfast for your dog. 2274 N. Clybourn Ave.; 773/935-3853; www.citizencaninechicago.com.

Cruisin' Canines: 773/327-4419; www.cruisincanines.com.

Danny's Dog Walkers: 773/728-4422; www.dannysdogwalkers.com.

DogoneFun!: Boarding and daycare in the South Loop with taxi service. 1717 S. State St; 312/765-9DOG (312/765-9364); www.dogonefunchicago.com.

D.O.G.S. Inc. of Chicago: 773/868-WOOF (773/868-9663); www.dogs-inc.com.

A Dog's Life: Has an indoor pool where you and your pooch can swim together. 4810 N. Clark St.; 773/271-5577.

Heathcliff's Doggie Daycare: 773/235-8893; www.ruff-ruff.net.

Hounds Unleashed: Serves the South Side, South Loop, and Near West Side. 773/251-5411; www.houndsunleashed.com.

K9-5 Dog Walking: Serves the North Side from Old Town to Evanston and out to Western Ave. 773/865-9516; www.K9-5.com.

Mid-Day Dog Walking: Heather Cajo and her staff walk pups in many neighborhoods in the city. 773/391-6102.

PeekaBoo's: Serves Evanston to UIC. 773/330-8368.

Pet Care Plus: Downtown location with a Webcam, so you can watch your puppy while you're apart. 312/397-9077; www.petcp.com.

Pet Depot: Boarding, day care, and pet taxi. 3618 N. Lincoln Ave.; 773/248-2022; www.petdepot.com.

Pet & Home Pros: South Loop dog walking and pet sitting. 801 S. Wells St.; 312/697-1013.

Pooch Chicago: Chic boarding with saltwater lap pool, organic food, and spa products. 2307 W. Belmont Ave.; 773/525-4006; www.poochhotel.com.

Rolling Bone: Dog walking in most neighborhoods. 1406 N. Western; 773/616-DOGS (773/616-3647); www.rollingbone.com.

Urban Canine: 2336 W. North Ave.; 773/278-6888.

Urban Out Sitters: Cage-free boarding, offered 24/7. 729 W. Randolph, 3241 N. Dayton St, and 161 N. Halsted.; 312/651-PETS (312/651-7387); www.urbanoutsitters.com.

Urban Pet Sitters: Service to the North Side. www.urbanpetsitters.com.

Urban Tailblazers: 773/388-9800; www.urbantailblazers.com.

Valerie's Pet Service: Natasha and Cooper's home away from home. 773/871-1446.

WatchDogs: Pet sitting and dog walking in the north suburbs from Evanston to Highland Park. 847/877-3004; www.watchdoggies.com.

West Loop Canine Club: 1328 W. Lake St.; 312/666-8910.

Wicker Pet: Also has a retail store for gifts to assuage your guilt for leaving your pup. 2029 W. North Ave.; 773/489-2050; www.wickerpet.com.

Windy Sitters: 3501 N. Southport Ave.; 773/909-PETS (773/909-7387); www.windysitters.com.

SUBURBS

B. C. Dog Training, Boarding, and Daycare: 872 Tower Rd., Mundelein; 847/566-1960; www.bcdogtraining.com.

Carriage Hill Kennels: 2218 Waukegan Rd., Glenview; 847/724-0270; www.carriagehillkennels.com.

The Crate Escape: 500 Industrial Dr., Naperville; 630/579-1220; www.thecrateescape.com.

Kiss My K9: 1640 Orrington Ave., Evanston; 847/424-0517; www.kissmyk9.com.

Pet Au Pair, Inc.: Dog walking in the western suburbs. 630/234-6501.

Shirley's Pets: Serves the North Shore and Rogers Park. 847/322-1977.

Spike's: 725 Madison St., Oak Park; 708/386-9881; www.spikeshotel.com.

Tails A Waggin' In-Home Pet Care: P.O. Box 3793, Oak Park; 708/650-1386; http://tailsawaggin.net.

Trainers and Behaviorists

Sometimes a problem needs a professional's touch. These obedience experts often offer classes at a variety of locations in the city and suburbs.

AnimalSense: Group and individual sessions tailored to your dog's needs. 773/ASK-DOGS (773/275-3647); www.animalsense.com.

Anti-Cruelty Society: Low-cost, high-quality classes. 510 N. LaSalle St.; 312/644-8338; www.anticruelty.org.

Bob Andrysco: Private lessons for tough problems. 847/604-0132; www.petshrink.net.

Anything is PAWsible: 773/919-7297; www.anythingispawsible.com.

Call of the Wild: Private and group lessons. 3027 N. Rockwell St., Chicago; 773/539-1088; www.callofthewildschool.com.

Canine Obedience College: 4667 W. 120th St., Alsip; 708/389-3110.

Canis Sapiens: Jane Masterson offers force-free, reward-based training in the Hyde Park area. 773/913-2030; www.canissapiens.com.

Chicago Paws: Jeff Millman. 4502 N. Dover St.; 773/818-5570; www.chicagopaws.com.

A Closer Bond: Training with boarding, day care, and grooming services. 842 W. Northwest Hwy. Rd.; 847/358-7312; www.acloserbond.com.

Dog Obedience Group: 1943 W. Estes Ave.; 773/973-2934; www.dogobedience group.com.

Dogs Best Friend Ltd.: Certified applied animal behaviorists. 1039 Mills St., Black Earth, WI; 608/767-2435; www.dogsbestfriendtraining.com.

Elizabeth Hammond, CPDT: Specializes in puppies and dogs, group classes, in-home training, behavior problems, clicker training, and reward-based method. 773/610-5634.

Going to the Dogs: 630/887-9437.

Good Dog! Great Bod!: Summer sessions have you and your pet work out together with games and strength exercises. 847/905-1700; doggreatbod@ gmail.com.

Grateful Dog: 2640 Green Bay Rd., Evanston; 847/869-9738.

Il Cane Dolce: 2227 W. Belmont Ave., Chicago; 773/661-0135; www.ilcanedolce.com.

In-Home Dog Training by Janet Contursi: 773/851-0869.

King's Kennels: Provides training, boarding, and veterinary services. 238 Sanders Rd., Riverwoods; 847/945-9592.

MarKay Dog Training: Owner Kathy McCarthy specializes in private lessons. P.O. Box 34-364, Chicago; 773/282-4464; www.markaydog.com.

That's My Dog: Owner Marilyn Anderson also offers play sessions. 773/973-5217.

Kim Thorp: 773/443-6308; k9professor@aol.com.

A Treat to Train: 773/610-5634; www.treattotrain.com.

Two Paws Up Dog Training, Inc.: In-home obedience training. 847/341-1024.

Wet Nose Obedience and Behavior Training: Offers private training and classes at animal hospitals and park districts throughout the suburbs. 708/453-DOGS (708/453-3647); www.wetnoseobt.com.

Dog Bakeries

Not only do dog bakeries whip up something better than what comes out of a box, they're the pooch's version of a coffee shop—a great place to meet other dogs and find out the neighborhood scoop.

Barker's Gourmet Bakery: 5527 S. Harlem Ave., Round Lake Beach; 847/356-6750.

Bulldog Bakery: People bakery that sells dog treats. 1955 W. Belmont Ave., Chicago; 773/248-2934; www.bulldogbakery.net.

Cody & Carl's Blvd.: Among many other things, Cody & Carl offer cakes for dog birthday parties, showers, and even weddings. 756 W. Northwest Hwy., Barrington; 847/304-7140; www.codyandcarlsblvd.net.

The Down Town Dog: 111 N. State St, Chicago; 312/782-4575; and 57 E. Scranton Ave., Lake Bluff; 847/295-BARK (847/295-2275); www.shopthedog .com.

Fido Food Fair: Deli and Happy Tails grooming all in one. 5416 N. Clark St., Chicago; 773/506-9063; www.fidofoodfair.com.

The Furry Beastro: A bakery, spa, and more. 1600 N. Wells; 312/932-WOOF (312/932-9663); www.thefurrybeastro.com.

Galloping Gourmutts: All-natural treats for canines. 2736 N. Lincoln Ave., Chicago; 773/477-5959; www.gallopinggourmutts.com.

Happy Dog Barkery: 5118 Main St., Downers Grove; 630/512-0822; www.happydogbarkery.com.

Healthy Hounds Dog Barkery & Boutique: No wheat, corn, additives, pre-servatives, or dyes in these food items. Also has classes and events for own-ers. 2550 Central Dr., Flossmoor; 708/922-2910; www.healthyhoundsdog barkeryandboutique.com.

The Hungry Pup: 941 Chicago Ave., Evanston; 847/866-9355.

It's a Dog's Life Bakery: 3576 W. 95th St., Evergreen Park; 708/424-3993.

K9 Cookie Company: Also offers delivery. 723 South Blvd., Oak Park; 708/848-K9K9 (708/848-5959); www.k9cookiecompany.com.

Off the Leash: 4955 N. Damen; 773/728-PUPS (773/728-7877); www.offtheleashpets.com.

Tails in the City: Check out the "dogsticker" (a potsticker-shaped treat). 1 E. Delaware Pl., 312/649-0347; www.tailsinthecity.com.

Très Bone Bakery & Boutique: 508 N. Seymour Ave., Mundelein; 847/837-8901; www.thepetgourmet.com.

Two Bostons: Pet boutique and gourmet bakery. 232 S. Washington St., Naperville; 630/357-7621; www.two-bostons.com.

Whisker Licken Pet Pastries: P.O. Box 72972, Roselle; 630/351-4558.

Waste Removal Services

It doesn't matter if you scoop the poop or pay someone else to pick it up: Just do it.

Doggy Detail: North and northwest suburbs. 847/212-5616.

Have Doggie, We'll Do: Will clean up at your place or sell you biodegradable bags to help you do it yourself. 773/286-4727; www.masterscoopers.com.

K-9 Poop Patrol: 847/414-8543; www.k-9pooppatrol.com.

Poopatrol: 826 N. Ellsworth St., Naperville; 630/428-7806.

Poop B' Gone: 847/670-8099; www.poopbgoneinc.com.

Poopbusters: Chicago and south suburbs. 877/766-7425; www.poopbusters.com

The Poop Zone: 5825 Washington St., Downers Grove; 630/969-3241.

Pet-Friendly Real Estate

Finding a place to live that allows a pet can be a pain. Below are a few real estate experts who know that pet owners make good neighbors.

Coldwell Banker, Yvonne Treacy: 773/467-5314.

Habitat Co., Betty Cook: 312/980-1552.

Rubloff Residential, Suzy Thomas: Finds pet-friendly condos from the South Loop to Evanston. 312/368-5957; www.realtorstotherescue.com.

Eleni Mathias Sudler: Makes a donation to a pet charity on each closing. 312/981-2579 or 312/520-7313.

Agility, Flyball, and Other Sports

A park is a park, but sometimes pups like a little more challenge in their exercise routine. Below are some of your options for more organized athletic activities.

Agility Junkies: 22073 Pepper Rd., Lake Barrington; 847/381-2222; www.agilityjunkies.com.

All for Doggies: Home of the indoor dog park for cold days. Also offers day care an boarding. 1760 N. Kilbourn, Chicago; 773/395-0900; www .allfordoggies.com or www.bestfriendspetcare.com.

The Barking Lot: Has space for open play on cold winter days and a retail store, in addition to classes. 2442 W. Irving Park Rd., Chicago; 773/583-0065; www.barkinglot.com.

Best Friends Windy City K-9 Club: One of the city's first such facilities. 1628 N. Elston Ave., Chicago; 773/384-k9k9; www.bestfriendspetcare.com.

Black Sheep Squadron: Flyball instruction. 773/736-5172.

Camp Dogwood: 3501 N. Southport Ave., Chicago; 312/458-9549; www.campdogwood.com.

Anne Copeland: Tracking instructor. Palatine; 847/358-0497.

Flydogs: Frisbee and tricks instruction in the city and suburbs. 630/820-1703; www.flydogs.ws.

Fox Valley Dog Training Club: www.fvdtc.org/events.

Hawk City K-9: Agility at various locations throughout the city. 773/348-2832; staceyhawk@ameritech.net.

Magic's Legacy Stock Dog Training: With herding instructor Shannon Wolfe. 262/279-9917; www.magicslegacy.com.

Of Mutts and Men: 2149 W. Belmont Ave.; 773/477-7171.

Playful Paws: 680 Milwaukee Ave., Prospect Heights; 847/419-1110; www.playfulpaws.com.

Tucker Pup's Dog Activity Center: 219 N. Carpenter St.; 312/829-TPUP (312/829-8787); www.tuckerpups.com.

Windy City Agility Club: Stages events across the city suburbs. 630/415-3022; www.windycityagility.org.

INDEXES

Accommodations Index

Restaurant Index

General Index

QR

Acknowledgments

Since the first edition of this book, my springer spaniel/retriever mix Natasha and I fostered various puppies and dogs who ate our wallpaper (Woodward), iBook cord (Iris), leather mules (Olive), steak knives, soap, coffee-table legs, and mini-cassette recorder (Roger, Roger, Roger, and Roger). When we brought home an American foxhound mix who waited several weeks before eating a copy of Ken Foster's book, *The Dogs Who Found Me*, we knew Cooper was the one to keep. He joined us in sniffing out Chicago's canine corners. They both will be disappointed not to see their bylines on the binding of this book. But that's what happens when you don't have opposable thumbs.

We couldn't have finished without our faithful research assistants, particularly, Alexis Crawford, who fact checked more facts than there are leaves in a park. Thanks to our ghostwriters, cheerleaders, and editors: Paul Rogers and Watson and Rockstar, Cat Auer, Emily Hagedorn, Leslie Mann and Mikey, and Kristine Hansen, as well as everyone who helped us with the first edition. Thanks to Kevin McLain, Kevin Anglin, Kay Elliot, Cinnamon Hearst, and the rest of the Avalon staff, a book publishing team of whom my author peers are envious.

Extra treats to Dan Parmer, Jessica Faulkner, Stacey Hawk, Barb Royal, Valerie Carlson, and all the park district officials, police officers, DFA organizers, hotel, restaurant, and tourism employees, and other dog lovers who gave me tips, time, and answered my questions. Continued thanks to Judy Sutton Taylor, who proves to me daily that being a "dog person" does not have to have the adjective "crazy" in front of it.

Keeping Current

Note to All Dog Lovers

While the information in these pages is as current as possible, changes to fees, regulations, parks, roads, and trails are often made after we go to press. Businesses can close, change their ownership, or change their rules. Earthquakes, fires, rainstorms, and other natural phenomena can radically change the condition of parks, hiking trails, and wilderness areas. Before you and your dog begin your travels, please be certain to call the phone number in each listing for updated information.

Attention, Dogs of Chicago

Natasha, Cooper, and I explore Chicago so your people will get you out of your apartment and into the parks. Since we first started working on these books, we've heard from many wonderful pups and their people about new dog-friendly places or old dog-friendly places we didn't know about. If we missed your favorite park, beach, outdoor patio, hotel, or other dog-friendly destination, please let us know. We'll sniff out the suggestion, and if it turns out to be a good one, we'll include it in the next edition, with a thank you to the canine who led us to it.

> *The Dog Lover's Companion to Chicago*
> Avalon Travel Publishing
> 1400 65th Street, Suite 250
> Emeryville, CA 94608, USA
> email: atpfeedback@avalonpub.com